Group Games

in early education

Implications of Piaget's Theory

by **Constance Kamii**
University of Illinois
   at Chicago Circle
University of Geneva
Switzerland
and
Rheta DeVries
The Merrill-Palmer Institute

Foreword by Jean Piaget

The National Association for the Education of Young Children
Washington, DC

Masculine and feminine pronoun references in this book are used only for editorial simplicity and are not intended to reflect stereotyped concepts of children or adults.

Cover design and illustrations by Caroline Taylor
Photographs by the authors, except for pp. 193-194, by Elizabeth DeBeliso

Second printing 1981. Third printing 1984. Fourth printing 1988. Fifth printing 1991. Sixth printing 1992.

The National Association for the Education of Young Children attempts through its publications program to provide a forum for discussion of major issues and ideas in our field. We hope to provoke thought and promote professional growth. The views expressed or implied are not necessarily those of the Association.

Library of Congress Catalog Card Number: 80-80178
ISBN Catalog Number: 0-912674-71-7
NAEYC #317

Printed in the United States of America

About the Authors

CONSTANCE KAMII is Professor of Early Childhood Education at the University of Alabama at Birmingham. A major concern of hers since the mid-1960s has been the conceptualization of goals and objectives for early childhood education on the basis of scientific research about children's development of knowledge. Convinced that the only theory in existence that explains this development from infancy to adolescence was that of Jean Piaget, she studied under him as a postdoctoral research fellow and, later, on a joint appointment with the University of Geneva and the University of Illinois at Chicago. She has

been working closely with teachers for 20 years to develop practical ways of using Piaget's constructivist theory in the classroom.

Arkansas born RHETA DE-VRIES completed a B.A. at Baylor University in Waco, Texas, and then taught for four years in Illinois public schools (second grade, eighth-grade language arts and social studies, and a combination fifth-sixth grade). This experience raised the educational issues that motivated her to do graduate work in child development at the University of Chicago. There she studied Piaget's theory under Lawrence Kohlberg and was invited to be his research assistant.

Following her Ph.D. in Psychology in 1968, DeVries began to ask the question: What are the educational implications of Piagetian research

and theory? Now calling this approach "constructivist education," DeVries has recently focused on research to study its effects on children's sociomoral development, in comparison with Montessori, DISTAR, and eclectic approaches. Her recent research is also concerned with the sociomoral atmosphere that produces differences in children's development, and she focuses especially on the nature of teacher-child interactions in classrooms.

As a research psychologist, she has been concerned with how children think and reason. As a teacher of teachers, she has been concerned with the practical implications of such research for education and childrearing. As Director of the Human Development Laboratory School at the University of Houston, she is concerned with implementing a living demonstration of, and continuing to develop, constructivist education. DeVries and Kohlberg wrote the most definitive work on constructivist education in another NAEYC publication, *Constructivist Early Education: Overview and Comparison with Other Programs.*

Contents

vii Foreword by Jean Piaget
ix   Acknowledgments
xi   Introduction

Part I. Rationale

1   Chapter 1. Good Group Games: What Are They?
11 Chapter 2. Why Use Group Games?
35 Chapter 3. Types of Group Games

Part II. Examples

87   Chapter 4. Block Race
95   Chapter 5. Tag
111 Chapter 6. Back-to-Back
119 Chapter 7. Marbles by Candace Arthur
131 Chapter 8. Pin the Tail on the Donkey
147 Chapter 9. Kitty Wants a Corner
173 Chapter 10. Making Families (A Card Game)

Part III. Teaching

189 Chapter 11. The Issue of Competition
201 Chapter 12. Principles of Teaching
231 Appendix: Piaget's Theory, Behaviorism, and
     Other Theories in Education
246 References
250 Index
255 Ideas for Using This Book in a Workshop or Class

Foreword

CERTAIN EDUCATORS say sometimes that my theory is only "cognitive," and that I neglected the importance of social aspects of the child's development. It is true that most of my publications have dealt with various aspects of cognitive development, particularly the development of operativity, but in my first works I emphasized the importance of interindividual exchanges sufficiently not to feel the need afterwards to return to it. In fact, it is clear that the confrontation of points of view is already indispensable in childhood for the elaboration of logical thought, and such confrontations become increasingly more important in the elaboration of sciences by adults. Without the diversity of theories and the constant search for going beyond the contradictions among them, scientific progress would not have been possible.

This is what the authors of this volume understood well in placing the discussion on such an important terrain as play, where the confrontation of points of view is constantly at work. Play is a particularly powerful form of activity that fosters the social life and constructive activity of the child. I wrote a preface to another book by the same authors, *Physical Knowledge in Preschool Education: Implications of Piaget's Theory*, in which these factors were already emphasized, but in another type of play. This is a second volume focusing on group games inspired especially by the game of Marbles that I studied myself by questioning children more than 50 years ago.

The authors must be congratulated for having pursued such research and for having known so well how to draw pedagogical consequences from it, with their rich personal experience.

Jean Piaget
May, 1979

Acknowledgments

MANY PEOPLE have contributed to the work that led to the writing of this book. The one person to whom we owe the greatest debt is Professor Hermina Sinclair of the University of Geneva. Professor Sinclair has influenced us in many ways for over a decade through her critiques of our manuscripts, her observations of our classrooms, our numerous discussions, and the support of her friendship. Without her assistance, publication of this book would not have been possible.

We also owe a large debt of gratitude to the teachers with whom we have worked. We ourselves are not classroom teachers, and without their perspective and insight, we could never have approached any level of practical application. To the administrators of the institutions in which these teachers worked, we also express thanks for enabling us to try our ideas in classrooms. We are especially grateful to the teachers and former Director of Circle Children's Center, a day care facility at the University of Illinois at Chicago Circle. It was there that most of the activities of Part II were carried out. The former Director, Ms. Patricia Chronis, created an organizational and interpersonal milieu which made our research and teacher-training seminars possible. The teacher with whom we worked the longest and most intensively is Ms. Maureen Ellis, and we would like to express our particular appreciation for all we learned from her. The other teachers making significant contributions are Mr. Sargent Aborn, Ms. Candace Arthur, Ms. Colleen Blobaum, Ms. Nancy Fineberg, Mr. Thomas Gleeson, Ms. Laura Gross Weinberg, Ms. Kathleen Harper, Ms. Jeanne Klauber, Ms. Ruth Rauter, and Ms. Talitha Sanders. The other teachers who also contributed to our research at Circle Children's Center are Ms. Robin Reser Burgess, Ms. Linda Chaplik, Mr. Mitchell Diamond, Mr. Thomas DiSalvo, Ms. Beverly Hanlon, Ms. Janice Hill, Mr. Ed Majewski, Ms. Debbie Markman, Ms. Sue Mosley, and Mr. Mark Thomma. We are grateful for their openness, their willingness to have us in their classrooms, their comments and questions, and their reactions to drafts of this book.

We would especially like to underline the assistance of Ms. Kathleen Gruber and Professor Lucinda Lee-Katz, our colleagues at the University of Illinois at

Chicago Circle. With their knowledge of teachers and children in the classroom, they spent many hours reading earlier drafts and made suggestions both about our ideas and about our writing. Professor Marianne Denis-Prinzhorn of the University of Geneva has also been a supportive but relentless critic for many years. It was she who insisted that card games and board games be included in this book. We would also like to acknowledge the contribution of students at the University of Illinois at Chicago Circle, University of Geneva, and the Erikson Institute for Early Education. They experimented with our ideas and helped us to grow with them.

The financial support from a variety of sources was indispensable. The bulk of the research reported in this book has been funded since 1971 by the Urban Education Research Program of the College of Education, University of Illinois at Chicago Circle. The Spencer Foundation also provided a grant during 1971-72 which made our work possible at the Evanston (Illinois) Child Care Center and the St. Barnabas Day Care Center of Christian Action Ministry in Chicago. Some of the material reported here was gathered in the course of our consultation during 1973-75 to a Title VII, Emergency School Aid Act, experimental kindergarten project in the District 65 Public Schools in Evanston, Illinois, under the direction of Ms. Corinne Kolen and Ms. Mona Golub.

Finally, we acknowledge the contribution of the children who are described in this book. This acknowledgment must also be extended to their parents, as this book could not have been written without their willingness to have their children photographed and discussed.

Introduction

HOW CAN TEACHERS of young children use Piaget's theory in the classroom? We have been trying to answer that question for more than a decade. During that period, our thinking evolved from one level to another as we studied the theory and experimented in classrooms. *Group Games* is our most recent attempt to address the question in one area of a total educational program. That program, or the context within which we envisage group games, has been described elsewhere (Kamii 1980; Kamii and DeVries 1977), and the reader interested in it is referred to those publications. Two books have also been written in other specific areas of the program: In *Piaget, Children, and Number* (Kamii and DeVries 1976), we discussed how the teacher can foster the development of early numerical quantification. In *Physical Knowledge in Preschool Education* (Kamii and DeVries 1978), we focused on an aspect related to science education. The present book cuts across many traditional disciplines. For example, as can be seen in Chapter 3, aiming games like Bowling involve physics and arithmetic. Many card games such as Go Fish and Rummy provide opportunities for development in logical thinking and arithmetic.

Group games have been around for a long time, but the educational value that people saw in them was much more limited than what we see from a Piagetian perspective. By reading about group games in all the early education texts we could find, we concluded that there is much more to group games than what they seemed to be saying. As we continued our research with teachers in classrooms, we became even more convinced that group games stimulate children's development in unique ways if used with the insights gained from Piaget's theory. The purpose of this book is to show what children can learn in these games and how the teacher can intervene in ways that maximize children's learning.

Although our emphasis is practical, we do not intend to present an encyclopedia of group games. Piaget's constructivism does not imply a cookbook curriculum or even a set of principles that can be used by all teachers to teach all children in the same way. Although children share basic similarities, constructivism implies that the teacher must make decisions by taking into account the way each child is thinking and feeling in each situation. We have tried to communicate a way of thinking about games so that teachers will become better able to choose, modify, or avoid old games and invent new ones. Just as each child has to reinvent knowledge to make it his own, each teacher must construct his or her own way of working with the ideas presented in this book.

In writing the book, we had in mind four audiences: classroom teachers, students of developmental and educational psychology, people in various administrative capacities concerned with curriculum, and parents. To teachers and prospective teachers, we attempt to present practical ideas that are solidly founded in a scientific theory. (A discussion of the scientific merits of Piaget's theory can be found in the Appendix.) We address ourselves particularly to those who are searching for alternatives to traditional, didactic methods. Although the book focuses mainly on children between four and six years of age, the ideas are also applicable to older children.

Students in developmental and educational psychology often ask about the educational implications of Piaget's theory. We hope this book will give more than a general answer such as the importance of the child's being active. Educational psychologists particularly overlook Piaget's insistence on the necessity of social interaction among peers. We hope the book will highlight that point at a time when the pendulum has swung too far from group instruction to overly individualized instruction. Piaget stated in *The Moral Judgment of the Child* (1932), *The Psychology of Intelligence* (1947), and in many other volumes that, without social interaction among peers, children can construct neither their logic nor their social and moral values.

We also hope that curriculum specialists, principals, and other school personnel influential in making decisions about curriculum, especially in the early grades, will find in this book a new and different way of thinking about *what* to teach, *how*, and *why*. It is also our hope that parents reading this book will recognize the educational value of games and support teachers who use them in the classroom. Many teachers and principals are afraid of using group games because parents complain when children play games and do not bring worksheets home. As stated in Chapters 2 and 3, we believe that children learn much more in group games than they do in many lessons and worksheets.

The book consists of three parts. Part I is a theoretical introduction to what we mean by good group games (Chapter 1) and why, according to Piaget's theory, games have tremendous educational value (Chapters 2 and 3).

Part II (Chapters 4-10) gives concrete examples of games and details the teachers' actions. Each of the games was selected from a different category discussed in Chapter 3. The purpose of these chapters is not to show how to teach each game but to give reality and precision to the principles of teaching given later in Chapter 12. For example, the first principle given in Chapter 12 is "modify the game so that it will be in harmony with the way young children think." The reader who has read a few chapters in Part II will understand what we mean by "the way young children think" in group games. Also, Piagetian teaching implies that a principle must be applied most of the time but not in all situations. It seemed necessary to describe several games in great detail to clarify the kinds of situations in which it is best for a teacher to intervene in one way rather than another.

Chapters 4-10 involve small groups of children, and we hope the teacher reading them will not conclude that these ideas are not usable in a class of 20 to 30 children. We worked with small groups because in a larger group it is difficult to imagine what is going on in each child's head. In a small group, we can better understand what happened and can later apply the insights in a larger group. Once the teacher understands the transition from noncompetitive to competitive play, he or she can use this understanding in all kinds of games.

Part III (Chapters 11 and 12), dealing with principles of teaching, begins with a chapter devoted to the issue of competition. Competition is an important issue for many teachers of young children, but many teachers avoid group games so as to avoid putting children in competitive situations.

Finally, the Appendix contains the major pedagogical concepts of Piaget's theory. Piaget's theory is compared with behaviorism and empiricism, which have dominated the mainstream of education. The reader unfamiliar with Piaget's research is urged to consult other books, as the Appendix is limited to certain points pertinent to education.

Although each chapter of this book is signed only by the person who took responsibility for writing the final version, the research, thinking, and earlier drafts were done together with many teachers in many settings since 1971 when Rheta DeVries conceived the idea of group games as a major part of a total program based on Piaget's theory. We are particularly pleased with Chapter 7 by Candace Arthur, who is now Laboratory Head Teacher-Lecturer at the Child and Family Study Center, University of Wisconsin at Stout. Arthur is a graduate of the Master's Program in Early Childhood Education at the University of Illinois at Chicago Circle, where she was also a teacher for two years at Circle Children's Center. As stated earlier, each teacher has to construct his or her own way of using Piaget's theory. Arthur's chapter testifies once again that the student can go far beyond what the teachers taught.

Part I

Chapter 1

Good Group Games: What Are They?

Rheta DeVries

THIS BOOK is about group games with certain characteristics which make them especially useful for children's education and development. Because the word "game" is commonly used in many ways outside the subject of this book, we begin by clarifying our restricted definition.

The most general definition of "game" given in dictionaries (such as Gove 1961; Murray et al. 1970; Morris 1973) is "fun," "amusement," or "pastime." Thus, "game" is used to refer to children's individual play at block building, and to group activities like singing and dancing. These uses, however, fall outside our focus in this book. The following dictionary definition of "game" is closest to what we mean by "group games":

> a physical or mental competition conducted according to rules in which the participants play in direct opposition to each other, each side striving to win and to keep the other side from doing so. (Gove 1961)

A better expression of what we have in mind is given by the *Encyclopedia Americana:*

> In games, . . . there are prescribed acts, subject to rules, generally penalties for the infringement of rules and the action proceeds in a formal evolution until it culminates in a given climax; which generally consists of a victory of skill, speed or strength. (1957, p. 266)

The group games discussed in this book conform to the above definitions except for the element of competition aimed toward winning. While the possibility of *competition* is always important in the games we describe, the possibility of *winning* is not essential. In a number of games we discuss, there is no possibility of winning (for example, Kitty Wants a Corner in Chapter 9). Even in games having the possibility of winning, we cite many examples of how children can profit from competing without trying to win. Because the issue of competition is such a delicate and important one, Chapter 11 is devoted to considering its dangers as well as its possibilities for children's education and development.

To clarify the definition of group games as used in this book, we refer to those in which children play together according to conventional rules specifying (1) some pre-established climax (or series of climaxes) to be achieved, and (2) what players should try to do in roles which are *interdependent, opposed,* and *collaborative.* In the game of Hide and Seek (p. 48), for example, the pre-established climax is finding/being-found or not-finding/not-being-found. The child who hides is supposed to try to avoid being found, and the child who seeks is supposed to try to find the hidden players. These arbitrary rules are fixed by convention and consensus. The hider and finder roles are inter-dependent because neither can exist without the other. "Hiding" implies "hiding *from* someone who will seek," and "seeking" implies "looking *for* someone who has hidden." These roles are opposed because the intentions of the hider and seeker are to prevent what the other is aiming to do. This implies the possibility of using strategy. Finally, these roles are collaborative because the game cannot occur unless players mutually agree on the rules and cooperate by following them and accepting their consequences.

By defining group games in this way, we exclude certain valuable group activities often referred to as games. For example, although dancing and singing songs with others involve conventional rules and complementary roles, no opposed intentions exist. Other good group activities also excluded are cooperative block building and pretend play because of the absence of conventional rules. In all these activities, there is no clear, specific, pre-determined end result to be accomplished which can be judged a success or a failure.[1] In addition, our definition also excludes many so-called "games" in education which are simply disguised didactic lessons. Consider the following example:

Number Recognition

Children are seated in front of a flannelboard. The teacher places a felt number on the board and calls on a child to tell its name. If the child is correct, the teacher lets him hold the number. The game proceeds in this manner, and the child with the most numbers is the winner. (Bureau of Curriculum Development, Board of Education, City of New York 1970)

Despite conventional rules which permit scoring, and despite a certain interdependence and opposition of roles, this activity is not a group game according to our definition. Although there is interdependence in the roles of the teacher as questioner and each individual child as responder, no opposition exists because the teacher does not try to win. Although children's intentions can be said to be opposed, there is no possibility for opposition in action and therefore no possibility for strategy. A child can do nothing to try to prevent someone else from getting a number or to influence his own chances of getting one. The teacher arbitrarily decides whom to call, and the child's success depends simply on whether he happens to know the correct answer when called.

The foregoing definition of group games is closely related to the educational rationale presented in Chapter 2. There the reader will find a discussion of why games having these particular characteristics can contribute especially

---

[1] The importance of children judging the success of their efforts is discussed on pp. 6-7 and in Chapter 2.

well to children's education and development. Nevertheless, not all group games are educationally valuable, and it is not enough that a game fit our definition. To introduce further the kinds of games discussed in this book, we present three general criteria of good group games that developed as we thought about published games and observed children playing them.

Criteria of Good Group Games

To be educationally useful, a group game should—
1. suggest something interesting and challenging for children to figure out how to do;
2. make it possible for children themselves to judge their success;
3. permit all players to participate actively throughout the game.

These criteria can be used as questions the teacher asks in the process of deciding whether to try or continue a particular game. Each is elaborated in the paragraphs that follow.

Is there something interesting and challenging for children to figure out how to do?

The value of a game's content must be considered in relation to children's developmental levels.[2] In Chapter 3, the contents of various types of group games are discussed theoretically in terms of specific cognitive advantages.

For example, one can analyze Drop the Clothespins (p. 36) in terms of how dropping clothespins in a container involves spatial reasoning, physical knowledge, logico-mathematical relations of correspondence, and the construction of number. However, we urge teachers to begin not at this theoretical level but at the practical level of what the experience is (or is likely to be) from the child's point of view. What is the child's notion of what he is trying to do? Is he interested in this goal? Is it difficult enough to be challenging but easy enough that he has ideas about how to go about it? In Drop the Clothespins, the basic idea of aiming and dropping is easily understood by four- and five-year-olds. When interested in this activity, they have spontaneous ideas about how they want to do it. The challenge of figuring out how and where to let go of the clothespin inspires a wide range of mental activity. When the child misses, he may decide to hold the clothespin closer to the container or in a more perpendicular position, to stand so as to look directly down at the target, to get a container with a larger opening, or to use a smaller object. If he finds it too easy or boring, he may decide to hold the clothespin at nose

---

[2] When we say that the teacher must consider the developmental levels of children, we do not refer to the abstract, formalized developmental stages examined by Piaget and other psychologists. Although Piaget's theory gives us great insight into the broad developmental stages from birth to adolescence, it provides little immediate help for teaching. Some teachers are surprised that they do not need to use Piagetian tasks to assess children's reasoning. However, once they begin observing within Piaget's theoretical framework, they can find in young children's spontaneous behavior the kinds of reasoning Piaget discussed in many of his books. It is not Piaget's formal stages, but other aspects of his theory, that enable us to look at children's behavior and make inferences about how they are thinking. Many examples of this kind of observation are found in later chapters on specific games.

level or arm's length, to stand on a chair, to use a container with a smaller opening, or to take a larger object. Older five-year-olds experienced with games may be able to figure out how to organize themselves to take turns and to regulate the play according to the rules they decide upon. Younger children will be more interested when everyone has his own container and pins. Interest in the basic actions can motivate them, with the support of the teacher, to think about such problems as how to distribute the pins fairly, what to do when people's pins get mixed up, and how to compare one's success with someone else's at the end by counting the pins in the containers.

By taking the child's perspective, the teacher can evaluate the degree to which a particular game might or does inspire children's reasoning and efforts to cooperate with others. This practical approach is usually much more fruitful in evaluating the potential or actual effectiveness of a game than beginning with theory. After thinking about what players are motivated to figure out, it may then be useful for the teacher to consider what those problems mean from the theoretical viewpoint discussed in Chapter 3.

In assessing whether a game meets this first criterion, the content should first be analyzed in terms of what it is the child has the possibility to do and think about. Games which involve little thinking at every developmental level are not even worth trying. An example is the following game which involves only the recall of a linear arrangement:

Arranging Colored Balls

One child arranges six colored balls in a row. Another child looks carefully at the arrangement and closes his eyes while the first child rearranges them. Then he "wakes up" and has to rearrange the balls the way they were originally. The teacher begins with three balls and gradually works up to six. (Palmer 1968, p. 67)

In this game, the child can do nothing to figure out the order if he does not remember it. The challenge to memorize such relationships does not arouse spontaneous interest or appeal to natural curiosities. Children play this game more to please the teacher than to enjoy thinking about the content of the problem. This does not deny the importance of memory in children's intellectual development. However, the ability to memorize meaningless content is of little value in and of itself. Its value is in its functioning within the intelligence as a whole with regard to particular meaningful content. Simply to exercise the memory is trivial. Rather, it is best exercised in the context of activities in which the child has his own reason for remembering something. For instance, in a card game a child may be motivated to try to remember that a particular player has a certain card because he wants it to complete a pair or book in his own hand.

It is fairly easy to eliminate many games such as Arranging Colored Balls which will not provide anybody with rich opportunities for activity. The value of others, however, depends on children's developmental levels and cannot be judged as good or bad without trying them. Sometimes a game which is expected to be appropriate turns out to have unexpected difficulties. We thought the following game might be good for four-year-olds until we tried it:

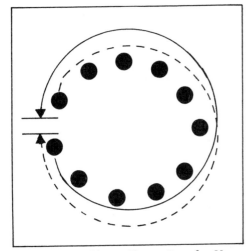

Figure 1.1. *Tom, Tom, Run for Your Supper.*

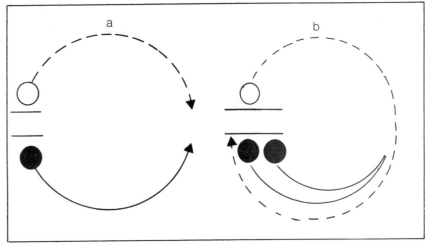

Figure 1.2. *Tom, Tom, Run for Your Supper. Some children had difficulty knowing what to do when they met face to face halfway around the circle.*

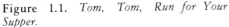

Tom, Tom, Run for Your Supper

"It" walks around a circle formed by other players. He stops and extends an arm between two players, saying, "Tom, Tom, run for your supper." The two players run in opposite directions around the circle, away from "It," and then back to touch "It's" arm (see Figure 1.1). The first player to touch "It's" arm becomes the next "It."

Only some of the four-year-olds we watched knew which way to run when "It" stopped beside them. After the teacher got them going in the right direction, most did not know where to stop running and failed to touch "It's" arm. Some had difficulty knowing what to do when they met face to face halfway around the circle (see Figure 1.2a). Often, upon meeting, they stopped in surprised puzzlement, clearly unable to anticipate this event. One player usually reversed direction, and the two ended up in a parallel race back to "It" (see Figure 1.2b).

We concluded that the game did not elicit reasoning because the basic rule was so difficult that children had no way of figuring out what to do on their own. The teacher ended up pushing them around, telling them constantly when to run, which way to go, where to stop, and what goal to touch. As a result, children seemed to feel confused and incompetent. Because we could not think of any satisfactory modification, we eliminated the game for our particular group of four-year-olds. This decision was made *not* because children were unable to play the game correctly, but because their particular difficulties made it impossible for them to play without substantial teacher regulation. These children tended to act because the teacher pushed them or told them what to do, and the teacher's corrections did not seem to lead them to know what to do later. They had little idea of why they were running a particular way, and their action was a mindless response to teacher direction.[3]

---

[3] The opportunity to play a game several times often results in a dramatic change in children's grasp of what they are doing. It is usually a good idea to try a game more than once before rejecting it.

In contrast, when the same difficulties arose in a group of five-year-olds experienced in playing games, they were not as helpless. When someone started to run in the wrong direction, other players excitedly yelled to tell them to go the other way and afterwards tried hard to explain how they were supposed to play. Children who did not understand the game simply did not do what they were told. Confronted by other children's protests and explanations, they felt a need to think about what they did and try to figure out how to play differently. Thus, these problems provided the five-year-olds with an excellent context for spatiotemporal reasoning and cooperating in mutual regulation.

Ideas for modifying games often occur to the teacher in the process of considering a game from the viewpoint of this first criterion. For example, in the game of Charades (p. 54), we observed that children frequently go through periods of frustrated inactivity because it is difficult to think up something to imitate out of the entire universe of possibilities. Seeing this problem, the teacher can try to figure out how to make the game more interesting and challenging by limiting the possibilities. By suggesting the category of "animals" or "something you do every morning," the teacher gives children a common framework within which to think. Another modification is to provide a set of pictures to be imitated. This not only gets children past the difficulty of dreaming up what to imitate, but also extends the possibilities beyond what they would think of spontaneously.

Some games which are too easy need not be eliminated if they lend themselves to being made more difficult. In Chair Ring Toss (p. 37), for example, children themselves often suggest standing further away when success becomes boring. Ideas already mentioned for making Drop the Clothespins more challenging may occur to children spontaneously or can be suggested by the teacher.

The criterion that a good game provide children with "something interesting to figure out how to do" does not imply that a good game is necessarily one that children can master. Many examples are given throughout this book of group games which are valuable experiences even for children who do not understand the game as a whole and who therefore do not play it "correctly." Nevertheless, there is a limit to which children can profit from a game they only partially understand. The teacher's use of this first criterion must be a blend of content analysis of a game's possibilities, coupled with behavior analysis of its significance to children.

Can children themselves judge their success?

The second criterion of a good group game involves assessing the possibilities for children themselves to evaluate the results of their actions. When the child tries to produce a desired result, he naturally is interested in the success of his effort. A result must be clear and unequivocal to enable a child to evaluate his success. In Drop the Clothespins, he knows for sure when he hits or misses the target. In Hide and Seek the hider knows without being told whether or not he is found, and the seeker knows whether or not he finds the hider. In Musical Chairs (p. 43), the result is clear as the child does not need anyone's help to know whether or not he is successful in getting a chair.

In contrast, the result of action is ambiguous in the game of Bull's-eye (p. 37) when children try to hit a paper wall target with a ball. The ball touches the target for only an instant and makes no lasting trace for the child to see. Even an adult finds it difficult to judge exactly where the ball hit. To improve the possibility of children getting clearer information, in Chapter 3 we suggest certain modifications of the target or of the object aimed. Instead of the paper target, the teacher might use a board with a large hole (or several holes) so that children can see for sure whether or not the ball went where they wanted it to go. Another possibility is to use suction or sticky darts which remain on the target. Children can judge for themselves the success or failure of their actions and can thereby exercise their intelligence in constructing relationships between variations in their actions and variations in the reactions of objects.

This criterion helps eliminate games in which the evaluation of a child's action is an imposition of adult authority. For example, in Arranging Colored Balls, described earlier, the child rearranges the balls in their original order as he remembers it, and the teacher tells him whether this is correct. Because the original arrangement of balls is destroyed and no duplicate model exists, the child cannot see for himself whether or not his memory was correct. [4] From the teacher's perspective, the evaluation is not capricious, but from the child's viewpoint, this is one more occasion when he is forced to rely on authority and accept on faith the adult's word as "truth." His only other alternative is the impasse of a difference of opinion. Because the child cannot decide for himself whether or not his attempt was successful, what he learns may be that right answers come from teachers in an unpredictable way. If a child's experience is heavily characterized by such encounters, he may become excessively dependent on adults and generally insecure about his own ability to figure things out. [5]

An even more extreme form of unverifiable adult evaluation can be found in the game of I Saw (p. 54) where the teacher judges a child's imitation as good or poor and the child loses his turn as "It" if the teacher says the performance was poor. Such subjective teacher evaluation of the imitation is unnecessary to the game's value, and we suggest omitting this rule.

This second criterion closely relates to the first because there is little interest or challenge in doing something if one cannot judge how well one has succeeded. When the results of a child's actions are clear to him, he is more likely to be interested and to find sense in investing effort in a game. It is possible, of course, for a game to meet this second criterion without meeting the first. One can find games in which children can judge the success of an action which is not interesting or challenging. It is important that both criteria be used in assessing a game's value.

---

[4] We do not suggest modifying this game with a duplicate model which the child could use to check his rearrangement. Although this would make it possible for the child to judge his success, the game still lacks interest for children.

[5] The way in which the child's development is critically affected by the nature of his relationships with adults is one of the main topics discussed in Chapter 2 and is a recurrent theme throughout this book.

Do all players participate actively throughout the game?

Assessing the active participation of all players in a game involves considering its possibilities in relation to the degree that children's development enables them to be active. When a player has nothing to do in a game, his mental activity is not inspired. For example, the child who is eliminated from the game of Musical Chairs (p. 43) often sits in frustrated passivity, feeling that others are having all the fun. In contrast, Tag is excellent because all players have the possibility of something to do at every moment in the game.

By "active participation" we mean mental activity and a feeling of involvement *from the child's point of view*. Whether a child finds something to do in a game depends on his developmental level. For young children, having "something to do" usually means physical activity because thought has not yet been completely differentiated from action.[6] The possibility for mental activity relates closely to the possibility for physical activity.

Four-year-olds tend to care only about what they themselves do, and for them the game of Musical Chairs is over when they are put out. We know many sensitive teachers who have modified this game to enable all children to participate throughout. One modification is to play as usual with one less chair than the number of players, but without eliminating the child who does not get a chair. Another possible modification is to begin a separate group for the losers with the chairs that are removed from the original group. Similar types of modifications are suggested in Chapter 3 for other games to avoid eliminating children from the game as prescribed in the unmodified versions.

Consideration of developmental levels is especially important in assessing active participation in games having "star" and "supporter" roles. In Dog and Bone (p. 206), children enjoy the supporter role only when they see possibilities for action in this role. In some games like Duck, Duck, Goose (p. 46), such possibilities for action do not exist. Players spend a brief time in the star roles of "It" and goose, and considerable time as supporters in the circle waiting for a turn. In such situations the teacher needs to be alert to the involvement of the supporters. If they begin to wiggle around and show other signs of restlessness, it is time to quit. Continue the game only if the supporters maintain their interest.

Our experience with four-year-olds is that they briefly watch others, especially while they anticipate being chosen as the goose. After a turn at being the star, however, they tend to lose interest and pay no attention to what is happening in the game. This is often partly due to teacher insistence that "It" choose someone who has not already had a turn. After being the goose and "It," children know they will not have another turn and feel that the game is over. When children are at this level, the teacher usually ends up trying to keep them from lying down and rolling into the middle of the circle or from disrupting the play in other ways. Sometimes this game can be used well with a group of only five or six four-year-olds. Having such a small number of players reduces waiting time and eliminates the need for iron-clad insistence on choosing someone who has not yet had a turn.

---

[6] This topic is discussed further in Chapter 2 in relation to Piaget's theory.

Five-year-olds, in contrast, can enjoy playing the game in larger groups because they tend to be genuinely interested in the chases of others. They watch "It" with anticipation and cheer and clap while the stars run. Older children can also begin to understand that in order to have the fun of the star roles, they need to cooperate by also giving others the chance for this fun.

When deciding whether a particular game does or does not meet this third criterion, the essential concern should be the active nature of the child's experience. Frustrated passivity and boredom are not pleasant states at any age, and children do not develop by being passive. The criterion of active participation for all players throughout a game closely relates to the first criterion of good group games. A game which gives the child something interesting and challenging to figure out how to do involves mental activity. Conversely, if a game does not insure a child's active involvement throughout, it has failed to give interesting and challenging content. However, a game may meet this third criterion while violating the first. A game can permit all players' active participation in dull and unchallenging content. A good game meets all three criteria.

The three criteria of good group games discussed above could have been given simply as criteria for good activities. Young children often play group games as if they were individual activities. For example, it was pointed out in relation to the first criterion that Drop the Clothespins is more interesting and challenging for younger children when everyone has his own container and pins. Such a modification can (although it does not necessarily) completely eliminate the interdependence, opposition, and collaboration of roles, thus ceasing to be a group game according to our definition. As discussed in Chapter 12 on principles of teaching, it is often an excellent idea to begin an aiming game as an individual activity, and later introduce children to the collective game. As an individual activity, children often want to set their own aims (for example, trying to get a certain number of pins in the container), and their intentions may differ from those specified by the rules. For example, young children frequently want to be *found* in Hide and Seek!

While we begin with a strict definition of group games, this does not imply that the educational value of children's play should be judged in terms of its conformity to this definition. Group games are not advocated here merely for the sake of children's learning to play these games. It is important that the game, whether or not played strictly according to the rules, provide a stimulating context for children's mental activity, and to the extent of their capability, for their cooperation.

As the reader considers our own and teachers' thinking about many games in this book, he or she will see more specifically how the foregoing definition and criteria can be used together as general guidelines for selecting and modifying group games, and evaluating their success. Chapter 2 discusses the theoretical orientation which led us to our definition and criteria of good group games.

Chapter 2

Why Use Group Games?

Constance Kamii

AS STATED in Chapter 1, we do not advocate group games merely for the sake of children's learning how to play these games. To explain why we believe in the use of group games in early education, it is first necessary to discuss the objectives of early education that we conceptualize based on Piaget's theory. It will then be argued in this chapter that group games are a particularly good form of activity in relation to these objectives.

Objectives

Long-range objectives

The goals of early education must be conceptualized in the context of long-range goals extending through high school. The circle in Figure 2.1 representing "development as long as development is possible" refers to the long-range goals that can be derived from Piaget's theory.[1] In a book on education, Piaget (1948) stated that it is a rare adult who is truly moral and capable of critical, logical thinking. This view has been supported by recent research (McKinnon and Renner 1971; Schwebel 1975) on the ability of college freshmen to engage in formal operations.

The researchers found 25 percent or slightly less to be capable of solid formal operations. In the moral realm, we do not need any research evidence to tell us how underdeveloped average adults are compared to their potential. We have only to open a newspaper to be reminded daily of corruption in public life and various immoral acts in private life. Most adults stopped developing at a level far below their intellectual and moral potential.

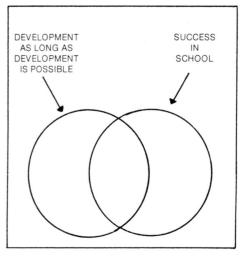

Figure 2.1. *Long-range objectives of education.*

---

[1] Credit goes to Dewey (1902) and to Kohlberg and Mayer (1972) for originally conceptualizing development as the aim of education.

The other circle in Figure 2.1 indicates the long-range objective of "success in school." The part that does not overlap with the circle to the left refers to the "right" answers students learn only to satisfy teachers and get through examinations. Most of this kind of "learning" is forgotten as soon as the examination is over. The result of "success in school" is findings such as those reported by McKinnon and Renner and by Schwebel showing the low intellectual level of those who were successful enough in high school to get into college.

Success in school is not entirely unrelated to the development of the individual. The overlap between the two circles in Figure 2.1 refers to things that are taught in school that mesh with and support development. For example, reading, writing, and arithmetic can mesh with and support the development of intelligence. When learning is personally meaningful, useful, and interesting, it is not forgotten after each examination. Young children can use these skills immediately to keep score in a bowling game, put up signs saying "do not disturb," and know how much money to take to go to the store. The study of physics, history, geography, and other subjects can also be part of our development and adaptation to the environment.[2] The better we know our environment, the more intelligently we can adapt to it. Piaget's theory implies a need to revise fundamentally the objectives of education so as to maximize the overlap between the two circles.

Objectives for early education

Within the perspective of "development as long as development is possible" as our long-range goal, I conceptualize the following three objectives for early education. The three will be delineated first and explained in the following discussion:

1. *In relation to adults,* we would like children to develop their autonomy through secure relationships in which adult power is reduced as much as possible.
2. *In relation to peers,* we would like children to develop their ability to decenter and coordinate different points of view.
3. *In relation to learning,* we would like children to be alert, curious, critical, and confident in their ability to figure things out and say what they honestly think. We would also like them to have initiative; come up with interesting ideas, problems, and questions; and put things into relationships.

This is a short and general list compared to my earlier conceptualizations (Kamii 1971, 1972a, 1972b, 1973a, 1973b; Kamii and Radin 1967, 1970; Sonquist and Kamii 1967; Sonquist, Kamii, and Derman 1970). If young children have all these qualities, I believe that the rest will naturally follow. For example, language development is absent from the above list, but when adult power is reduced as much as possible, negotiations emerge.[3] When children participate in the decision-making process, they have to talk often and articulate their ideas as logically and convincingly as they possibly can.

---

[2] Piaget refers to adaptation in a biological sense. All organisms use their intelligence to adapt to their environment and die when they cease to adapt.

[3] If the class is used to being tightly controlled by the teacher, chaos emerges first.

The meaningful use of language encourages its development. By negotiating compromises with adults and peers and by expressing their ideas and listening to others, children develop both their language and intelligence.

For example, when it starts to rain unexpectedly during nap, the adult in charge usually decides that the group will stay inside after nap. The children who protest this decision by saying, "But you promised we could go outside," are using their language and intelligence to fight what they consider arbitrary adult power. They are putting the adult's previous promise and the subsequent reversal into a relationship, and arguing that the relationship between the two must be one of sameness. The adult may argue that the promise was made under different circumstances, whereupon the children may argue that all the ifs and buts should have been spelled out previously and that the teacher's credibility is now on the line. It is by using their intelligence and language actively that children develop both of these.

If language development were included explicitly in our list of objectives, it would be included hierarchically in the context of the above three objectives. Language development independent of social relationships with adults and peers, and independent of children's thinking, is an untenable objective from the Piagetian point of view.

Social and affective objectives such as trust and a positive self-concept are likewise absent from the above list. Trust and a positive self-concept are bound to develop if children are respected and their ideas are taken seriously in relationships that foster the development of their autonomy.

I used to conceptualize social and affective objectives separately from cognitive objectives. However, the more I thought about constructivism and observed children, the more I became convinced of the inseparability of social, affective, and cognitive development, particularly in early childhood and with respect to the definition of goals for education. Children who are confident in their ability to figure things out construct knowledge faster than those who do not have this confidence. In the experiment on the learning of passive sentences (e.g., changing "The boy pushes the girl" to "The girl is pushed by the boy"), Sinclair (personal communication) observed that children who try many expressions make more errors but end up producing the correct form faster than those who are afraid of trying various expressions. Individuals with confidence try harder to figure out an answer. When they have an answer, they are not afraid to express it, and if their opinion turns out to be in disagreement with other views, they try to convince others or admit to being wrong. By contrast, children who are afraid of being wrong keep their mouths shut and their minds devoid of opinions, thereby remaining passive.

Reading, writing, and arithmetic are also absent from the above list of objectives. Children cannot be alert and curious without becoming interested in cultural objects in their environment such as the on-off sign on a switch, street signs, and labels on boxes and cans. Alert children are also interested in how many children are present or absent, what the teacher writes on the board when voting takes place, and the list of names that tells whose birthday is coming up next or when their turn will come to be the cook.

Many parents and teachers wonder how some children learned to read without any conscious teaching on the part of either. Recently, Ferreiro (1977, 1978) has shown that young children have many ideas about written words and sentences at ages four and five. There is a time when children think that nouns are written in sentences but that verbs are not written independently of nouns. There is also a time when children think that an article (such as "a") is not a word and that there has to be a certain minimum number of letters (3 ± 1) for letters to be "for reading." Ferreiro showed that children's ideas evolve through a number of levels and that they have various ideographic notions before figuring out that letters correspond to the sounds they utter.

Objectives must be conceptualized hierarchically and within a developmental framework. If children's alertness and curiosity are encouraged, the 3 R's have a high probability of developing to the fullest extent possible. If, in contrast, the 3 R's are singled out and taught in ways unrelated to the ways children think, the result will not be "development as long as development is possible." Many parents have remarked that their children were eager to learn when they began school, but that their enthusiasm soon died. If children learn to read "c-a-t" and 100 other words but also acquire the habit of passively waiting for the teacher to tell them what to learn, we unintentionally hinder their development.

A vast difference exists between the approaches represented by the two circles in Figure 2.1. Piaget's theory differs fundamentally from the theories on which education has been based for centuries. As stated in the Appendix and in Kamii (1980), education has traditionally been based on empiricist assumptions according to which knowledge and moral values are believed to be learned by internalization from sources external to the individual. On the basis of this assumption, educators have concentrated on how to present materials and reinforce "right" answers that show "correct" internalization.

Constructivism is the most basic principle of education that I derive from Piaget's theory. Constructivism refers to the view that knowledge and moral values are learned not by internalization from the outside but by construction from the inside in interaction with the environment. (See the Appendix for evidence and an explanation of constructivism.) Anyone who has been around children can give countless examples of constructivism. When my niece believed in Santa Claus, for example, she surprised her mother one day by asking, "How come Santa Claus used our wrapping paper?" She was satisfied for a few minutes by the explanation supplied by her mother, but then came up with the next question: "Then how come Santa Claus has the same handwriting as Daddy?" This example illustrates how children construct their knowledge by putting things into relationships. They may seem to internalize what they have been told, but they keep putting the bits and pieces into relationships and often construct knowledge that is different from what they have been taught.

In another example of constructivism, a five-year-old child was surprised to discover that a unit block floated in water. She then tried a longer block and a third one that was even longer than the second one. She seemed to believe that she would eventually find a block heavy enough to sink, but each longer block gave her a negative answer. This example shows how children construct beliefs about the physical properties of objects and modify them as they gain further knowledge. It also illustrates the necessity of each child's going through one level after another of being "wrong" before becoming able to construct "correct" knowledge. Piaget's view of learning is that new knowledge develops by the child's active modification of his own knowledge, and not by an additive process like the laying of bricks.

An analogy clarifies the difference between the traditional empiricist-associationist view and the Piagetian view of learning. The empiricist view resembles the pouring of water into empty glasses. In traditional education, each teacher tries to fill all the glasses up to a certain level and passes them on to the next teacher at the next grade level. The Piagetian view, in contrast, compares to plants growing out of seeds. Each leaf grows not by being pasted from the outside but by differentiation and coordination of already developed elements. The constructivist view of teaching is, therefore, an indirect one. Water and a certain level of temperature are necessary for the growth of a plant, but these can work only indirectly through the seed or plant that has its own biological nature. Fertilizers help, but they do not directly turn into leaves, flowers, or fruit.

The difference between the two views of learning can also be seen in the following tendency among educators. When educators succeed in teaching something, they believe that this success is due to their teaching. When they do not succeed in teaching the same thing to other children, however, they tend to say that it is the child who is not "mature" or "ready." If our failure to teach is attributed to the child, our success must also be attributed to the child. Constructivism shows that instruction helps the child construct more knowledge if and only if he has already constructed the elements that are necessary to benefit from the instruction.

The three objectives of early education delineated earlier all flow out of one general principle: to foster whatever maximizes the constructive process. Let us examine each of them more closely.

1. In relation to adults, we would like children to develop their autonomy through secure relationships in which adult power is reduced as much as possible. Autonomy was originally a political term which meant self-governing, the opposite of heteronomy, which means being governed by someone else. Autonomy is not the same thing as complete freedom to do anything one pleases. It involves the mutual regulation of desires, or negotiations, to work out decisions that seem right to all concerned.

In *The Moral Judgment of the Child,* Piaget (1932) made an important distinction between the morality of autonomy and the morality of heteronomy. The morality of heteronomy can be seen in blind obedience and conformity, as well as in the repetition of immoral acts with calculation of risks. The person who blindly follows rules without questioning them is not more autonomous than the one who repeats immoral acts after calculating the risks involved. In either case, the person is governed by other people rather than by himself.

Heteronomy can be seen in the example of the seven-year-old who says no to the question "Would it be bad to tell lies if you were not punished?" Autonomy, in contrast, can be seen in the example of the 12-year-old who said, "Sometimes you almost have to tell lies to a grown-up, but it's rotten to do it to another fellow (Piaget 1932, p. 173)." Autonomous people have their own convictions about what is right or wrong under a particular set of circumstances. Their judgments are not governed by reward and punishment.

Autonomy is sometimes confused with independence as the ability to hold a job, pay one's bills, and live in society as a responsible citizen. One way of clarifying the difference between autonomy and independence is that the autonomous individual goes beyond conventions and views conventions as a set of rules among many other possibilities, and adopts conventional rules only under certain circumstances when they make sense to him.

Piaget states that the morality of heteronomy is maintained by sanctions, that is, by reward and punishment.[4] Coercion, or the threat of punishment, is the most common tool adults use to make children obey. Coercion works only as long as it is maintained, or when children have become docile and dependent on adult approval. The pursuit of reward in behavior modification may be more pleasant than the avoidance of punishment, but rewards do not make children more autonomous than coercion.

All children begin by being heteronomous, and as they grow older, some become more autonomous. According to Piaget, cooperation with other individuals permits the development of the morality of autonomy. The term *cooperation* here means something different from its customary meaning referring to consent. When we are told, "Your cooperation will be appreciated," we usually understand that our consent is requested. When Piaget uses the term *co-operation*, he means "co-operating (with a hyphen in the word)," "operating together," or "negotiating" to work out an agreement which seems right to all concerned.

An example of cooperation is the teacher's saying, "I am trying to read this story, and some of you are bothering us by talking and punching other people. What do you think we can do about this?" Some children may suggest stopping the story and going outside. Others may suggest, "Tell Johnny and Suzy to be quiet." Still others may say, "Put Scotch tape on their mouths." Cooperation sometimes involves clashes and arguments. If there is a relationship of mutual respect among the parties involved, the noisy children may in time voluntarily construct a rule about being reasonably quiet. When children come to their own conclusion by decentering and seeing other people's points of view, they construct a rule for themselves. In contrast, when ready-made rules such as no talking are imposed and enforced, the rule remains external, something to obey only when someone enforces it with sanctions.

Adults maintain their power through the use of reward and punishment. As long as adult power reigns, children are not free to cooperate with adults and voluntarily construct rules for themselves. This is why I said earlier that we would like children to develop their autonomy through relationships in which adult power is reduced as much as possible.

Reducing adult power as much as possible is not the same thing as eliminating it completely. Piaget realizes that it is often impossible to avoid sanctions, for instance, when we do not want children to touch dangerous objects. He states that while sanctions are inevitable, certain types are more conducive than others to the child's construction of moral rules. For example, letting the child experience the natural consequence of telling a lie is more effective than depriving him of dessert. If the adult says, "I don't know if I can believe you next time you say something . . . ," this sanction gives the child reason to construct the value of honesty. If, however, the child is deprived of dessert, the punishment has no inherent relationship to the act sanctioned,

---

[4] The translator of *The Moral Judgment of the Child* unfortunately changed the French word "sanctions" to the English word "punishment," thereby changing Piaget's writing considerably. Sanctions can be positive or negative. Punishment, however, is always a negative technique.

and all the child can think about when he is again tempted to tell a lie is the chance of being punished again.

Exclusion from the group is another example of an effective sanction. Piaget points out that children often use this technique in group games when they say, "You can't play with us because you cheat." Wise parents and teachers also use this technique when they send children to their room, their bed, or a corner and say, "When you think you can sit quietly with us, then you can come back."

Piaget notes that none of these sanctions works without a positive relationship between the parties involved. If the child has no desire to be believed, the adult's saying, "I don't know if I can believe you next time," is not likely to make any difference to him. Likewise, the adult's saying, "Come back when you can behave," is not likely to work if the child does not have a desire to maintain certain relationships in the group. Piaget further comments that the effectiveness of any sanction depends on the attitude of the adult. If the adult merely orders the child to march to his room, the child is likely to serve his sentence mechanically and come out ready to repeat the sanctioned act.[5]

All children are made to obey adults at least sometimes, but most are included in the decision-making process sometimes. The proportion of this cooperation in adult-child interactions is important in determining the extent to which the child will develop the morality of autonomy. In homes characterized by high adult power, the child cannot develop autonomy. In homes in which the child can participate in the decision-making process, his autonomy has a chance of developing. The more his autonomy develops, the less his heteronomy will exist.

Unfortunately, many schools tend to demand "right" answers and use sanctions that reinforce children's heteronomy. Among the positive sanctions are grades, gold stars, the teacher's approval, and citizenship awards that are used to encourage "good" behavior. Among the negative coercive sanctions are deprivation of recess, the detention hall, and the use of shame or even physical punishment. If some children come out of the nation's schools with autonomy, it must be attributed to factors other than adults who run schools, such as parents, siblings, peers, and other significant individuals.

Autonomy is not only social but also intellectual. Just as social and moral rules must be constructed by each child to become his own, knowledge must also be constructed by each individual. When knowledge is imposed in ready-made form, as can be seen in the Appendix in Engelmann's attempt to teach specific gravity to kindergarten children, this knowledge becomes both an overlay of "right" answers and a source of confusion for children. More seriously, when "right" answers are not understood by the child, he loses confidence about his own ability to figure things out. When children think that right answers can come only from the teacher's head, they become more heteronomous than before coming in contact with teachers.

Teaching in the nation's schools consists basically of presenting knowledge and insuring its internalization by getting children to give "correct" answers. What children honestly think is usually not considered the most important terrain where learning occurs.

[5] In various parts of *The Moral Judgment of the Child*, Piaget mentions the following three kinds of outcomes of sanctions: (a) repetition of the act sanctioned, with calculation of risks (p. 225), (b) becoming a submissive, conventional person, who is safe from sanctions (p. 324), and (c) revolt, usually in adolescence (pp. 138 and 324).

We will return to the issue of intellectual autonomy when we discuss the third objective. Let us proceed to the second objective regarding the child's relationships to his peers.

2. In relation to peers, we would like children to develop their ability to decenter and coordinate different points of view. This objective is an extension of the first one, and to "coordinate different points of view" means to "cooperate." For Piaget, social interactions among peers are indispensable for the child's social, moral, and intellectual development.

Interactions with peers are indispensable for the child's moral development because the child is on an equal footing only with peers. No matter how much adults may reduce their power, children have no illusion that adults are still more powerful than children. Cooperation with other children helps children to construct moral values much more freely than cooperation with adults.[6]

Adults never completely overcome the egocentric tendency of young children to see things only from one point of view—usually one's own. An example of egocentrism can be seen in children's answers to Piaget's question as to why there were a Big Salève and a Little Salève, two mountains close to Geneva. Young children replied that there was a big Salève for long walks and a small one for short walks. When he asked them what the moon did when they walked and when they stopped walking, young children replied that the moon followed them when they started to walk and stopped when they stopped. It is not surprising in view of this general egocentricity that when children fight over a toy, they can see only their own viewpoint.

Cooperation, or the coordination of points of view, cannot begin without decentering. Decentering refers to viewing something from a point of view that differs from one's original viewpoint. To see the situation from the standpoint of the other child who also wants the toy is an example of decentering. When decentering happens, the child is on his way to coordinating different points of view and eventually constructing a solution based on this coordination.

Interactions with other children are important for two additional reasons. First, another child's viewpoint is more similar to any child's view than an adult's. Therefore, it is much easier for children to decenter and coordinate points of view with other children. Second, a large part of children's social life will be increasingly more with peers, and not with adults.

For Piaget, interactions with other children are indispensable also for the child's intellectual development. In *The Psychology of Intelligence* (Piaget 1947), he stated that the child's logic could not develop without social interactions because it is in interpersonal situations that the child feels an obligation to be coherent. As long as he is by himself, the child can say whatever he pleases for the pleasure of the moment. It is when he is with others that he feels a need to be consistent from moment to moment and to think about what to say to be understood and believed. While logical thinking cannot be taught directly, especially to children at the preoperational level, social interactions have the powerful effect of making the child feel obliged to make sense and be logical.

[6] It is true that not all children are equal because some are stronger and/or more popular than others. While some children can coerce or charm others into compliance, their power is still limited compared to adult power.

Perret-Clermont's (1976) work adds empirical support and precision to the above argument. Extending the work of Inhelder, Sinclair, and Bovet (1974), Perret-Clermont studied the effects of exchanges of ideas among children in small groups. In one of the experiments, she gave Kool Aid in an opaque bottle to a nonconserver and asked him to give exactly the same amount to drink to two other children. The two were given glasses of different shapes, B being wider and shorter than A. A third glass, A', which had the same dimensions as A, was then casually given as something to use if it were helpful. The children were told that they could drink their Kool Aid only when they could all agree that the two with different glasses had exactly the same amount.

The children usually began by pouring the liquid into A and B. (No one used A and A' first, to transfer the content of A' into B afterwards.) The exchange of opinions continued for about ten minutes, accompanied by many actions. For example, one child might pour some liquid from B back into the bottle, asserting that B had more. Another might then insist on pouring the liquid into B again to reestablish the same level. The third child might then suggest that the content of B should be emptied into A'.

Whether the group consisted only of nonconservers, or the nonconservers were in the majority or minority of the threesome, significantly more of them made progress on the post- and/or post-post-test than in the control group. (The only difference between the control and experimental group was that the latter had the ten-minute session described above.)

The pre-, post-, and post-post-test consisted not only of the conservation-of-liquid task but also of tasks involving the conservation of number, quantity of clay, and length. Among the significant findings of this study were the following two:

1. More than 70 percent of those who made progress in the conservation-of-liquid task also made progress in conserving the quantity of clay. The benefit of social interaction can thus be said to extend beyond the specific content of liquid in containers. The clashes among children indeed can be said to have stimulated their ability to coordinate other relationships as well.

2. The children who showed progress in the post-test were those who were already at a relatively high level of development before the experiment. In the pre-test, they had been found to be either conservers or intermediary cases in the conservation-of-number task. Social interaction results in a higher level of thinking only when there already exist in children's heads the elements that need to be coordinated to produce a higher level of reasoning.

3. In relation to learning, we would like children to be alert, curious, critical, and confident in their ability to figure things out, and say what they honestly think. We would also like them to have initiative; come up with interesting ideas, problems, and questions; and put things into relationships. This objective, too, is derived from constructivism. If knowledge is constructed actively by the child, by differentiation and coordination of what he already has, and not by having knowledge poured into an empty glass, qualities such as alertness, curiosity, and critical thinking are essential. The five-year-old cited earlier who looked for a block large and heavy enough to sink was alert and curious and had the initiative to come up with an interesting question. She was also putting things into relationships when she looked for a larger and larger block to put in the same water. She expected a different reaction from a heavier block but found the same one each time.

As stated earlier, one of the most important qualities for the construction of knowledge is confidence in one's own ability to figure things out. The five-year-old described in the above paragraph can be said to be building this confidence. The six-year-old taught by Engelmann, discussed in the Appendix, can be said to be losing it. The "right" answer always came from the teacher, and most of the answers were beyond the child's ability to understand. Teachers are generally not as extreme as Engelmann, but they are no different in imposing ready-made, adult knowledge and demanding "right" answers. As a result, many university students do not say anything in class because they are afraid of sounding stupid.

Constructivism implies the importance not only of the child's figuring out the answer in his own way but also of his coming up with his own questions. Starting with the child's own question insures starting the constructive process where the child is, rather than where the teacher is. The five-year-old cited earlier who looked for a block heavy enough to sink was answering her own question. Encouraging children to come up with problems of interest to them has the further advantage of producing a long attention span. When children work on their own projects, they concentrate for a surprisingly long time.

It is important for Piagetians that children put things into relationships because it is by putting things into relationships that children construct their knowledge. An example of this construction is the relationship between Switzerland and Geneva that the six-year-old in the Appendix had yet to coordinate. Another example is the relationships my niece established between Santa Claus and the wrapping paper he used, and between his handwriting and her father's. Knowledge is acquired by creating relationships, and not by being exposed to isolated facts and concepts.

2.1. *The object of this game is to keep one's balloon up the longest. Three-year-old children do not pay attention to what others are doing, while six-year-old children would compare their performances with others.*

Chapter 2

2.2. *Who Is Gone? One child hides while the guesser has her head down. When the children understand the game, the children, instead of the teacher, choose the child who hides.*

2.3. *In this balance game, a ball rests in a cup, and a cardboard disc is balanced on top. The disc is marked off into numbered segments. Players take turns throwing a die and then choose an object to place in that segment on the disc. (Objects vary in size and weight.) Players try to keep the disc from falling off. Using two dice makes addition necessary. While the primary value of this game involves physical knowledge, the reading of numerals also plays a role.*

Alertness, curiosity, and initiative extend naturally into academic subjects. Children love to count objects in their play and daily routine such as snack time. They also love to copy words to put on greeting cards. Examples such as the four-year-old who asked why there was no "z" in "eggs" can be multiplied. The child had asked her mother how to write "eggs" which she wanted for supper. When the mother wrote the word, the child surprised her by asking why she had not used a "z." Neither the mother nor the teacher at the day care center could recall having taught the child to read anything. Children who are alert and curious pick up a great deal of knowledge by putting things into relationships. The characteristic feature of babies and young children is their curiosity and alertness. *The Origins of Intelligence* (Piaget 1936) and *The Construction of Reality in the Child* (Piaget 1937) contain many examples showing how much young children learn without a single lesson.

The above discussion concerning learning can be summarized by referring to intellectual autonomy. Young children are spontaneous investigators who are insatiably curious and proud of their accomplishments. If we meet them where *they* are and encourage them to think in *their* way and put things into relationships in *their* way, rather than making them give "right" answers, they will construct knowledge in ways that lead to development as long as development is biologically possible. Knowledge that makes sense to the learner is likely to lead to further learning. "Right" answers that do not make sense and are not interesting cannot be expected to result in intellectual autonomy or further development.

The three objectives discussed above are not free of values. However, the way empiricists define educational objectives based on their values fundamentally differs from the way Piagetians conceptualize them on the basis of constructivism. Empiricists use what Kohlberg and Mayer (1972) call the "bag of virtues" approach. In this approach, the educators select out of a bag of virtures those they particularly value. If they value the 3 R's, for example, rather than critical thinking, creativity, or children's social development, they decide on the 3 R's as their objectives. If two or more goals are contradictory, these contradictions usually go unnoticed because virtues are always stated with terms having positive connotations. Kohlberg and Mayer give as examples the objectives of "self-discipline" and "spontaneity." While everybody can agree on the desirability of both, the cultivation of one may well be incompatible with the other.

The three objectives discussed above were derived not from a "bag of virtues" but from constructivism—a scientific theory based on research that showed how human beings develop as individuals and in history. These are the three general groups of factors that enhance the process of construction in the child. Adult power must be reduced because the child can construct moral rules and knowledge only when he is free to come to his own conclusions autonomously. Children should develop social relationships with other children because a scientific theory shows that these are indispensable for their moral and intellectual development. Curiosity, alertness, initiative, and honesty of expression are qualities that are essential for the child to construct his own knowledge.

If a person is against the morality of autonomy, intellectual autonomy, and "development as long as development is possible," that person's objection must be discussed in the realm of values. Piagetians are thus not entirely free from ideological controversies. I agree with Piaget about the desirability of the morality of autonomy, intellectual autonomy, and development as long as development is possible.

The Value of Group Games

Many parents and school administrators object to group games and other types of classroom play. Some parents say, "Why should I send my child to school if all he does there is play?" These parents are often more pleased when their children bring worksheets home as evidence of work and learning. To people who believe that learning is proved by reading tests, play seems to be only for amusement and recreation. I would like to discuss the value of group games, considering this objection.

Children have a strong, natural tendency to engage in group games. Opie and Opie (1969) have documented the variety of street games older children play in their free time. All elementary school teachers know that children's favorite activity during recess is group games. A casual inspection of toy stores, especially at Christmas time, also convinces us that group games such as Checkers and Chutes and Ladders are highly attractive. Adults, too, seek partners to play tennis, golf, bridge, chess, and bowling for recreation.

The prevalence of group games as a natural and satisfying human activity does not need further proof. What is needed is a justification for their use in the classroom. I argue below that group games have a different significance for young children than for older children and adults, and that young children often learn more in group games than in lessons and a multitude of exercises.

The significance of group games for young children

In his study of the game of Marbles, Piaget (1932) found that children were not able to play this game until sometime between the ages of five and eight. In Switzerland, the game of Marbles is usually played by drawing a square on the ground, putting a pile of marbles inside it, and trying to knock as many as possible out of the enclosure by shooting one marble from a certain distance. Piaget found many variations in the details of this game, but the basic idea was to try to win by knocking more marbles out of the enclosure than anybody else.

The reason for the late appearance of ability to play this game can be found by examining the behavior of younger children. Piaget found the following four levels in the way children played:

1. motor and individual play
2. egocentric play (ages 2-5)
3. incipient cooperation (appears between 7 and 8 years of age)
4. codification of rules (appears between 11 and 12 years of age)

At the first level, motor and individual play, the child plays alone, doing a variety of things with marbles that cannot be called a game. For example, Piaget describes what one of his daughters did at age three. She dropped marbles on the carpet, put them in the hollow of an armchair, put them back on the carpet, dropped them from a certain height, and piled them into a pyramid (pp. 29-30). There is no resemblance between these behaviors and the game of Marbles. This motor and individual play is all that the child's intelligence permits her to do at age three because three-year-olds are cognitively unable even to feel the need to follow the rule of aiming at a pile of marbles.

At the second level, egocentric play, children typically imitate their elders but play either alone without bothering to find a playmate or with others but without trying to win. They eagerly draw a square, pile marbles inside, and shoot at the pile time after time without paying attention to anyone else. When asked with whom he played, one child replied, "All by myself." When asked whether he liked to play alone best, he answered,"You don't need two. You can play only one (p. 38)." The marbles are handled perfectly well at this level, but from the child's point of view, other players are irrelevant.

The term *egocentric* is sometimes confused with *selfishness,* which refers to doing something for one's own benefit, with the knowledge that this action inconveniences or even hurts someone else. Egocentrism differs from selfishness in that it refers to the total inability to see another viewpoint. Three- and four-year-olds are interested only in what *they* are doing, and it does not occur to them to compare their performance with somebody else's. For these children, the point of the game is the fun of knocking marbles out of the enclosure. Therefore, the game can be played either alone or alongside somebody else. To become interested in comparing one's performance with somebody else's, the child has to decenter and think about himself *in relation to* another player. This relationship does not exist in the way very young children view the situation.

Between about five and six years of age, children begin to decenter and view themselves in relation to other children. When this happens, they begin to compare performances and coordinate players' intentions. Without this comparison and coordination, there can be no "game" as the term is defined in Chapter 1. The ability to compare performances and eventually try to outdo or outwit the opponent is a cognitive ability involving decentering. It is this decentering that children cannot do at a very young age.

The third level, incipient cooperation, is characterized by each player's trying to win. As long as no one is trying to win, there is no need for rules to make people's performance comparable. But when competition appears, children have to cooperate to agree on rules. To quote Piaget,

> . . . no child . . . ever attributes very great importance to the fact of knocking out a few more marbles than his opponents. Mere competition is therefore not what constitutes the affective motive-power of the game. In seeking to win, the child is trying above all to contend with his partners (opponents) *while observing common rules.* (1932, p. 42)

The essence of cooperation lies in the making of rules that govern competition. As stated earlier, the term "cooperation" here does not mean "consent." It means to operate together to negotiate rules that are acceptable to all concerned.

Despite their effort to establish and follow mutually agreed upon rules, children at the third level still retain much egocentricity, and each player insists on the rules that *he* understands. It is only at the fourth level, codification of rules, that children cooperate in an attempt to unify the rules. They even take a peculiar pleasure in anticipating all possible situations and codifying complicated rules that apply to every situation that can arise.

Games have a special function for young children. When older children play group games, they are having fun repeating a form of activity they already know. Parents would therefore be justified in complaining about 12-year-olds' playing Marbles in the classroom. For young children, however, group games are a new form of activity never possible before. The budding ability to play group games is a major cognitive and social achievement of five-year-olds which must be fostered before age five and further promoted after this age.

Fostering the child's ability to engage in group games is not the same thing as training him to perform at a higher level on a Piagetian task. In the first place, the game of Marbles is not a Piagetian task, and many children play group games outside the classroom anyway. Second, the purpose of using group games is to foster the development of autonomy, not to teach children how to play these games.

It may seem contradictory to say that games are not possible before seven or eight years of age and to say that games are good for children younger than this age. But children become more able to decenter and coordinate points of view by being in situations that require this coordination. Two-year-olds cannot learn to coordinate viewpoints by playing group games. But four- and five-year-olds can, by playing at *their* level. It is not by avoiding games or waiting to be "ready" that five-year-olds become better players.

Piaget thus showed that young children's increasing ability to play games is due to their increasing ability to decenter and coordinate points of view. We therefore believe that group games should be used in the classroom not to teach children how to play these games but to promote their ability to coordinate points of view. Egocentricity is a characteristic of all aspects of young children's thought, and that thought develops by becoming more decentered, socialized, and coordinated. Let us take a few examples from language development and children's ideas about the material world.

In *The Language and Thought of the Child*, Piaget (1923) discussed young children's egocentric speech. Egocentric speech evolves from monologue to collective monologue. In the former, the child goes on announcing what he is going to do even when he is alone. Here are a few examples of statements made by LEV (whose age is somewhere between 5;0 and 7;6):

> LEV sits down at his table alone: *"I want to do that drawing, there . . . I want to draw something, I do. I shall need a big piece of paper to do that."*
> LEV knocks over a game: *"There! Everything's fallen down."*
> LEV has just finished his drawing: *"Now I want to do something else."* (p. 37)

A collective monologue differs from the above examples by taking place in the presence of other people. While the presence of other people is necessary in a collective monologue, the others only furnish an occasion for talk, and their point of view is not taken into account. As can be seen in the following example, the others are expected neither to attend to nor to understand the speaker. They are only loosely associated with the speaker's action or thought of the moment. The teacher had told a group of children that owls cannot see by day, and LEV made the following statements as he went from one activity to another:

> *"Well, I know quite well that it can't."*
> (At a table where a group was working) *"I've already done 'moon' so I'll have to change it."* . . .
> *"I say, I've got a gun to kill him with. I say, I am the captain on horseback."* (p. 41)

The child here does not succeed in making his audience listen because he is only talking to himself in front of other people.[7]

To engage in a conversation, and communicate with others, the child has to decenter and adapt his speech to what he thinks the listener will pay attention to and understand. For example, he has to decenter and decide whether to say "I'll have to change it" or specify what he means by "it." The egocentric child is unaware that communication requires a common frame of reference. As he talks to others and puts into relationships what they seem to understand, he gradually becomes better able to figure out what goes on in their heads.

Many parallels can be found between the young child's egocentric speech and his egocentric way of playing group games. Egocentric speech occurs because the child cannot take into account other people's points of view. Egocentric play likewise takes place in group games because young children cannot take into account what goes on in other people's heads. As the young child seeks the company of other children and interacts more with

---

[7] Piaget (personal communication) recognizes that according to later research, collective monologues occur less frequently than what he had found in his early research. The high percentage he found was due to some condition that existed in the Maison des Petits at the time of his study. The phenomenon of collective monologue itself, however, remains undisputed.

them, he is stimulated to decenter and begins to coordinate his point of view with that of others. Becoming able to play group games demonstrates a major transition from egocentricity to a higher, more socialized level of thinking.

Egocentricity can also be seen in young children's ideas about the material world. In *The Child's Conception of the World,* Piaget (1926) describes what children think about the movement of the moon (or moons). Below is an excerpt from a conversation he had with a seven-year-old:

> "You've seen the moon, haven't you?—*Yes.*—What does it do?—*It follows us.*—Does it follow us really and truly?—*Yes.*—...—Why does it follow us?—*To show us the road.*—Does it know the road?—*Yes.*—...—Does it know the Geneva roads?—*Yes.*—And the Salève roads?—*No.*—And the roads in France?—*No.*—Then what about the people in France? What does the moon do?—*It follows them.*—...—Is it the same moon as here?—*No, another one.*" (p. 217)

As their ideas become more decentered and better coordinated with other points of view, children come to think that the moon only appears to follow them.

The history of science is the history of continuous decentering, coordination of points of view, and objectification. Primitive people thought as young children still do. In *The Child's Conception of the World,* Piaget says that young children believe the sun, moon, earth, and mountains were made by some person, and that objects that move have a will. Below is an excerpt from his conversation with VEL (8;6):

> "When the wind blows against the Salève (a mountain near Geneva), does it feel there is a mountain there or not?—*Yes.*—Why?—*Because it goes over it.*"—"Does a bicycle know it goes?—*Yes.*—Why?—*Because it goes.*—Does it know when it is made to stop?—*Yes.*—What does it know with?—*The pedals.*—Why?—*Because they stop going.*—You think so really?—*Yes* (we laugh).—And do you think I think so?—*No.*—But you think so? Can the sun see us?—*Yes.* ... What does it see us with?—*With its rays.*—Has it got eyes?—*I don't know.*" (p. 175)

These childish ideas are examples of the child's egocentrism as well as of artificialism and animism. Before human thought became scientific, primitive people believed that the sun, moon, and earth were made by somebody (artificialism), and that objects such as the wind have feelings and a will (animism). Even some adults today retain some elements of these beliefs. But scientific thought has developed over the centuries as ideas became more decentered, socialized, and coordinated in more objective ways.

The development of ability to decenter and coordinate points of view can be seen in every other area studied by Piaget, including classification and seriation (Inhelder and Piaget 1959), conservation (Piaget and Inhelder 1941; Piaget and Szeminska 1941), the construction of spatial relationships (Piaget and Inhelder 1948; Piaget, Inhelder, and Szeminska 1948), and the coordination of temporal relationships (Piaget 1946a). The transition from egocentricity to a more coordinated way of thinking characterizes the development of all aspects of thought.

Adults who distinguish play from work and believe that school is made for work are trapped in their own egocentrism. For young children, there is no distinction between work and play. Anyone who has watched babies in terms of *The Origins of Intelligence* (Piaget 1936), *The Construction of Reality in the Child* (Piaget 1937), and *Play, Dreams and Imitation in Childhood* (Piaget 1946b) is convinced of the importance of play and the amount of work and learning involved in play. Older children's and adults' math clubs, ski trips, and tennis games are other examples of how hard human beings can work in their play. Work and play are not necessarily mutually exclusive, and educators should find ways of teaching that maximize the overlap between the two.

For parents who believe that forced efforts and joylessness are necessary parts of learning, my counterexamples are skiing, rowing, and tinkering with old bicycles and cars. Children learn about physics while they ski and row boats. The amount of physics and mathematics that can be learned while tinkering with bicycles, cars, and other machines is almost unlimited. The fact that *we* went to schools that forced a ready-made curriculum on us and that way *we* could succeed in the system only by forcing ourselves to study does not prove that education must forever remain in this state.

I am not against efforts. To this day, for example, reading Piaget's books requires enormous efforts on my part. What makes me discipline myself is not the fear of failing an examination but personal interest in the content. It is one thing to study out of the fear of getting a bad grade and quite another thing to study out of the conviction that the learning is personally worthwhile.

Human beings seem to have an intrinsic desire to grow as can be seen in babies learning to walk and talk and young children's pride in their accomplishments. Human beings also seem to like being mentally active. In prisons, when adults do not have to do anything, they often play card games and engage in sports. In more normal life, adults work hard and learn a great deal in various hobbies. School curricula too often destroy this intrinsic desire to work and grow by imposing lessons and exercises that do not mesh with the learner's way of thinking. As stated before, many parents have observed that their children were eager to learn when they first went to school, but this eagerness died soon afterwards. These are the parents who can perhaps be convinced that group games are one of the more natural ways to preserve and foster children's capacity for development.

Social, political, moral, emotional, and cognitive development

As stated earlier in the discussion of objectives, children's social development vitally matters in a Piagetian program because, according to Piaget, social interactions are indispensable for both the child's moral and cognitive development. Children develop not only socially, morally, and cognitively but also politically and emotionally through games involving rules. A game cannot begin unless the players agree on the rules. Once it begins, it cannot continue unless the players agree on how to interpret the rules. Because young children usually want to play group games, games constitute a natural context in which children are motivated to cooperate to make rules and live by them. I will elaborate below on the statement that children can develop socially, morally, politically, emotionally, and cognitively around the rules of games. This section focuses on the making of rules and then proceeds to the enforcement and modification of rules.

If the teacher proposes rules rather than imposing them, children have the possibility of making rules. Making rules is a political activity, involving making decisions. If some children want to play Musical Chairs with enough chairs for everybody and others want one chair fewer, a decision has to be made before the game begins. Children develop socially and politically by engaging in legislation.

The moral side of this legislation relates to the political aspect (although not all political issues are moral issues and vice versa). Moral issues involve questions of right and wrong. For instance, if there is a minority of four-year-olds in a multiage class of older children, we want the majority to become able to think in terms of what is right and fair for the powerless minority. The Golden Rule of "Do unto others as you would have them do unto you" is a rule that takes many years to construct. Partly by suffering injustices, children come to be able to see a situation from the underdog's point of view and eventually construct the Golden Rule for themselves. Practice in legislation provides opportunities for children to develop morally by handling moral issues. Children do not construct moral convictions about minority rights from listening to a lesson or sermon on minority rights. Children have to see for themselves the consequences of the rules they make. Group games provide many opportunities for making rules, seeing their effects, modifying them, and comparing what happens.

Cognition is involved in the above comparisons. In exchanging ideas to come to an agreement about rules, children have to decenter and coordinate points of view. As we saw earlier in Perret-Clermont's (1976) study, the co-ordination of points of view is a cognitive process that contributes to the development of logical thinking. In this cooperation, children use previously acquired knowledge to construct new rules. Chapter 7 (Marbles) is a clear example of this coordination of points of view in the process of making rules. The children argued a great deal, but they also accepted each other's ideas and invented one game after another, together. The first one was completely unplayable, but the last one was a sensible game resembling pool.

Let us go on to the enforcement of rules. When I played the card game of War (p. 68) with two first graders in an inner-city school, I observed the following incident: I noticed that one of the children was getting away with taking the cards, even though he knew that he had the smaller of the two numbers. I turned to the other child (who also knew that he was entitled to the cards) and asked, "Are YOU going to let so-and-so cheat you like THAT?" The child sat there looking at me, as if to say, "Of course, because YOU are the adult, and YOU are in charge." I understood this attitude as the result of an education that had kept him heteronomous. The child showed no initiative and no sense of responsibility. He was passive and waited for me to take care of the situation. He was probably quite tough outside the classroom, but inside, in my presence, he remained meek and inactive. This passivity is the opposite of what we would like children to learn by playing group games.

The responsibility of enforcing rules encourages the development of initiative, alertness, and confidence to say what one honestly thinks. These are some of the cognitive-emotional qualities included earlier in the discussion of objectives derived from Piaget's theory. The responsibility of enforcing rules also leads to the invention of sanctions. By having to invent solutions such as sanctions, children become more inventive.

A major aspect of the enforcement of rules is the judgment as to what rule applies to what situation. In Tag 1 (Chapter 5) Anita is an example of a three-year-old who could not cognitively apply the rules. When she was tagged, she did not know that she became "It." When she was told that she was "It," she did not know that meant she had to chase someone. And when she tagged someone, she did not understand that she ceased to be "It." These examples illustrate the kind of cognition that is exercised when children enforce rules. In applying rules, children have to make categories. The categories are simple in Tag (such as "It" vs. "all the other players" and "tagging" vs. "being tagged"), but they become very complicated in many card games such as Crazy Eights (p. 69). Intelligence develops by being used, and the enforcement of rules requires its active use.

Sometimes children decide to modify a rule rather than enforce it. In a room of young five-year-olds, for example, the teacher introduced Pick-Up Sticks in the usual way, demonstrating how each player was to pick up one stick after another, trying not to make any other stick move. If a player made another stick move that ended his turn. The person who picked up more sticks than anybody else would be the winner. After playing this game for a while, the teacher left the room for a few minutes, and when she returned, she found the children playing by different rules. They were taking short turns, each child picking up only one stick each time. When a player made another stick move, he put that one down and picked up another one.

The above example of Pick-Up Sticks contrasts sharply with the first graders in the game of War. Instead of blindly obeying the teacher, the five-year-olds initiated a modification of the game. They had cooperated among themselves because otherwise there would not have been such agreement about this modification. Their version maximized the potential of the game for their development. Short turns permitted each player to be more active, and the token penalty made better sense to the children, for whom winning was irrelevant.

Autonomy has not only intellectual, moral, and political aspects but also an emotional aspect. Without a strong self, there can be no intellectual, moral, or political autonomy (and vice versa). When the child only obeys the rules made by someone else, he remains undifferentiated from that person. His will is only an extension of that person's will. In conflicts involving rules, if the teacher intervenes in ways that foster the development of autonomy, she also contributes to the child's development of a strong sense of self.

Back-to-Back (Chapter 6) is an example of a situation that worked in this way. The game broke down because two players wanted to be "It." The teacher asked the group what could be done about the problem, and the children made a series of suggestions. Each one was considered seriously, and the search for a solution took so much time that the children did not have much time to play the game. The solution came in the end when one of the two children decided to give up wanting to be "It."

The teacher could have suggested the same solution from the beginning, but that would have helped neither the development of autonomy nor the emotional development of the children. From the child's viewpoint, a large difference exists between giving up a desire voluntarily and giving it up under orders. The child's ego was not violated because she gave up her desire voluntarily. She could convince herself that this was necessary and desirable to do under the circumstances. All the other children, too, had an experience in which they were respected as individuals. Every idea suggested by individual children was carefully considered, and each child's idea was respected. Above all, the teacher communicated to the children that she believed they were capable of coping with the problem. If the teacher had proposed the solution from the beginning, the children would not have had these experiences that contributed to their emotional development.

Aside from the advantage of involving rules, group games also have the advantage of involving physical actions that encourage children to be mentally active. As stated in Chapter 1, for young children the possibility for mental activity closely relates to the possibility for physical action because young children's thought cannot yet be differentiated completely from their actions. In Pick-Up Sticks, we saw an example of mental activity that paralleled the possibility of physical actions. By trying to pick up a stick without making another one move, the children engaged in spatial reasoning. They also mentally grouped the sticks that were not in contact with any other stick because they knew the advantage of concentrating on this category first.

The games in Chapter 3 are categorized in terms of the child's actions, such as, aiming, chasing, hiding, and guessing. Each kind of action encourages a slightly different kind of thinking, but all the group games stimulate mental actions by involving physical actions. In aiming games such as Ring Toss (p. 37), for example, the child can put into relationships the variation in his action and

Figure 2.2. *A typical worksheet in first grade.*

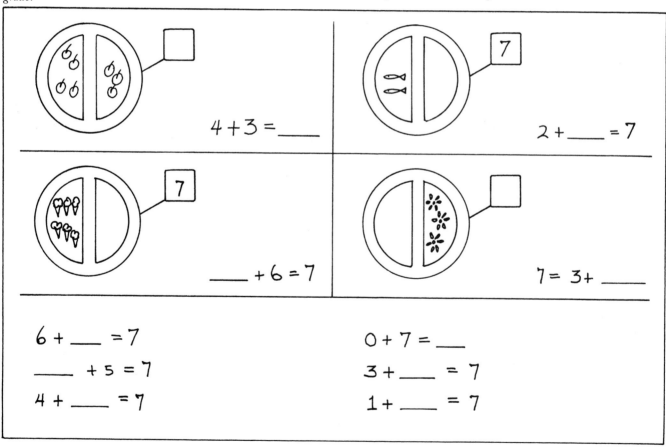

the variation in the object's reaction. (For example, throwing the ring in one way made it go too far. Throwing it in another way made it go too far to the right.) In chasing games such as Duck, Duck, Goose (p. 46), "It" can try to maximize (or minimize) the distance between the chaser and himself. In hiding games such as Hide and Seek (p. 48), the hider can try to think of a clever place to hide to be found with difficulty (or with ease).[8]

Finally, I would like to elaborate on the statement made earlier that young children can often learn more in group games than in lessons and worksheets. The point has already been made that children develop socially, politically, morally, and emotionally in group games but not in lessons. Set partitioning is an example which shows that specific intellectual content can also be learned better in group games than in lessons and worksheets. Figure 2.2 is a typical example of a first-grade worksheet designed to teach set partitioning. Many teachers and parents believe that this is the way children learn the different combinations that make "7." Teachers spend hours correcting these papers, and parents are generally pleased when children bring these worksheets home.

In a class of "slow" third graders in an inner-city school, however, one of the many things the children seemed unable to learn was this lesson. The teacher corrected the same errors day after day, and one day she decided to introduce the card game of Sevens (p. 71).[9] Below is a description of this game:

Sevens

Twenty-four cards from A through 6 are used (6 cards $\times$ 4 suits $= 24$). The A card counts as 1. All the cards are stacked as a drawing pile except the top three cards which are turned up and placed on the table in a row. The object of the game is to find two cards that make a total of seven ($1 + 6$, $2 + 5$, or $3 + 4$). When his turn comes, each player picks up two cards if possible and replaces them with two from the top of the drawing pile. If he cannot, he passes. Each time a player cannot pick up two cards that make a total of seven, the next player takes the top card of the drawing pile and tries to make seven with it. If she cannot, she starts a discard pile. As soon as a player can take two cards, the discard pile is put back in the drawing pile at the bottom. The winner is the person who ends up with the most cards.

To the teacher's amazement, a few children came back the next day with all the combinations memorized. In this game, a player is better off knowing all the combinations possible because, otherwise, he has to count the symbols on cards endlessly by trying the cards out two by two at random. Besides, a person who does not know all the combinations cannot tell immediately that 4

---

[8] The point made in this paragraph is different from one of the points made in Chapter 11, that group games have the advantage of involving strategies. It is true that strategies stimulate cognitive development by involving decentering and the coordination of many relationships. While strategies thus make group games particularly desirable for children's cognitive development, this is not the point I am trying to make in the present discussion. Ring Toss, for example, does not involve much strategy. It does involve physical actions, and physical actions are important for young children to be mentally active.

[9] The exact line of demarcation between a group game and a lesson in disguise (such as Number Recognition, which was alluded to in Chapter 1) is admittedly not easy to draw. We must be careful not to sugarcoat every dull, didactic lesson into a so-called game. I nevertheless conclude from this situation and many other similar observations that children seem to view Sevens as a genuine game.

$+ 2 \neq 7$, and therefore cannot pounce on a player who picks up a 4 and a 2. Worksheets and teaching machines do not have the same motivating force. Moreover, correction by another player is far more conducive to the development of autonomy than is correction by the teacher.

Furthermore, in a game, the players are mentally more active than when they are working on worksheets. They are motivated to supervise what others are doing from one moment to the next. With worksheets, the child works alone, and the feedback comes from the teacher much later. In a card game, by contrast, the feedback comes from peers and is immediate. If a player does not notice a 5 and 2 that can be picked up, for example, the others are aware of this combination and can hardly keep quiet. They sometimes chant, "I see one, I see one," and even say, "Dummy!" A teacher would not use such language, but children often accept such remarks from other children.

The element of chance is another factor that renders the game of Sevens attractive. In this game, the three or four cards that the child can choose from come up by chance, and even the teacher does not know which card will turn up next. In worksheets, the problems are already printed, and the teacher chooses the ones he gives from day to day. In lessons and exercises, the teacher knows everything and is the only judge of right and wrong. In a card game, by contrast, truth comes from the children. Piaget's theory shows that in logico-mathematical knowledge truth does not have to come out of the teacher's head.[10] If first graders argue long enough about the result of adding 5 and 2, they are bound to construct the truth without any instruction. Lessons and worksheets give to children the message that truth can come only out of the teacher's head and that the learner's task is to give the "right" answer the teacher wants. This message undermines children's confidence in their own ability to figure things out. Instead of spending his time correcting worksheets, therefore, the teacher will do better to enable his group to play games in more autonomous ways.

As implied in the preceding paragraph, group games can contribute greatly to children's emotional development if they are handled well. The development of confidence has already been discussed in the section on objectives as being essential for children's further development in all areas. In Back-to-Back (Chapter 6), the reader will find the example of some children loudly laughing and yelling, "We can't do it!" when they could not do "knees to knees" and "foot to foot." This attitude of fun and confidence is far more conducive to the use of the mind than the feeling of incompetence and insecurity children get when they cannot produce the "right" answer. Children who are confident can win games without becoming boastful and lose them without being traumatized. They also tackle difficult tasks without being discouraged easily.

Photograph 2.4 shows two kindergarten children playing War. Not only the two players but also the spectators here are supervising everybody's thinking. Kindergarten children can be much more autonomous and mentally alert than were the first graders described earlier playing the same game of War. If the teacher is clear about his objectives and his theory of how children reach these objectives, he can teach in ways that make kindergarten children much more advanced than many first graders. Ironically, the teacher in

[10] See the Appendix for a definition of logico-mathematical knowledge.

Photograph 2.4 does not seem to be working harder than the first-grade teacher trying to keep 30 children under tight control.

Everything that has been said in this chapter about the value of group games depends on how the teacher intervenes while playing the game. If a game is taught to teach children how to play it "correctly," its value will disappear completely. If, in contrast, the game is used to achieve the three broad objectives of early education discussed earlier, it can contribute to children's social, political, moral, cognitive, and emotional development. Group games are not indispensable for children's development in these realms, as children can exchange ideas and make decisions with adults and peers in many other situations throughout the day. However, games are a particularly desirable form of activity for young children. Because they are a highly satisfying activity outside the classroom, they are worth bringing into the classroom to make education more compatible with children's natural development. While *in*struction becomes increasingly more necessary and desirable as the child grows older, careful attention to the *con*structive process will permit the meshing of instruction with the way children learn. By teaching in ways that are in harmony with the child's natural development, we will maximize the overlap between the two circles shown in Figure 2.1.

2.4. *Two kindergarten children play War.*

Chapter 3

Types of Group Games

Constance Kamii

THE USE of group games in preschool is not new. The new element for us is that Piaget's theory provides a tool for analyzing them as a type of activity that is particularly good for children's social and intellectual development. Having discussed the rationale for group games in general in Chapter 2, we now turn to examples of eight types and their educational value. Although we give many examples, our purpose is not to write an encyclopedia or cookbook. Our hope in discussing the educational value of specific games is to help teachers develop a way of thinking about games so that they will become able to select, modify, and invent other games which do not appear in this chapter.[1]

The examples cited in this chapter were culled from many different sources. Most came from observations of teachers in classrooms. Many came from books, especially those on party games. Some came from our own and others' childhood memories.

In categorizing group games, we were influenced by Piaget's emphasis on the role of action and his insistence that mental action and physical action are inextricably related. Our categories are defined primarily in terms of what players *do*. We present examples of the following categories:

1. aiming games
2. races
3. chasing games
4. hiding games
5. guessing games
6. games involving verbal commands

---

[1] In this chapter, we usually focus only on the cognitive aspects of each game because the social and affective considerations apply to all good games with little variation from one game to another. The importance of games for children's social and affective development was discussed in Chapter 2.

7. card games
8. board games

Some games such as Hopscotch (p. 59) and Kitty Wants a Corner (p. 59) do not fit neatly in the foregoing categories. Those that combine various kinds of actions are discussed between the sixth and seventh categories. I see a difference between the last two types of games and the first six that include Hopscotch in that card and board games are played sitting down with special materials.

The eight types of games can also be divided into two general forms: parallel-role and complementary-role games. In parallel-role games such as races and most aiming games, the players all do the same thing. In complementary-role games, such as chasing (and running away), players do different, complementary things. Complementary-role games also include hiding (and finding), guessing (and giving hints), and following commands (and giving them).

While easy and difficult games can be found within each form, complementary-role games are generally more difficult for four-year-olds than are parallel-role games. This is so because decentering and coordination with other players' actions are necessary for playing complementary parts. Try to imagine a game of Hockey in which everybody directs the ball to the same goal! Most of the other aiming games are much easier because coordination with other players' actions can be minimal.

Aiming Games

In these games, players aim objects at a target. Most of the aiming games described here involve knowledge of how objects move when one acts on them in various ways. Examples of actions frequently found in aiming games are dropping an object, throwing it, pushing it, rolling it, kicking it, and blowing it.[2] Some games such as aiming while blindfolded are slightly different and involve special kinds of actions that will be described shortly.

Aiming by dropping

Drop the Clothespins

Players try to drop clothespins into milk cartons placed on the floor. They stand over the carton, take aim, and drop each clothespin. The person who drops the most into the container out of ten trials is the winner.

As can be seen in Chapter 11, very young children are usually not interested in comparing their performance with anybody else's. It is best for the teacher not to introduce the idea of winning and, instead, wait until some of the children talk about it. This and many other principles of teaching are given in Chapters 11 and 12 to help the teacher adapt the games to the particular group he has. For example, four-year-olds cannot be expected to take

[2] Refer to the Appendix (p. 231) and to Kamii and DeVries (1978) for a discussion of how children acquire physical and logico-mathematical knowledge by acting on objects and seeing how they react.

turns in this game, and therefore, each child needs to be given his own milk carton. In contrast, older five-year-olds can take turns and enjoy watching others, especially in games such as Bowling and Basketball which are described later.

Drop the Clothespins may be varied by having children hold the clothespins with a hand at chin level or at arm's length, by having them hold it with their teeth, or by using a narrow-necked plastic bottle.

Aiming by throwing

Chair Ring Toss

Players stand behind a line drawn on the floor and throw rings toward the legs of an upturned chair. If the player rings a chair leg, she scores a point.

A variation of this game is tossing beanbags into a container. Another modification is to give children six or more plastic blocks to arrange in any way they like as a target (see Figure 3.1).[3] The child who knocks the most blocks out of his arrangement is the winner.

Another version of Ring Toss can be played with a basketball net hung at a height suitable for young children to throw balls into. A similar piece of equipment is a board in which a large hole (or several of them) have been cut out.

The use of such a board or basket is much better than the following game, because in Bull's-eye children cannot clearly see the results of their actions.

Bull's-eye

A plastic or paper target is attached to a wall. Children attempt to hit the bull's-eye with a large rubber ball. (Bureau of Curriculum Development, Board of Education, City of New York 1970, p. 149)

In this game the ball bounces off the wall instead of disappearing behind a board or staying in a container for a while. A ball that bounces off the wall does not give enough time for young children to ascertain whether or not it hit the bull's eye.

Darts with various safety features are also widely available, with a target that can be hung on a wall. The target and darts having surfaces of nylon threads woven in a special way stick well and are easier for young children to throw than darts with suction cups.

Unlike all the preceding aiming games, Dodge Ball is a complementary-role game. It is also different in that the target consists of people who run.

Dodge Ball

Three or four children are chosen to go in the center of a circle formed by the other players. A player forming the circle throws a volleyball, trying to hit one of those in the center. The players in the center try to dodge the ball. If a child is hit, he exchanges places with the person who hit him.

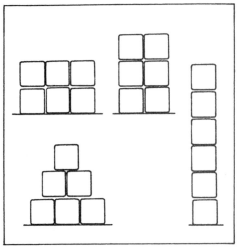

Figure 3.1. *Variation of Chair Ring Toss. Children can arrange six or more plastic blocks in any way they like as a target.*

---

[3] See Kamii and DeVries (1978, Chapter 6) for a description of how three-year-olds play with these objects before they become able to organize themselves sufficiently to play a group game.

Dodge Ball can be modified into a game we call Don't Get Hit by the Ball by tying to the end of a light rope a sponge ball (or a pillow case stuffed with crumpled newspaper). "It" tries to hit someone by swinging the ball, while the other children run around trying to avoid being hit. Those who get hit have to do a forfeit (such as hopping three times).

Aiming by pushing, rolling, kicking, and blowing

These are all basically the same actions of pushing an object to make it move on the floor or ground. (When thrown, the object moves in the air.) In Shuffleboard, the object pushed slides. In every other game in the present category, the object rolls. In Bowling, the target gets knocked down, but in Billiards and Marbles the target rolls. Hockey is different in that it is a complementary-role game.

3.1. *Bowling.*

Shuffleboard

Single unit-sized blocks and long blocks can be used to play shuffleboard.

Bowling

Ten bowling pins (or blocks, tall empty cartons, or plastic bottles) are set up-right in a *v*-shaped arrangement. Players take turns rolling a ball from a line to see who can knock down the most pins (see Photograph 3.1).

An adaptation of Bowling is to bounce the ball off a wall.

Billiards

A rectangular area is enclosed by blocks as the area of play. Each child takes a long block as his cue. Balls varying in size and weight (marbles, ping-pong ball, styrofoam ball, ball bearing, wooden balls) are scattered in the enclosed area. Players take turns trying to hit one ball with another.

Marbles[4]

In one of the many versions of this game (Piaget 1932, Chapter 1), players try to hit marbles out of a square by shooting from a line drawn outside the square. The marbles which are knocked out become the property of the player who hit them. The winner is the player with the most marbles.

Hockey

One ball and two goals are used on a table or on the floor as shown in Figure 3.2. One player (A) tries to roll the ball through the goal at the other end (near B), and the other player (B) tries to prevent A. Player B tries to roll the ball through the goal close to A, and A tries to prevent this accomplishment. Usually, the players have short sticks like in ice hockey.

Figure 3.2. *Hockey. One ball and blocks are used on a table or on the floor.*

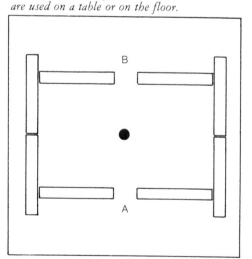

[4]Chapter 7 is a detailed account of a modification of this game.

Aiming while blindfolded

Pin the Tail on the Donkey[5]

A picture of a donkey whose tail is missing is mounted on a wall. Each player is given a paper tail. One by one, the players are blindfolded and try to pin their tail to the proper part of the picture. The player whose tail is most accurately placed is the winner.

This game can be modified by making the donkey with corrugated paper so that children can feel the outline and figure out where to put the tail (rather than aiming haphazardly).[6] It can also be varied by turning the donkey at various angles to make it necessary for children to think about the relationships among parts of the animal. Examples of additional variations are putting wheels on a truck and a stem and leaves on a flower. (See Photograph 3.2.)

The cognitive value of aiming games

All aiming games are good for the structuring of space because children think about spatial relationships when they try to direct an object toward a specific spot. As they see the result of an attempt, they put it into relationship with the correspondences they established previously between variations in actions and variations in results. All aiming games thus involve reflective abstraction in addition to perceptual-motor coordination.[7]

In the first category the child drops objects into a container from a certain distance. Immediate success requires that the child mentally create a vertical

3.2. *Make a Pig.*

---

[5]Chapter 8 is a detailed account of a modification of this game.

[6]Corrugated paper has the advantage of being light and, therefore, of not falling off the wall when masking tape is used to make a body part stay on the donkey. In addition, it has the advantage of feeling very different from the wall when children explore the donkey tactilo-kinesthetically.

[7] Reflective abstraction is explained in the Appendix (p. 240).

line above a specific spot. This is easier to do when his eyes can be directly above the container. When he tries to drop a clothespin into a plastic bottle with a narrow neck, the child has to further figure out how to hold the clothespin to maximize his chances of getting it into the bottle. When every child is given ten clothespins, this game can encourage numerical quantification. Young children love to count the ones they succeeded in dropping into the container.[8]

While the first category, dropping, involves only figuring out the spot from which to release the object, the second and third categories involve figuring out the direction of the throw and the amount of force necessary to hit the target. In Ring Toss, for example, a longer distance from the target requires more force, and the throw must be adjusted to the weight and size of the ring.

When the target has to be constructed as shown in Figure 3.1, the child has an opportunity to compare the advantages and disadvantages of different constructions. For example, he may ask himself whether a tall, skinny tower is easier to knock down than a broader, shorter one.

In Dodge Ball, the person aiming the ball has a chance to decide whether to aim at one child who is close or a group of children who are farther away. The children inside the circle must also decide where to situate themselves, either far away to be safe or near the ball to have the excitement of a narrow escape.

Don't Get Hit by the Ball requires anticipation of the ball's path. Sometimes "It" suddenly reverses direction, and the alert player is ready to duck or run to the middle of the circle where the ball cannot reach him. The rope constitutes the radius of an imaginary circle beyond which the ball cannot go.

The third category, pushing, rolling, etc., also involves putting into correspondence variations in direction and amount of force and variations in outcome. This group of aiming games offers the advantage of movement on a solid plane, which is easier to "read" than movement in air.

Shuffleboard is an opportunity to think about friction. On a waxed floor, the same block slides much better than on concrete.

Bowling, which was described in our book on physical knowledge (Kamii and DeVries 1978, pp. 302-305), provides many possibilities for spatial and numerical reasoning. Children compare the advantages of arranging the pins in a line, with lots of space between them, with those of bunching them together in various forms. Some six-year-olds take special pleasure in arranging and rearranging the pins. The many ways in which a group of six-year-olds arranged nine pins are shown in Figure 3.3. What these children learned about the partitioning of "nine" is a matter of speculation, but the arrangement and rearrangement of pins was in itself an absorbing activity.

When the ball accidentally bounces off the wall behind the target, children sometimes decide to change the rule of the game to this way of aiming. According to Inhelder and Piaget (1955, Chapter 1), the law of the equality of angles of incidence and reflection is not constructed as a necessary relationship before the period of formal operations. However, success may be obtained by trial and error, and the angle of reflection can be found in certain situations

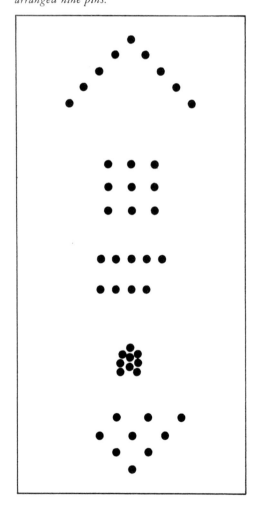

Figure 3.3. *Bowling. The many ways in which a group of six-year-old children arranged nine pins.*

---

[8] When one child announces "I got five in," and another says "I've got six," this does not necessarily mean that the second child is saying he got *more* in. Each child may simply be announcing the result of counting without making any comparison.

at a much younger age. This way of playing Bowling seems good for young children as a general experience on which they will build later on.

Bowling has the further advantage of offering an occasion for keeping score. The progress a group of first graders made in this regard can be seen in our book on physical knowledge (pp. 303-305). Two score sheets are reproduced and presented as Figures 12.1 and 12.2 (p. 213) of the present book. In such a game, the written sign is used in a much more natural and meaningful way than in empty exercises.

In Billiards, children first choose the ball they want to use as the means and the one they want to use as the target. As they compare the reactions of various balls, they have a chance to decide which ball is good for what purpose. For example, a ping-pong ball may be good as a target, but not as the one with which to hit the target. In choosing two balls, the players also consider the distance between them. The best spot from which to take a shot is likewise an important consideration.

The game of Marbles is particularly good for numerical quantification when children can keep the ones they knocked out.

As can be seen in Chapter 8, Pin the Tail on the Donkey requires the construction of a mental image without the help of direct visual perception. When children think about where the tail should go, they explore the cutout tactilo-kinesthetically and construct a mental image of the object by coordinating the spatial relationships among the other parts of the body.[9]

Races[10]

In the simplest type of common race, the players start at the same time and run as fast as possible toward a goal, and the first one to reach the goal is the winner. In such a race, the players run literally in parallel paths. More elaborate races can be grouped into three categories. One involves various tasks such as running with a ball in a spoon or a book on one's head. A second category involves more latitude with respect to space and time. In Musical Chairs, for example, the child can decide which chair he wants to sit in when the music stops. He can also work out how to be the first to start running. A third category includes relays, which repeat the same action and involve teams. Examples of each of these types are given here, followed by a discussion of their educational value.

Races involving various tasks

Some tasks can be carried out alone, while others require two or more people. The first two here are examples of individual tasks:

Spoon Race

Each player balances a tennis ball in a teaspoon and races to the finish line. The first one who puts the ball in the container at the finish line (without dropping the ball en route) is the winner. (See Photograph 3.3.)

---

[9] Refer to Piaget and Inhelder (1948, Chapter 1) for a discussion of tactilo-kinesthetic exploration, perceptual activity, and the mental image.

[10] Chapter 4 is a detailed account of one kind of race.

3.3. *Spoon Race. Two children chose tennis balls, and the other two chose smaller balls. The one sitting on the floor is running the show. It occurred to him after this photo was taken that he should tie the rope to the leg of the chair and hold the other end. That way, he said, the starting line would be straighter.*

Blowing Race

Each child has a balloon of his choice inflated as much or as little as he wants, and the object of the game is to blow the balloon across the finish line. The first one across is the winner.

Blowing races can be modified by using an instrument such as a straw or folded newspaper fan. The children can also blow objects of their choice. Both of the above games involve knowledge of certain physical properties of objects, and the child tries to produce a desired effect by acting on objects in a variety of ways. The tasks can be varied almost infinitely. For example, running to a sweater, putting it on, buttoning it, and returning to the starting line can be fun for young children.

We now turn to two examples of tasks involving coordination between two (or more) people:

Wheelbarrow Race

One player holds the ankles of another who walks on his hands. Pairs of players race to a finish line.

Three-Legged Race

Two players stand side by side as the teacher ties together the right ankle of one to the left ankle of the other. Pairs of players race to a finish line.

Races in which spatial and temporal constraints can vary

The previous examples given involve equal distance in parallel paths for all the players to run, starting at the same time. The following examples are different in that the paths are neither parallel nor necessarily equal in distance. They are different also in that, if some children figure out how, they can start running before the others.

Musical Chairs

Chairs numbering one less than the number of players are placed back to back. When the music begins, children march in a line around the chairs. When the music stops, everyone hurries to get a chair. The player left without a chair is out of the game. A chair is removed, and the remaining players march until the music stops, and one more player and chair are removed. This procedure is repeated until the winner gets the last chair.

We recommend that this game be modified so that all the players can participate throughout. Examples of such modifications can be found in Chapter 12 (pp. 217-218).

Poison Seat

"It" stands in front of all the players, who are sitting in chairs. When he calls, "Change," all players must change seats. "It" also attempts to get a seat. The player failing to get a seat becomes "It."

Tom, Tom, Run for Your Supper

"It" walks around a circle formed by other players. He stops and extends one arm between two players, saying, "Tom, Tom, run for your supper." The two players run in opposite directions around the circle, away from "It," and back to touch "It's" arm. (See Figure 3.4.) The first player to touch "It's" arm becomes the next "It."

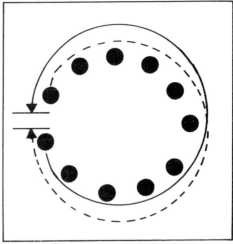

Figure 3.4. *Tom, Tom, Run for Your Supper.*

Races in which the same action is repeated many times

As can be seen in Peanut Race, the rule can specify that each player run the same distance three times.

Peanut Race

The teacher lays out a course with three peanuts in front of each child at the starting line and a bowl at the goal. Each player picks up one peanut at a time with his spoon, races with it to the bowl, puts it in the bowl, and returns to the next peanut. The race ends when everyone has placed three peanuts in his bowl. The first one finished is the winner. (Kohl and Young 1953, p. 30)

Relays are similar to Peanut Race, but they involve teams which must be equal in number.

The cognitive value of races

All races provide opportunities for making comparisons. Some offer the possibility of ordering people's arrival in time. If competition remains casual, races provide excellent natural situations in which to use terms such as "first, second, third, . . ." and "fast, faster, fastest." In some races, the relationships the child establishes involve a classificatory scheme rather than a seriation scheme—"people who got chairs vs. those who did not" and "people who dropped their balls vs. those who did not."

Races such as Spoon Race and Blowing Race have all the advantages described in our book on physical knowledge (Kamii and DeVries 1978, Chapter 2). Like many aiming games, these races provide opportunities for making serial correspondences between variations in one's actions and variations in the effects produced. For example, the child can notice that the more he blows in one direction, the more the balloon moves in the corresponding direction. He can also notice that the harder he blows on a can, the faster it rolls, and that when he empties it of its contents, it rolls more easily. In the social context of a game, interest in such phenomena is stimulated. Spoon Race likewise motivates children to work out how to hold the spoon and how to run without dropping the ball. These tasks are good not only for the development of motor coordination but also for the construction of physical and logico-mathematical knowledge.

Wheelbarrow Race and Three-Legged Race provide opportunities for children to coordinate actions. Each child is encouraged to decenter to a certain degree as he tries to get the other person to do what he wants, precisely at the right time. The other person's response immediately lets him know how long the desired effect lasted and what other agreement must be made for the fun to continue.

Musical Chairs and Poison Seat help children work out one-to-one numerical relationships, especially when they play on their own without needing the teacher to organize the game. The most valuable part of these games from an educational viewpoint may be the preparation when certain decisions have to be made such as how many chairs to get. The game may or may not help numerical reasoning, depending on the child's developmental level. If the child observes that somebody did not get a chair, he may understand no more than that so-and-so did not get a chair. This understanding does not necessarily mean that the child has any idea that there are more children than chairs.

In games such as Musical Chairs and Poison Seat, children can look for possible seats to grab and who else is likely to want them. Sometimes, they decide that it is better to try for a distant seat that no one else is likely to want.

Relays are similar to Peanut Race except that a different person runs each time. Relays must be used sparingly with young children for the following reason: When there are only 10 to 12 children, many five-year-olds can keep themselves organized in two teams, but some wait for the corresponding child on the other team in order to start running with him simultaneously! This behavior indicates five-year-olds' inability to understand the competition between two teams, in which each member contributes a part to the final outcome.

The teacher can invent variations of Peanut Race by suggesting that each player carry three different things with a spoon—a block, a straw, and then a fork. In this variation, children have different problems of weight and balance to handle, as well as a sequence to remember.

Chasing Games

Chasing games are complementary-role games in which one child runs to catch another, and the other runs away to avoid getting caught. If either player lacks the intention expected of him, the game may break down, or it may not even get started. It is no fun for "It" to tag a player who makes no effort to run away, and there is no point in running away if "It" makes no effort to catch anyone. At age four, children begin to understand the challenge of these games as they become able to coordinate opposite intentions.

Chasing games may be grouped as follows according to what players do. In games belonging to the first category, "It" tries to catch any one of the other players, and the others all run away. In the second category that includes Duck, Duck, Goose, "It" chooses the one who will chase him while the others sit waiting for him to make a choice. In the third category typified by Cat and Mouse, "It" has to catch a specific person, and the others try to prevent him ("It") from catching that person.

"It" tries to catch any one of the other players

Tag[11]
Everyone runs away from "It," who tries to tag someone. A safety zone may be designated where "It" cannot tag anyone. When "It" catches someone, that person becomes "It."

Shadow Tag is a version of the same game that offers abundant possibilities for children to put into relationship the position of the sun and the position and length of shadows.

Wolf
A safety zone is marked off. One player is chosen to be the wolf. The other children form a circle around him and call out, "Wolf, are you ready?" He replies, "No, I just got up. I have to put on my socks," pantomiming the action. Those in the circle again ask, "Are you ready?" Each time they ask, the wolf invents some new delay, until, finally, he tries to take them by surprise and shouts, "I am ready! Here I come!" He tries to catch one of the children before he reaches the safety zone. The child who is caught is the new wolf. McWhirter 1970, p. 31)

"It" chooses the one who will chase him, and the others sit waiting

Drop the Handkerchief
Players form a circle. One is chosen to walk around the outside of the circle while they all sing:
A tisket, a tasket
A green and yellow basket,
I sent a letter to my love,
And on the way I dropped it.
I dropped it, I dropped it.
As they sing, "It" drops the handkerchief behind one of the children and then runs around the circle. When the child discovers the handkerchief behind him, he grabs it and tries to catch "It" before "It" reaches the empty place. The chaser then becomes "It." (Kohl and Young 1953, pp. 38-39)

[11] Chapter 5 is a detailed account of this game.

> ### Duck, Duck, Goose
>
> Players are seated in a circle. "It" walks around the outside of the circle, tapping each child on the head as he says, "Duck, duck, etc." When he dubs one "Goose!" the goose jumps up and chases him around the circle. If "It" gets to the goose's empty spot before being tagged, the goose becomes the next "It." If "It" is tagged, he is "It" again.

Drop the Handkerchief and Duck, Duck, Goose are about the same game, but the former requires more vigilance, as the players are not told who has been chosen to chase "It."

A similar game is one that we do not recommend but present here to clarify the criteria of good games by contrasting them with undesirable ones.

> ### Squirrel with a Nut
>
> All the children except one sit with their heads resting on an arm as though sleeping, but with a hand outstretched, palm open. The odd child is the squirrel who quietly drops a nut into the open hand of a child. That child jumps up and chases the squirrel, who is safe only when he reaches his "nest" (chair, tree, or other goal). If the squirrel reaches his nest without being caught, he may be the squirrel again. If caught, the tagger becomes the squirrel.

In this game, all the children except the squirrel have to keep their eyes closed most of the time and cannot know what is going on. The game provides most players with nothing to think about except a sound "It" might make.

"It" tries to catch a specific person, and the others try to prevent him

> ### Cat and Mouse
>
> Players hold hands in a circle. One child is chosen to be the cat who stands outside the circle, and another is chosen to be the mouse who is inside. Those forming the circle raise their hands to help the mouse run away from the cat and lower them to prevent the cat from catching the mouse.

Hyena and Sheep (McWhirter 1970) is similar except that the hyena tries to pass under or climb over the clasped hands, or to break their grip. We do not generally recommend this game because success depends on brute force, and some children get physically hurt. In addition, when they are openly blamed for letting the hyena break the circle, sensitive children feel guilty for not resisting brute force until the bitter end.

> ### Dragon's Tail
>
> Players form a line one behind another, and hold their arms around the waist of the person in front of them. The child at the front is the dragon's head, the ones behind, his body, and the player at the end, his tail. When the leader gives the signal, the head tries to catch the tail by swinging the line around so he can tag the child at the end. The line must not break as the players try to circumvent the efforts of the head. As soon as the head tags the tail, the child at the end of the line is out. The head then becomes the tail, and the second child in line, the new head. The game continues until only two players are left. After several children are out, they may form another dragon and continue playing. (McWhirter 1970, p. 16)

Dragon's Tail can be modified by adding an "It" who tries to catch the tail as the head holds his arms out to guard the tail. When "It" catches the tail, the head becomes "It."

The cognitive value of chasing games

When children are able to play chasing games, these games encourage decentering. In Tag, for example, "It" may try to catch someone off guard as he suddenly pounces on him in the course of pursuing someone else. He may also chase a child around a tree in one direction, and suddenly reverse direction to catch him in a frontal collision. These surprise moves all reflect decentering, looking at the situation from someone else's point of view and doing what the opponent does not expect. When a child tries to avoid getting caught, he also decenters as he tries to imagine what surprise move "It" may be up to.

All complementary-role games involve a classificatory scheme where one person tries to do something and the others try to produce the opposite result. In Tag, "It" tries to catch someone, and everybody else tries to avoid getting caught. While playing Tag, the players constantly have to remember who is "It" and who is *not* "It." As "It" tags someone, "It" becomes a "non-It."

Tag is also an opportunity for children to engage in spatial reasoning. The example of chasing someone around a tree and suddenly reversing direction is a sign of spatial reasoning. As "It," children also work out the shortest distance to a point in situations such as the one shown in Figure 3.5.

As can be seen in Chapter 5, when there are areas of safety, where children cannot be tagged, Tag also involves quantification and categorization of objects. The children in Tag 2 designated so many objects all over the room to be safety that "It" ended up having nobody to chase.

Wolf is different from Tag in that "It" remains stationary for a long time. The game requires the wolf to think about various things he might do after getting up and describe them in the correct order. (For example, he cannot put on his socks after putting on his shoes.) The wolf may make up a long string of details, such as "I have to put milk on my cereal," or he may decide to give chase without even getting out of his pajamas. To take everybody by surprise, the wolf has to imagine what other people expect. For example, he may decide to give chase while he is supposedly naked.

The value of the second category of chasing games is problematic. When the teacher does not intervene in Duck, Duck, Goose, children tend to choose only their friends and the game quickly becomes monopolized by a few. In contrast, when the teacher suggests the choice of someone who has not had a turn, young children become bored and restless as soon as their turn is over. In spite of this problem, Duck, Duck, Goose is popular, perhaps because of certain features. What other game permits a four-year-old to continue saying, "Duck, duck, duck, duck, . . ." making all the other people wait eternally while he retains the privilege of being the only one running the show deciding who will be the next goose?

Duck, Duck, Goose and Drop the Handkerchief offer to "It" the opportunity to decenter so as to maximize the distance between himself and the person who will chase him. One way to increase the distance is by getting the

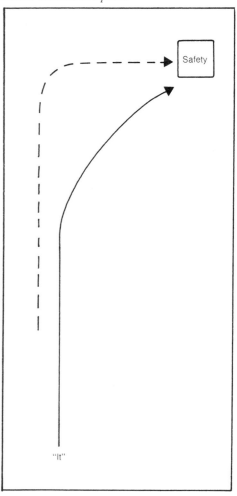

Figure 3.5. *Tag. Children work out a shorter distance to a point.*

opponent to take a long time to start running. By trying not to give any clue as to whom he will choose, "It" can catch his opponent unprepared. In Duck, Duck, Goose, this may be done by saying, "Duck, duck, duck, . . ." in monotone and then, goose, in the same monotone. In Drop the Handkerchief, "It" can drop the handkerchief without starting to run immediately afterwards, catching unawares the player who is watching for this clue. "It" can also keep pretending to drop the handkerchief to make the others tired of looking behind without finding the handkerchief.

Watching young four-year-olds play Duck, Duck, Goose makes it possible to appreciate the many opportunities for thinking presented by this game. Four-year-olds often skip some players when they go around tapping them on the head saying, "Duck, duck, duck, . . ." This skipping shows their difficulty in mentally putting *all* the elements (the players) into a relationship of order in space and time. All the players are in plain view, but some are not noticed by "It" if he does not put *every one of them* in a well-structured order. Four-year-olds also tend to take a deep breath before yelling "GOOSE!" thereby letting the goose get up and run immediately. The goose may then run in the wrong direction and even collide with "It." Frequently, "It" does not know when the chase is over and keeps running around the circle many times. (Sometimes, however, "It" knows exactly when he should sit down but does not want to!) These "errors" in games show how many decisions children have to make while playing simple games like Duck, Duck, Goose. Because each decision requires thinking, or putting things into relationship and deciding what to do with them, the "wrong" decisions four-year-olds make indicate the opportunities these games provide for thinking.

Dragon's Tail requires the collaboration of all the players. If the players in the middle do not coordinate their efforts, the tail may try everything possible but fail to achieve his objective. The game provides many opportunities for cooperation. In the modified version involving an "It," when "It" suddenly changes direction, all the other players must respond accordingly, in unison.

Hiding Games

In hiding games, the hider tries to conceal an object in a clever place which the finder is not likely to think of. In some of these games, the hider hides himself (as in Hide and Seek). These games are described here.

Hiding oneself

Hide and Seek
"It" covers his eyes and counts to ten while other players hide themselves. "It" searches until he finds someone. The player found becomes "It."

> ### Mother Hen
>
> A blindfolded child is the mother hen who searches for her "lost" (hidden) chickens. When mother hen says, "cluck, cluck," the hidden chicks must respond, "peep, peep." The last chick found becomes the new mother hen. (Tiemersma 1952, p. 40)

Games such as Old Mother Cat, which is described here, are variations of Mother Hen. Such a verse can increase both the fun and educational value of the game.

> ### Old Mother Cat
>
> Children (kittens) sit in a circle, with one player (old mother cat) sitting in a chair in the center, eyes closed. The kittens hide while they recite the following verse:
>
> Old mother cat lies fast asleep.
> Her babies, too, make not a peep.
> But little kittens like to play.
> So they softly creep away.
>
> When all have found a hiding place, they say:
>
> Old mother cat wakes up to see
> No baby kittens. Where can they be?
> Softly she calls, "Meow."
>
> Kittens must answer once each time the mother cat meows, until they are found. As mother cat finds each kitten, she says, "I found you, _____ (child's name)," and each child then returns to the floor close to mother cat's chair.

Hiding an object

> ### Doggy, Doggy, Your Bone Is Gone
>
> While the doggies are out of the room, the hider hides the bone (a unit block). When he calls, "Doggies, doggies, your bone is gone," the dogs return and search for it. The one who finds the bone becomes the hider in the next round.
>
> Another version of this game is to have one dog leave the room while the rest of the players hide his bone. When the dog approaches the hidden bone, the others say, "You're hot." When the dog is looking in the wrong places, he is told, "You're cold."

Another version consists of asking who would like to be hiders and who would like to be finders. There will then be a group who hides the object and a group who tries to find it. There can also be two blocks to hide.

> ### Button, Button
>
> Children sit in a circle or semicircle with the palms of their hands pressed together. "It" has a button, coin, ring, or similar small object pressed between the palms of his hands. "It" walks around the circle pressing his hands between those of each child. He surreptitiously lets the button fall into the hands of one child, without letting the others see or guess that he has done so. When he has gone around the circle, he chooses a child to guess who has the button. (Tiemersma 1952, pp. 37-38)

In another version of the same game, "It" is the guesser, and the children forming the circle make the object go around it. As A presses his hands between those of B, and B between the hands of C, and so on, one of the players keeps the object, and the rest of the children pretend to pass it on from one player to another.

The cognitive value of hiding games

All hiding games encourage decentering. In Hide and Seek, the hider has an opportunity to think about how the finder is likely to think, in order to select a spot the other person is not likely to think of. A spot that no one else has thought of before is always a good one. The finder, too, may imagine how the hidden person might have been thinking when he selected a spot. If the person is found immediately, he can tell clearly that his idea was not so clever. If he remains unfound for a long time, he can conclude that his idea was very clever.

It is generally harder to hide oneself than to hide an object. When one hides oneself, one cannot see whether or not one is concealed. (See Photographs 3.4-3.6.) If three-year-olds cannot *see* the finder, they tend to believe that they cannot *be seen* either. (In trying to hide themselves, two- and three-year-olds even put their hands over their eyes and think that others cannot see them!)

3.4. *Hide and Seek. Before thinking of putting the blanket over himself, this child opened the toy stove and tried to get into it.*

3.5 and 3.6. *Hide and Seek. One child decided to hide in the bookcase and got a friend to push it back to its original position. As can be seen in the photo opposite, the friend did not evenly line up the two bookcases. The finder noticed this gap and went straight to the child inside.*

3.7 and 3.8. *Doggy, Doggy, Your Bone Is Gone. Unable to find the bone, the finder was frustrated and engaged in random guessing. The bone was larger than a unit block and could not have been in this box. Some children in Photograph 3.7 are saying "It's ice cold," while others are saying, "We wouldn't have put it in a place like THAT!"*

Hiding an object provides many opportunities for the finder to use clues from other players. For example, in Doggy, Doggy, Your Bone Is Gone, (Photographs 3.7 and 3.8) the finder uses the clues of "hot" and "cold" to figure out where to try next. These often become elaborated into expressions such as "You're boiling," "You're lukewarm," and "You're ice cold." These expressions involve serial correspondences and contribute to language development. ("You are ice cold" corresponds to "You are far away," and "You are boiling" corresponds to "You are very close.")

Giving clues also requires decentering. For example, a child may be trying to find the object, standing close to it but looking in the wrong direction. Conversely, he may be far from the object physically but looking sharply at the closet in which the object is hidden. The players who give clues must give them in terms of what is going on in the finder's mind.

3.9. *Doggy, Doggy, Your Bone Is Gone. Symbolic play often appears in group games. The children here are pretending to pet the dog, saying, "Nice little doggy, you have to wait just a little bit more. Your bone is not ready yet."*

Types of Group Games

3.10.
*Button, Button.
"It" is going in a
clockwise direction.
The child who has
had his turn does not
realize the
desirability of
holding his hands
together like every-
body else.*

In Button, Button, the finder can study people's hand movements and expressions. For example, he can watch for a look of disappointment or elation as "It" leaves each player. He can also watch closely to see if the hider presses his hands differently or for a longer time between any player's palms, and if anyone holds his hands differently after the button has apparently changed hands. Knowing that these are the clues the finder looks for, the others may purposely produce all of them to confuse the finder.

Mother Hen does not make any sense to older children for whom saying "peep-peep" is too obvious a clue. For younger children, however, these clues do not make the game silly. When three-year-olds hide themselves or an object, they want it found immediately and even cry out, "Here I am," as soon as the search begins. Saying "peep-peep" makes perfectly good sense to three-year-olds.

Hiding games are good also for thinking about relations of size. The child must sometimes decide whether or not a space is big enough to contain him. Frequently, young children try to get into a small space such as a toy refrigerator and then conclude that the space is too small. (For older children, the relative size is so obvious that this action is superfluous.) In Hide and Seek, it is sometimes possible to avoid being found by moving around a tree in such a way that one is always behind the tree in relation to "It."

Guessing Games

Hiding games have an element of guessing, but involve guessing only *where* something is hidden. Guessing games differ by involving guessing *who* or *what* from limited clues. In Mystery Bag and Fourteen, Stand Still, the child cannot see the object, and must mentally construct it out of tactilo-kinesthetic clues by feeling it with his hands. In It Is I and Zoo, the clues are auditory, and the blindfolded child must guess who or where from the sounds he hears. In The Orchestra Conductor, Charades, and I Saw, the guesses are based on visual clues, namely movements. In Police Officer and Teapot, the child guesses the answer on the basis of verbal hints. These four kinds of games are described in the following paragraphs.

Guessing from tactilo-kinesthetic clues

Mystery Bag

Each child feels an object which he cannot see, and must guess what it is. The object may be presented in a bag or behind his back. Rules about taking turns, how many guesses are allowed, etc., are to be specified by the teacher.

Fourteen, Stand Still

Blindfolded, "It" stands in the middle of a circle formed by the other players. He counts slowly to fourteen and then calls out, "Stand still!" During the counting, the other players each take 14 steps. At the command, "Stand still!" all must stop where they are and remain quiet. "It" then gropes in search of them. When he locates a player, he must identify him on the first guess by feeling his body and clothing. The first player to be identified becomes "It" in the next game.

For four-year-olds, the number of steps needs to be reduced, depending on spatial considerations and children's ability to grope with a blindfold on. Pin the Tail on the Donkey, which was presented as an aiming game, could also have been discussed here as a guessing game.

Guessing from auditory clues

It Is I

One child sits on a chair, and another comes from behind to tap on the chair. "It" asks, "Who is tapping?" and the tapper responds, "It is I," in a disguised voice. "It" then tries to guess who tapped. If he guesses correctly, the tapper becomes "It." If he guesses incorrectly, another player takes a turn at tapping on the chair.

Zoo

The players form pairs, and each pair chooses an animal whose voice they want to imitate. Everyone is blindfolded, and the players are scattered about the room. On a signal, everyone begins to make the sound of the animal chosen. Partners try to find one another, and when they do, they remove their blindfolds and run to the goal. The first pair to get there wins.

Zoo works only when the children can blindfold themselves. If the teacher has to put all the blindfolds on, this preparation takes such a long time that children become restless, especially those who cannot see anything.

Guessing from visual clues (body movements)

The Orchestra Conductor

"It" goes out of the room while the rest of the group sitting in a circle selects the conductor. After "It" returns, the conductor does a variety of actions for the other children to imitate, such as waving both hands symmetrically, then conducting with one hand, and then pointing to one person. By watching the group who imitate the conductor, "It" has to guess which child is the conductor.

Charades

One child performs some action, such as pouring juice. The other children try to guess what he is doing. The child who guesses correctly may be the next performer. (Bureau of Curriculum Development, Board of Education, City of New York 1970, p. 150)

This version of Charades can be modified for four-year-olds by having "It" draw from a pile of cards on which there are pictures of people (such as a crossing guard and a violinist). Another way of limiting the choice, thereby improving the game, is to play Animal Charades.

I Saw

"It" says, "On my way to school this morning, I saw . . ." and imitates what he saw. Other players guess what he saw. If no one guesses correctly, "It" tells what he saw. If the imitation was poor, he loses his turn as "It." If it was good and no one guesses correctly, he is praised and allowed to imitate something else.

The preceding game is essentially the same as Charades, but it seems worth describing because it lends itself to productive variations. For example, children can decide to play "When I Went to the Apple Orchard, I Saw . . ." or "When I Went to the Airport, I Saw. . . ."

We suggest modifying this game by letting each child take a turn and eliminating the teacher's evaluation of good and bad imitations. The teacher's evaluation invokes adult authority, which reinforces the child's heteronomy.

Guessing from verbal hints

Police Officer

While the "police officer" is out of the room, the rest of the group decides who will be the "lost child." When the officer is invited back, he calls for someone to describe that person without naming him (for example, "She is wearing a red dress"). After each description, the officer has a chance to take a guess. The player who gave the hint that led to the correct guess becomes the new "It."

> **Teapot**
>
> While "It" is out of the room, the rest of the group decides upon some object in the room for "It" to guess. When "It" is invited back, he calls on someone to describe the object. Each person called on says something such as "The teapot is on a table."[12] The player who gave the hint that led to the correct guess becomes the new "It."

This game can be played by four-year-olds by making the entire group "It." The teacher then tells something about the object and asks for guesses. She continues to give additional hints until someone guesses correctly. To make the task easier, she can reduce the scope of the guesses by putting pictures on the wall. One teacher, for example, used a large picture of characters from *Mother Goose*. Gradually, as the children became able, she encouraged them to give clues.

The cognitive value of guessing games

Guessing games are good for the guesser because they provide opportunities to make inferences that go far beyond the information available. Guessing games are good also for the person who has to come up with clues in light of those that have already been given.

Mystery Bag is widely played in nursery schools, but for unclear reasons, it is usually said that this game sharpens children's sense of touch. For Piaget (Piaget and Inhelder 1948, Chapter 1), the important thing is not the tactile sense but the mental construction of the object in the mind based on kinesthetic exploration. The perceptual *activity* involved in creating a mental image of the object makes Mystery Bag a good game. As can be seen in *The Child's Conception of Space*, (Piaget and Inhelder 1948) objects such as spoons are much easier to identify than cutouts of geometric shapes.

While Mystery Bag involves objects to identify, Fourteen, Stand Still involves people. In Fourteen, Stand Still, it is often enough for a blindfolded four-year-old to feel a friend's hair to identify her. The game also has the advantage of requiring spatial reasoning. Those who want to be caught take tiny steps, or they may even think of walking in a circle. In It Is I, the child gives a clue by disguising his voice as much as possible. In Zoo, in contrast, the clue he gives must be as undisguised as possible.

Young children playing The Orchestra Conductor do not think of the importance of subtly changing their actions. As orchestra conductor, they often switch suddenly from moving both hands, for example, to conducting with one hand. The Orchestra Conductor is an opportunity not only for the conductor but also for all the other players to decenter. When the players forming the circle know that the guesser is trying to determine which person everybody else is looking at, they may try to confuse the guesser by looking at someone other than the conductor. They may also try to make the task difficult by looking at one person after another instead of focusing on one person.

In Charades and I Saw, four-year-olds often do not know what movements particularly characterize the object in question. In Animal Charades, some begin

---

[12] In playing this game children say, "It is . . . ," rather than "The teapot is. . . ." It seems unnatural for them to speak of a teapot when they know that they are not talking about a teapot.

by jumping on both feet. This behavior shows the difficulty of choosing a unique characteristic and/or the difficulty of representing a well-chosen characteristic. A typical imitation of a four-year-old can be seen in Photograph 3.11. The child finds out that other people say "a dog" when he wants them to get the idea of a horse.

Games involving verbal hints promote classificatory thinking and the structuring of categories already given. In Police Officer, for example, when both a boy and a girl are wearing red sweaters, four-year-olds tend not to notice the foolishness of saying, "He is wearing a red sweater."

Teapot is a simplified version of Twenty Questions. In Twenty Questions, the guesser has to come up with questions, and only the smart guesser thinks of using categories well (such as "Is it an animal?"). In Teapot, in contrast, the teacher begins by giving categories such as "It is something to eat." This game is more appropriate for four-year-olds not only because the categories are given by the teacher but also because the clues can be given in positive terms. As shown by Piaget (1974c, 1974d), negative characteristics (such as "It is *not* an animal") are hard for four-year-olds to handle. In Twenty Questions, after learning that the object in question is *not* an animal, four-year-olds often ask, "Is it a dog?" The teacher who is sensitive to the way a group is thinking and feeling in a particular situation comes up with just the right statement at the right time. For example, if he or she says, "The object is on a table in this room," the children can look around and consider one object after another. When she senses that the children are frustrated, she might make the clue even easier by saying, "You use it to call people and talk to them."

Games Involving Verbal Commands

Commands can be simple and straightforward, and very young children find enough challenge in merely doing what "It" says. For example, Simon Says

3.11
Animal Charade.

can at first be a game of following straightforward commands. As they go on playing this game, however, the complementarity has to be sharpened for the activity to be fun. Simon Says thus has to be modified into a game in which "It" tries to trick the others into doing things at the wrong time. Another way of heightening the complementarity is by introducing the rule that the players can "cheat" as long as they can get away with it. The third type of game described here involves partners.

Following tricky commands

Simon Says

The leader, Simon, gives orders such as "Simon says, 'Thumbs up,'" or "Simon says, 'Raise your right hand.'" The players must do what Simon says only when the order begins with "Simon says." A child who follows the command when the order is not preceded by "Simon says" or who fails to follow a command is out of the game.

To allow all the players to be active, a losers' group might be formed on the side. This statement also applies to the following two games:

I Say Stoop

The leader stoops or stands, saying with each action either "I say stoop" or "I say stand." Occasionally, he stoops when he says to stand and vice versa. Players must do what "It" *says* rather than what he *does*. Children who make a mistake must sit down. The last player to remain standing is the leader the next time.

Ducks Fly

The leader calls out, "Ducks fly, birds fly, horses fly, ..." When he names something that flies, the players flap their arms. When he names something that does not fly, they must keep their arms at their sides. Anyone who makes a mistake is out of the game. The last player becomes the new leader. (McWhirter 1970, pp. 12-13)

Following commands and trying to get away with "cheating"

Giant Steps

"It" is at one end of the room behind the finishing line. All the other players are at the other end behind the starting line. "It" gives commands such as "Two giant steps," or "Three baby steps backwards." The players do what they are told, but, in addition, they try to creep up without being caught by "It." If "It" catches someone moving, he orders that person back to the starting line. As long as "It" does not object, the "cheaters" get away with it. The first person to reach the finishing line is the new "It."

Following commands with a partner

Back-to-Back[13]

The players are in pairs. "It" can name only body parts, and each pair must touch each other on that part. Examples of commands are "back to back," and "foot to foot." When "It" says, "Change," everybody including "It" must find a new partner. The player left without a partner becomes the new "It."

---

[13] Chapter 6 is a detailed account of this game.

The cognitive value of games involving verbal commands

All the foregoing games of following commands, particularly tricky ones, are good for children to listen attentively to verbal instructions. If they make a mistake, they get a clear and immediate reaction from their peers. These games are also good for the child who has to think up one command after another. The advantages of such games for language development are obvious.

In games such as Simon Says, I Say Stoop, and Ducks Fly, talking fast is one way to get the opponents to do the wrong thing. To talk fast, children have to think fast. Another way is to catch the opponents off guard by consistently beginning the command with "Simon says" and then omitting it unexpectedly—with the same voice and dead-pan expression as before. Tricking opponents thus requires decentering.

Giant Steps also encourages decentering. For example, "It" may pretend to be looking at someone else while using peripheral vision to catch another person. This game can be good or bad for certain children because "It's" authority plays a large role. Some children refuse to go back to the starting line, insisting that they did not move illegally. What constitutes a "baby step" can also be the subject of an argument. For children who can cooperate in an argument, this game is excellent. For others, however, it may be a game to avoid.

As can be seen in Chapter 6, Back-to-Back can also be an occasion for arguments and cooperation, as young children want to be "It" and sometimes refuse to accept a partner. (The same phenomenon of children insisting on being "It" can also be observed in Poison Seat, p. 43.) This game is also good for figuring out different ways of following the same command. For example, the command "foot to foot" is hard when the players are facing each other and lose balance. Some children come up with the idea of standing back to back, locking arms, and keeping their toes on the floor as they touch each other with the bottoms of their feet. Photograph 3.12 illustrates knees to knees.

3.12.
Knees to Knees. In trying to do "knees to knees," some partners thought of the desirability of getting into a sitting position.

Chapter 3

Before going on to the next category, card games, which differs from the preceding six, I would like to say that there are many other games which do not fit neatly into the previous classification, such as Hopscotch and Kitty Wants a Corner. These are described here, with only one version of Hopscotch.

Hopscotch

Each child finds a stone as his "potsie," and the hopscotch diagram is drawn on the ground (see Figure 3.6). The first player throws his "potsie" into space No. 1, jumps with the right foot into 8, with the left into 2, with the right into 7, and so on until he arrives at "Home," never putting both feet on the ground at the same time. At Home, he puts both feet down. He then returns, left foot into 5, right foot into 4, and so on, until he arrives at 1. Here he retrieves his "potsie" while standing on one foot, and then jumps out. If the "potsie" lands on a line, or when a player steps on a line, he is out and must start his next turn as before. But when a player completes the full round, he continues by throwing his "potsie" into space number 2, completes a full round of hopping as before, jumps out, and then continues until he has thrown his "potsie" into every space from 1 through 8, except Home, hopping the full circuit each time. If he completes all rounds without fault, he closes his eyes and throws the "potsie" aiming for Home. If it lands inside without touching a line, he goes through the diagram once more, eyes closed, first stepping into 1 and 8 with both feet at the same time, next into 2 and 7, all the way to Home and back again. If he completes this round without stepping on any lines, picking up his "potsie" on Home and finally jumping out, he has won the game.

Kitty Wants a Corner [14]

Four players occupy the four corners of a square marked, for example, with four pads. "It" (a fifth player) tries to get a vacant corner as the four other players exchange places.

Part of Hopscotch is aiming, and part of Kitty Wants a Corner is running. But we do not include Hopscotch among aiming games because it is much more than that. Kitty Wants a Corner likewise does not fit neatly into any one of the foregoing six categories. Many other games are left out of this chapter because our purpose is not to be exhaustive but, rather, to communicate a way of thinking about games.

Hopscotch encourages children's development in many ways:

1. It is a parallel-role game, which encourages comparisons.
2. The players do not all play at the same time. Comparisons are over time and may, therefore, encourage record keeping if different children have different memories of the facts that took place.
3. Aiming an object as well as oneself is involved, and both involve figuring out the right amount of force.
4. The rules are complicated, and children structure their actions in the following ways:
   a. They establish an unusual series within a series. The "potsie" goes numerically from 1 to 8. Within this sequence is the spatial sequence that corresponds to the numbers 8, 2, 7, 3, 6, etc.
   b. They alternate left and right feet except at Home (a dichotomy between *Home* and *every other space*).

[14]Chapter 9 is a detailed account of this game.

Figure 3.6. *Hopscotch.*

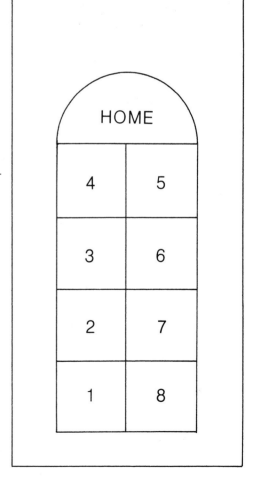

c. They apply rules that specify successful and unsuccessful rounds (another dichotomy).

d. When they have to throw the "potsie" or hop with their eyes closed, they have to mentally structure space with exactly the same dimensions.

This version of Hopscotch can be a good game for older children who can handle complicated rules involving a series within a series, categorization, and spatial reasoning.

The educational value of Kitty Wants a Corner is discussed in detail in Chapter 9.

Card Games

Many card games exist on the market, some of which claim to be "educational." Teachers often say that it is hard to determine their educational value, and they wonder about the difference between what children can learn with these "special" cards and with ordinary playing cards. This section focuses on simple games young children can play with ordinary playing cards. To show the similarities and differences between these games and those that can be played only with "special" cards, the discussion will also indicate how regular playing cards can be used to play the same games.[15]

The following classification is based on what children do:
1. recognizing certain cards
2. making sets of two, three, or four that are alike or identical
3. arranging cards in order
4. judging which card has "more" (or "the most")
5. matching two cards either by number or by suit
6. making "runs" of three or more and/or sets of three- or four-of-a-kind
7. addition and set partitioning

Again, we do not try to be exhaustive, as our purpose is to communicate a way of thinking about card games so that teachers will become able to generalize from this kind of analysis to other games that are not included in this section.

All the games in the first two categories and the fifth (recognizing certain cards; making sets of two, three, or four that are alike; and matching two cards either by number or by suit) can be played with regular playing cards as well as with picture cards. The other five categories require cards that have numbers. The relationship between games that can be played with regular playing cards and those that can be played with unnumbered picture cards is a part-whole relationship. All the games discussed here can be played with playing cards, but only some of them can be played with unnumbered picture cards. As long as children only have to make a dichotomy or sets of two, three, or four cards that are alike, the difference between cards does not have to be ordinal. The cards need to lend themselves only to classification. For War, in contrast, the cards have to lend themselves to seriation. (Classification entails *putting together* things that are alike and only *separating* those

[15]Some people object to regular playing cards on moral and/or religious grounds. This section is written to enable teachers to use only picture cards if they wish. Flinch cards may be an acceptable substitute.

that are different. Seriation, however, entails the *ordering* of differences. For example, five is not just *different* from three and four. It is *more* than four, and four is in turn *more* than three.)

The following discussion proceeds generally from the easiest to more difficult games.

Recognizing certain cards

Picture Cards (Court Cards)[16]

The dealer deals all 52 cards. Each player keeps his cards face down in a pile in front of himself. The player to the dealer's left starts the game by placing the top card of his pile in the middle of the table, face up. The other players take turns doing the same thing, placing each card on top of the preceding one. They keep doing this until a picture card appears (a jack, queen, or king). When this happens, the person who put down the picture card takes all the face-up pile and keeps it in a separate pile. Play continues until the players run out of cards. The person who gets more cards than anybody else is the winner. (Adapted from Giannoni 1974, pp. 40-41)

Slap Jack

All 52 cards are dealt, and each player keeps his cards face down in a pile in front of himself. Everybody turns his top card over at the same time, and as soon as he sees a jack, he slaps it. The first child to slap the jack takes all the face-up cards and keeps them in a separate pile. Play continues until the children run out of cards. The person who gets more cards than anybody else is the winner.

The cognitive value of card games involving the recognition of certain cards

Picture Cards is a simple game requiring little more than the recognition of pictures of people (as opposed to a number of hearts, spades, clubs, or diamonds). For very young children who have never played with regular cards before, this is an excellent way to begin, especially when they want to imitate adults' card playing but cannot handle more difficult games. Interest in the game is short-lived because it is so easy.

Slap Jack is a similar game, but it offers the challenge of requiring speed. When many claim to have been the first to slap the jack, the argument can be settled by seeing whose hand is at the bottom. Young children sometimes confuse the king and jack, but this is an educationally useful difficulty. This difficulty constitutes another advantage of Slap Jack over Picture Cards, in which the king, queen, and jack are undifferentiated.

Both of these games can be played with unnumbered picture cards. For example, Picture Cards can be played with cards of animals, and animals that fly (birds, bats, and bees, for example) can be designated as the equivalent of jacks, queens, and kings. Such content can enrich the educational value of these simple games.

---

[16] Because young children do not know what *court* means, two teachers at Circle Children's Center, Nancy Fineberg and Kathleen Harper, changed the name of this game to Picture Cards.

Making sets of two, three, or four that are alike (or identical)

The preceding games require the consideration of only one card at a time. In Picture Cards, it is necessary only to judge whether or not a given card is a court card. In Slap Jack it is necessary only to judge whether or not a card is a jack.

We now come to games in which children have to put two or more cards into relationship. As Piaget (Piaget, Grize, Szeminska, and Bang 1968) pointed out, complex logical relationships are built with those the child created earlier between two elements. It is not surprising that card games involving making pairs are among the easiest for young children. One type of such games, Concentration, involves *remembering* where the other card is. The second type includes Snap, Dominoes, and Old Maid, which involve *finding* two that are the same.[17]   The third type, which includes Go Fish and Making Families, involves *asking* for a card to make a pair.

Making pairs by remembering where the other card is

Concentration

The teacher selects a small number of pairs of cards that are easily distinguishable (such as aces, kings, queens, 5's, and 10's, each pair being of the same color). He arranges them face down in neat rows. The players take turns in turning up two cards, one at a time, trying to make pairs. When a player succeeds in making the second card match the first one, he can keep the pair and continue playing. When he fails, he must turn the two cards over so that they are face down again, and the turn passes to the person on his left. The winner is the person who makes more pairs than anybody else.

With young children, Concentration works best when pictures are used, especially when these pictures are glued on cardboard or plaques. The children at Circle Children's Center particularly like to play this game with pictures of fish and sea animals.

Making pairs by finding cards that are the same

Snap

The dealer deals all 52 cards. Without looking at them, each player takes his cards and holds them face down in one hand. Simultaneously, all the players take the top card of their respective pile and place it face up on the table. Anyone who finds two identical cards says, "Snap!" The first one who said it wins all the cards that are turned up and places them at the bottom of his pile. If a player says "Snap" by mistake (when all the cards are different), he must pay a penalty by discarding one of the cards he won. Play continues until one person wins all the cards (or until all the cards that were dealt are used up). (Adapted from Giannoni 1974, pp. 12-13)

---

[17]Dominoes is not a card game. Its inclusion here will be explained shortly. Domino cards can also be used.

Snap, as well as many other games described here, is easiest when only two people play. (Concentration, in contrast, can be played with many players from the very beginning, since it does not require much coordination of actions among players.)

Snap is an easy game to play. Children who are young enough to enjoy such an easy game tend to prefer picture cards to regular playing cards.

The next game, Dominoes, is similar to a card game. Young children have difficulty holding a large number of cards spread out in a way that permits them to look at all of them. Dominoes have the advantage of staying up by themselves in full view of only one person without having to be held in his hands.

Dominoes

The dominoes are all turned face down, and when they are well mixed, each player draws five. The remainder stay face down as the "bone yard." The first player places any domino of his choice face up in the middle of the table. The player on his left must match one of the numbers with one of his. If the first player puts down a 6-4 piece, the second player can play any domino that has either a 6 or 4. Each subsequent player must make a match with either end of the line. (That is, he must find a match for either 6 or 3 if the 6-4 piece is next to a 4-3 piece.) When a player does not have a match, he must draw from the bone yard until he draws something that matches. The winner is the first one to get rid of all his dominoes.

To facilitate matching, some manufacturers use a different color for each number. Dominoes can also be played with picture cards that are available commercially. Each card has two pictures, and the child finds a match, for example, for either a car or a flower.

When children grow "ears" out of sides, the rules can be modified to allow this if all the players agree.

Old Maid (Odd Card) [18]

The dealer takes all but one queen out of the deck before dealing all the cards. Each player looks through his cards and discards, face up, any pair he can make. The player on the dealer's left then starts by offering all his cards to the person on his left to draw one of them at random, without looking at them. If the person who drew the card can make a pair, he puts it down for everybody to see. If he is unable, he simply keeps this card, and lets the player on his left draw one. Play continues around the circle until one person is left holding the odd queen. (Adapted from Giannoni 1974, p. 33)

---

[18] Old Maid is a sexist term, but we use it here for ease of recognition. We prefer to call this game Odd Card, in which any card can be designated as the odd one. Another possibility is Joker, in which the joker is the odd card.

Making pairs or sets of four by asking someone for a card

Go Fish

Usually, 32 cards are used (4 each of 8 kinds, well mixed). If there are two players, each receives seven cards. If there are three or four players, each receives five cards. The rest are spread out on the table, face up, and are called the "fish pond." Each player first makes all the pairs he can find in his own hand and puts them down in front of himself, face up. (If he has three that are the same, he can put down only a pair, and must keep the third card.) The dealer then begins the game by asking someone for a card to make a pair. For example, if Mary thinks John has a 5, she may say, "John, do you have a 5?" If John has one, he must give it to her. If he does not, he says, "Go fish." Mary then takes a card from the fish pond and puts a pair down if she can. If she cannot, she simply keeps that card, and the turn passes to the player on Mary's left.[19] Each player can keep asking for a card as long as he gets one that enables him to make a pair. Play continues until all the cards have been put down in pairs. The person who makes the most pairs is the winner. (Adapted from Go Fish, Ed-U-Cards 1951)[20]

In another version of Go Fish, the players try to make sets of four instead of pairs. Another difference of this harder version is that the cards left over after the distribution are not scattered in the middle, face up. The remaining cards are stacked, face down, so that players who go "fishing" have to take the one on top of the stack.

Making Families is exactly the same as the version of Go Fish in which sets of four are made, except that all the cards are dealt, and there is no stack from which to draw cards.

Making Families[21]

All 52 cards are dealt. The first player begins by asking someone for a card, in an attempt to make a set of four of a kind. If the person asked has the card, he has to give it. As long as the first player gets cards he asked for, he can continue asking for more. If he fails to receive the card he requested, the turn passes to the person who said, "I don't have any." Play continues until all the cards have been put down in groups of four. The person who makes more families than anybody else is the winner.

Making Families has many advantages over Go Fish because Making Families does not involve any stack from which to draw cards. If the players know that all the cards are in people's hands, it is easier to structure and deduce information. For example, if a player has two flowers and is looking

---

[19] This is an adaptation of the usual way of playing Go Fish. In the standard version, the turn passes to the person who did not have the card requested. For young children, however, this rule seems more confusing than simply taking turns by going around the circle.

[20] The cards called Go Fish put out by Ed-U-Cards are particularly good for very young children because they consist of four each of eight different solid colors. These cards have the following advantage for very young children: Because very young children can usually not distinguish numbers, picture cards are better for them than playing cards. Pictures, however, have the disadvantage of having to be seen almost in their entirety to be recognized, and it is impossible to hold many cards without hiding most of them. Cards consisting of solid colors have the advantage of being distinguishable when they are held like a fan, with only the edges being visible.

[21] Chapter 10 is a detailed account of this game.

for two more, he does not have to wonder whether or not Suzy might have picked one up from the pile since the last time she said she did not have any. When he knows for sure that the other two flowers must be in the hand of one or two other players, he can find out where they are by asking questions systematically and/or making inferences. For instance, if Mary asks John for a flower and John gives it to her, he can infer that Mary now probably has the two flowers. The reader who has read *The Early Growth of Logic in the Child* (Inhelder and Piaget 1959) will understand why young children are not able to make such inferences.

Making sets of three that are alike (or identical)

Animal Rummy

The name of this game comes from the source referred to below, and it can also be played with playing cards. The reader will recognize this game as a simplified version of Rummy (described shortly). Usually, 36 cards are used (for example, all the cards from ace through 9). Six cards are dealt to each player. The remaining deck is turned face down, with the top card beside it, face up, which starts the discard pile. The object of the game is to make two sets of three identical cards. The player on the left of the dealer begins by drawing a card from either the discard pile (which in this case has only one card in it) or from the top of the deck. He then tries to make a set, if possible, and then discards a card on the discard pile (face up). Play continues until one person wins by being the first one to lay down two sets of three identical cards. (Adapted from Animal Rummy, E. E. Fairchild Corp. undated)

The source of this game uses pictures of animals—four each of nine different kinds. As usual, this game can be played with cards made by the teacher or the children. Pictures of anything can be drawn or glued on blank cards, and the only constraint is that there be four of everything.

The cognitive value of the second category of card games

Making sets of two, three, or four that are the same requires perceptual discrimination. Concentration also requires memory and logic. At first, young children not only turn the cards over randomly but also have a tendency to begin their turn by turning over the card that everybody has just looked at! When they begin to look for a match, they do not remember where a certain card is. Soon, however, they begin to go straight to the two that are the same by remembering the location of two flowers, fire engines, etc. (Trying to remember these objects involves a classificatory scheme.) When they know that all the cards turned over before are different, they go straight to one that they have not looked at. By thus structuring the cards into the "known" and the "unknown," and remembering the location of each card that has been turned up, they soon become able to beat the teacher.

Snap is like Slap Jack and does not contribute much to children's development of logic. However, these are both easy games which are good for beginners. In these games, children learn to coordinate with others the action of turning cards over at the same time. They also learn to invent rules when, for example, two people say "Snap!" at the same time. The speed of perceptual discrimination required by Snap is also an advantage of this game.

Like any other game, the educational value of Dominoes depends on the child's developmental level. Many three-year-olds insist on counting all the dots on the entire surface of a domino, since they are unable to structure it into two parts. Some are able to see two numbers but cannot find an obvious matching piece among those they have. Some children proceed only in one direction, limiting their choice to one end of the line. For instance, when the dominoes have been added always to the right in the following way, young children often look only for a 3 and not a 2: 2-4, 4-1, 1-5, 5-3. As they are reminded by other players of the possibility of going backward to the left, they are encouraged to decenter and think about both ends. As they draw from the bone yard, they may see the disadvantage of getting more pieces, which goes hand in hand with the advantage of having more possibilities of making a match later. Dominoes can be excellent for young children, especially when they become able to think of various strategies.

In Old Maid, children learn to make pairs out of more cards than in any other game previously presented. When one observes the pairs that young children fail to find, one appreciates that this game requires the systematic comparison of each card with every other card in one's hand. While playing this game, young children can learn to establish these relationships systematically.

In Old Maid, children learn to coordinate different actions, spatial relationships, and temporal order. They learn that after B takes a card from A, the turn goes clockwise, and B has to offer his cards to C to let him draw one. Each player does one thing first and its complement next. The coordination of drawing a card and letting someone else draw one with the right-left relationship is not easy for young children.

There are many versions of cards on the market called "Old Maid." Some are sexist. Others are too "busy" and/or of exceedingly bad taste. We do not need to saturate children's world with Bach and Beethoven's photographs, but neither do we need to accentuate grotesque humor. Young children's liking to play Concentration with cards of various fish and sea animals alerted us to the possibility of making cards that have more educational content.

Go Fish, Making Families, and Animal Rummy are the first card games presented that provide opportunities for children to use rather sophisticated logic. All the other games work more by chance than by intelligent decisions. In Go Fish, the child has to *ask for* a card, which means that he has to decide what pair he should try to make. If a player has one card each of a whole variety including a red card, and he hears Mary asking John for a red card, he might decide to make a pair with the red card(s) Mary seems to have. Young children do not make this kind of inference from the available empirical facts. While playing this game, they may become able to produce information by deduction if they can decenter enough to figure out that if Mary asks for a red card, she must have one or more of the four red cards.

As stated before, Making Families is particularly good, since it encourages logical thinking. (This statement, however, does not imply that Making Families is always superior. The relative value of these games depends on what the child does in the game. Go Fish can be said to be better than Making Families if the child cannot make inferences anyway, and he particularly likes to go "fishing." Go Fish has the further advantage of requiring the child to hold fewer cards than Making Families.) Following is a list of the kinds of thinking that Making Families can encourage:

1. When a player picks up the cards he received and approaches the game

logically to proceed in an economic way, the first thing he does is to put together the cards that are the same and separate those that are different (the beginning of classification).

2. To decide which set(s) to try to make, each player must categorize the groups he has just made, that is, he must identify groups of two, three, and four cards. If he finds four of a kind, he puts that family down. If he finds three of a kind, this is usually a better set to try to complete than a set of one or two cards.

3. To decide *whom* he should ask for a card, the child can try to get information by inference. As it was pointed out earlier, if Mary asks for a flower, some children can infer that Mary must have at least one flower. If John replies that he does not have any, there is no point in asking him for a flower. If John gives one to Mary, some children can infer that Mary now probably has two or three of them. If a player has reason to believe that Mary has three flowers and David has one, it is clever to try to collect all of them.

As can be seen in Chapter 10, young children's way of playing Making Families is far below the theoretical level discussed here. We see once more that while certain games offer the possibility of logical thinking, the benefit that a child can derive from playing these games depends on his level of development. The better his logic is already elaborated, the more he can benefit from the possibilities that are available in games such as Making Families.

Like Go Fish and Making Families, Animal Rummy requires that the child decide what goal he wants to pursue. If he has two of one kind, he might do well to try to complete that set—unless someone else is trying to do exactly the same thing. In Animal Rummy, a player makes sets by deciding which card to *pick up* and which one to *discard*. To pick up a card, the child must choose between a known card (which is visible on top of the discard pile) and an unknown card (which is at the top of the deck, face down). It is not easy to decide which card to throw away, and this is a feature that does not exist in any of the other games presented so far.

Arranging cards in order

Making a matrix

Card Dominoes

Face cards are removed from the deck before the cards are dealt. The players who have aces (1's)[22] put them all down in a column to begin the matrix. The children then take turns putting down one card at a time, to make the matrix by continuing the series without skipping any number. For example, the first player can put down any 2. If he puts down a 2 of hearts, the second player can put down either a 3 of hearts or a 2 of any other suit. Anyone who does not have a card that can be played must pass. The first player to get rid of all his cards is the winner.

---

[22] Young children are sometimes bothered by the series that begins with an A rather than a 1. They are also often confused by the fact that an A has three symbols (such as hearts), a 2 has four of them, a 3 has five of them, and so on. Telling them to count only the big symbols may or may not stop them from continuing to count both the big and little symbols. When these problems come up, the teacher may want to use liquid paper to erase the small symbols under each numeral and/or change the A to a 1. I am working on the publication of cards shown in Figure 12.4 (p. 223) that do not have these disadvantages.

This game can be modified by beginning with all the 10's and making the matrix in decending order. It can also be modified by beginning with all the 5's (or any other number) and going both "up" (6, 7, 8 . . .) and "down" (4, 3, 2 . . .). A third modification is to let the first player choose any card he likes and build the matrix around this card.

Making a series that no one can see

I Doubt It

All 52 cards are dealt. The first player puts an ace out, face down, saying, "one." The next player then places a 2 on top of the first card, also face down, saying, "two." Any player who does not have the card he needs uses another card, trying to get away with this substitute. Anyone who thinks that a fake card has just been played says, "I doubt it." If the doubt is verified, the person caught must take all the cards on the table and add them to his hand. If the doubt is not verified, the accuser has to take all the cards. Play continues until a person wins by getting rid of all his cards. (Giannoni 1974, p. 48)

This game can be modified for very young children by using only the suits instead of the number series (for example, putting out a heart, heart, heart . . .). For this version, any picture card can be used, and the players can put down, for example, a dog, dog, dog. . . .

The cognitive value of the above two games

In the preceding two games, children learn numerals and their order in ways that are incomparably easier, more fun, and more meaningful than lessons. In Card Dominoes, they also learn to make matrices and to plan strategies. For example, if a player has the 2 of hearts and the 2, 3, and 4 of spades, the better of the two 2's to play is the 2 of spades.

In I Doubt It, children may make inferences. Based on the cards one has, the number that everybody else has, and the cards that are on the table at a given point, a child can say, "I doubt it," with a high probability of being right. All these inferences are generally too hard for preschoolers, and this is, therefore, a game we do not recommend for them. Besides, they often say "I don't have it," and cannot play a fake card. Moreover, their small hands have difficulty holding a large quantity of cards.

Judging which card has "more" (or "the most")

War

All 52 cards are dealt. Without looking at the cards, each player puts his pile face down in front of himself. Then the players simultaneously turn up the top card of their respective pile. The person who turned up the card which has "more" takes both cards (when only two are playing). If there is a tie, each player turns over the next card, and the person who turns up the larger number takes all four of them. [23] The winner is the person who collects all the cards. (Adapted from Giannoni 1974, pp. 18-19)

---

[23] This is a simplification of the usual rule of dealing with a tie. In the usual way, each player takes the top card of his pile and places it, face down, on the card that made the tie. Each player then turns over another card from his pile and places it on the one he just put on the first card. The one who turns up the bigger number takes all six of the cards.

The easiest way to play this game is with only two players.[24] As can be seen in Photograph 2.4 (p. 33), spectators are often mentally active while watching a game.

The cognitive value of War

War is a popular game in which children have opportunities to judge which number is "more" or "the most." This is an incomparably better way of learning about "more (or greater) than" and "less than" than with worksheets that are supposedly part of "modern" math. For young children, it is best to eliminate the jack, queen, and king, which often cause confusion.[25]

Matching two cards either by number or by suit

Crazy Eights

The dealer deals five cards to each player and stacks the remaining cards face down in a drawing pile. The top card is turned over and placed face up beside the pile. Each player tries to get rid of his cards by playing them in turn, one at a time. The player on the dealer's left begins, and each person puts face up on the upturned card a card that matches either by number or by suit. (For example, a 2 of hearts can be matched with either a 2 or a heart.) All 8's are "crazy" (or "wild") and may be played on any card. Whoever plays an 8 tells the next player on his left what suit to play next. If a player cannot match the card or play an 8, he must draw from the pile until he finds a card he can play. When the pile is used up, he passes. The first person to get rid of all his cards is the winner.

This game can also be played with picture cards. For example, if there are four cards each of ten different animals, and each of the four cards represents a suit (indicated by a red, blue, green, or yellow edge, for instance), children who cannot handle numbers can play the same game by matching either an animal or an edge. For very young children, it is best not to introduce the idea of a wild card, and simply draw from the pile when one does not have any card to play.

The cognitive value of Crazy Eights

Having to match cards by either of two criteria means that each time his turn comes, the child may go through all his cards with two criteria in mind at the same time, or first with one and then with the other. These processes are good for the development of the mobility of thought. Also, having five cards to get rid of as quickly as possible but collecting more from the pile makes children see the advantage and disadvantage of having more cards. The best use of 8's, including knowing which suit to designate for the next player, is a question of strategy. For example, if a particular suit has been played a

---

[24] When there are more than two players, young children tend to insist that there is a tie when, for example, two 3's and one 5 turn up. When this is their idea of a tie, they often break it in the following way: The two who had the 3's play the next cards to break the tie, and the child who had the 5 automatically becomes the loser!

[25] Young children do not have transitivity (the ability to deduce from $A > B$ and $B > C$ that $A > C$, or to deduce $A = C$ from $A = B$ and $B = C$). When they are told that the queen is "more than" the jack (and comes after it), and that the king is "more than" the queen (and comes after the queen), they often cannot tell whether the jack is "more than" or "less than" the king.

great many times, that suit is the one that is hard to obtain and, therefore, the one that should be requested. Crazy Eights encourages children to structure past events to anticipate probable future outcomes.

Making runs of three or more and/or sets of three or four of a kind

Rummy

This game is similar to Animal Rummy, which was described earlier. The differences are—

1. Each player receives ten cards if there are two players, and seven cards if there are three or four players.
2. Runs of three or more cards within the same suit can be made as well as sets of three or four of a kind.
3. Once a player has put down a set of cards, he or anybody else can add any card(s) to that set when his turn comes.
4. The winner is the person who uses up all his cards first, and he collects forfeits from the others in the form of points. Each player who did not win adds up the number of points he has left in his hand according to the following point system:
   jacks, queens, and kings: ten points each
   ace through ten: according to the number on the card
5. A player may keep all his sets in his hand until he can throw his last card in the discard pile and wins by putting his sets down all at once. If he wins in this way, he doubles his score.

The cognitive value of Rummy

This is a difficult game which is generally not appropriate before the second grade. The game requires many decisions, and chance plays a very small part in this game. Each player first has to decide what to try for—a run or three of a kind—and these decisions have to be modified according to what the other players seem to be trying to do. In picking up a card, as in Animal Rummy, each player has to decide between a known card on the discard pile and an unknown card in the deck. In discarding a card, he has to think both about the desirability of getting rid of a card and the likelihood of that card's being useful to the next player. Another big decision involves when to put a set down. If a player keeps his sets to put down all at once, he increases his chances of doubling his score, but he also increases the chances of someone else's winning first, in which case he will be left holding many points against himself.

The addition of points at the end of the game is educationally worthwhile. As stated before, it is much better for the child's development to do arithmetic in such a meaningful situation than in empty exercises done only to comply with the teacher's request.

Sevens

Twenty-four cards (ace through 6) are used (6 × 4 = 24). All the cards are stacked as a drawing pile except the top three cards, which are turned up and placed on the table in a row. The object of the game is to find two cards that make a total of seven (1 + 6, 2 + 5, or 3 + 4). When his turn comes, each player picks up two cards if possible and replaces them with two from the top of the drawing pile. If he cannot, he passes. Each time a player cannot pick up two cards that make a total of seven, the next player takes the top card of the drawing pile and tries to make seven with it. If he cannot, he starts a discard pile. As soon as a player can take two cards, the discard pile is put back in the drawing pile, at the bottom. The winner is the person who ends up with the most cards. (Adapted from Elevens, Giannoni 1974, p. 8)

This game can be modified to require any other total, such as 11. The number of cards turned up can also be varied. For Elevens, 12 cards arranged in three rows of four cards each works well. When 12 cards are turned up, it is easier to find possible combinations than when only three cards are turned up.

The cards that equal or exceed the total cannot be used. For example, the cards that exceed ten cannot be used in Elevens. Many first graders are unaware of this fact and play with the entire deck without suspecting that *something* is wrong.

Ed-U-Cards makes a game similar to Sevens called Piggy Bank that can be found in variety stores. Following is a description of this game.

Piggy Bank

The deck consists of the following 30 cards that have pictures of coins:

7 cards showing 1 penny
6 cards showing 2 pennies
6 cards showing 3 pennies
7 cards showing 4 pennies
2 cards showing 5 pennies
2 cards showing 1 nickel.

The players put money in the bank, but they can do this only by depositing five cents at a time. All the cards are dealt. Without looking at them, each player puts his cards face down in a stack in front of himself. When his turn comes, he turns up the top card of his pile. If it shows either five pennies or a nickel, he can put it in his "bank" (a dish). If it shows any other number, he must discard the card in the middle of the table, face up. The next player who turns up a card that does not show five pennies or a nickel looks among the discarded cards trying to find one that gives a total of five cents. (If, for example, he is holding a 3 and he finds a 2, he can pick up the 2 and deposit five cents in his bank.) The winner is the person who saves the most money. (Piggy Bank, Ed-U-Cards 1965)

Piggy Bank should be modified to include dimes and quarters to be more versatile. The rules should also be changed so that the players can use any number of cards to make a total. [Number is logico-mathematical knowledge. Nickels and dimes, in contrast, belong to social (arbitrary) knowledge. It is by convention that a coin can stand for five cents while another smaller coin can stand for ten cents.]

The cognitive value of Sevens

As stated at the end of Chapter 2, card games such as Sevens are much more effective than worksheets in motivating children to master set partitioning, if they are already at a certain level of cognitive development.

Board Games

Board games, too, can be classified according to what players do. Among those that young children like, we found the following four types: those (such as Chutes and Ladders) in which all the children move their markers along a given path, those (such as Bingo) in which they try to fill spaces in certain ways, those (such as Hi-Ho! Cherry-O) in which they try to collect many pieces, and those (such as Checkers) in which they move many pieces along paths that depend on their strategies. Each one of these types is discussed in the paragraphs that follow.

Moving one (or more) marker(s) along a given path

In most of these games, the player makes his marker(s) advance the number of steps indicated by dice or a spinner. Candy Land is an exception by using cards that show one or two squares.

Candy Land

The board is a winding path divided into 136 squares mostly of five different colors. Some squares have pictures of an ice cream cone, candy canes, candy hearts, lollipops, etc. Each player chooses one of the four markers and places it at the beginning of the path. There is a stack of small cards most of which show either one or two squares of one of the five colors. Some cards show an ice cream cone, candy canes, candy hearts, etc. Each player begins his turn by turning the top card of the stack over. If it shows two blue squares, for example, he advances his marker to the second blue square from where he is. If it shows an ice cream cone, he either advances or goes back to the corresponding square. The player who gets his marker to the goal first is the winner. (Milton Bradley 1978)

Skipping Stones is a similar but boring game partly because it offers little variation in action and partly because it evokes no symbolic content. Candy Land evokes the story of the Gingerbread Boy, etc., but Skipping Stones is dry and without appeal. It is presented here (a) to point out some factors that may explain why games like Candy Land are appealing and (b) to clarify the difference between numbers used as categories and those used to indicate quantities. The 5 indicated by a die in Skipping Stones only means "Go to the first 5" in the same way that a red square in Candy Land means "Go to the first red square." In Skipping Stones, therefore, children do not have the possibility of counting the number of steps to take.

Figure 3.7. *Skipping Stones board.*

Skipping Stones

The board consists of 36 stones drawn in a linear arrangement around a square as shown in Figure 3.7. The first stone is numbered 1 and is both the Start and Finish stone. On the other 35 stones are numerals up to 5 in a random order. The players take turns throwing a die, moving their marker to the next stone having the corresponding number. For example, if the first player throws a 4, he puts his marker on the first stone in the sequence having that number. If a player throws a 6, he must go back to the stone with the same number as the number he is on. A player must throw a 1 to finish. The winner is the first player to move his marker to Finish. (56 Games 1975)

We now come to games involving dice or a spinner that indicate how many steps each player's marker(s) will take. In the first three games, all the players move in the same direction. In the fourth game, Forward and Backward, there are only two players, and they move in opposite directions on the same path. In the fifth game, Tug O' War, there is only one piece for the two players, and the two try to move this piece on a common path from the middle to their respective goals at opposite ends.

Chutes and Ladders

The board consists of 100 squares numbered from 1 to 100 as shown in Figure 3.8. As can be seen in this figure, the numbers begin with 1 in the lower left corner and go from 10 to 11 in the lower right corner. To move one's marker through the sequence, a player must move to the right on one row, to the left on the next, to the right on the third row, etc., as indicated by the arrow at the end of each row. The object of the game is to be the first to move one's marker to 100. The players take turns spinning a spinner that has numbers from 1 to 6 and move their markers the designated number of spaces. The characteristic of this game is pictures of ten chutes and nine ladders scattered over the board. If a player lands on a square at the top of a chute, he has to move the piece down to the bottom of the chute, thus going back to a square previously passed. If he lands on a square at the bottom of a ladder, he can move his piece up to the square at the top of the ladder, skipping ahead many squares. As in a race, the first marker to reach the goal wins the game. (Milton Bradley 1956)

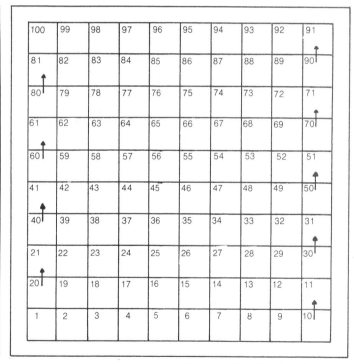

Figure 3.8. *Chutes and Ladders board.*

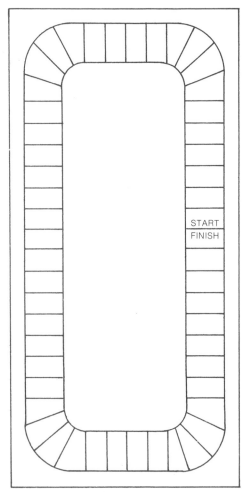

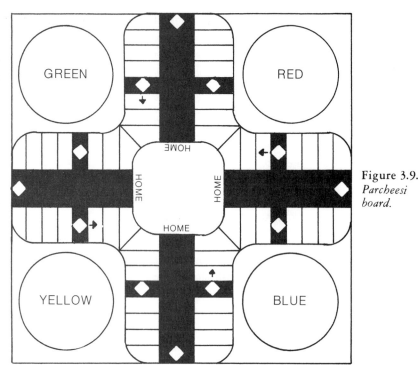

Figure 3.9. *Parcheesi board.*

Figure 3.10. *Track Meet board.*

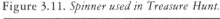

Figure 3.11. *Spinner used in Treasure Hunt.*

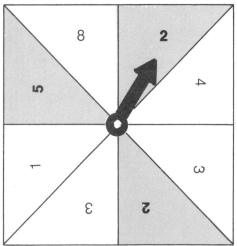

Parcheesi (Pachisi)

The Parcheesi board is shown in Figure 3.9. Each player selects one of the four colors (green, red, blue, and yellow) and begins by placing four pieces of that color in the corresponding circle. The object of the game is to move all four of one's markers around the board to Home. The players roll the dice in turn and move their markers as shown on the dice. If a player overtakes an opponent's piece, that piece is sent back to its starting point. If two markers land on the same space, they create a blockade which no one can pass. There are 12 safety spaces (indicated by diamonds) where a marker is safe from being sent back. (56 Games 1975)

Track Meet

The board shown in Figure 3.10 represents an oval track field divided into 52 segments, with a starting line which is also the finish line. Two markers and two dice are used (one for each player). Each player throws his die, and the one with the higher number moves. If one player throws a 5 and the other a 3, for example, the one with the 5 moves five spaces, and the other player remains at the starting line.[26] The winner is the one to get his marker across the finish line first. (56 Games 1975)

There are many other variations of the basic idea of advancing in parallel toward a goal as designated by a die or spinner. One variation is Treasure Hunt (Judy Company 1973) in which the piece must go backward if the spinner lands in a shaded area (see Figure 3.11). Cat and Mouse (Parker

[26] This game can be made harder by establishing the rule that the person who rolled the bigger number moves by the number of steps by which he exceeded the smaller number. In this situation, the player who rolled the 5 would take two steps.

Chapter 3

Brothers 1964), another variation, uses a board divided into 49 squares in a 7×7 arrangement. In each one of these squares (except the "traps") is the picture of a mouse drawn to indicate the direction in which the piece must move on the next turn (to the left, right, up, or down). Other variations are detours, signs indicating that the player loses one or more turns, and traps which eliminate a marker permanently. By the time they are in first grade, children enjoy making their own board games and playing with them.

Some board games are for only two players, who start at opposite ends of a path and move in opposite directions. The starting line of one player is the finish line of the other. The commercially made games of this type are easy to imagine and will not be cited here. The one made by a teacher called Forward and Backward is shown in Figure 3.12.[27]

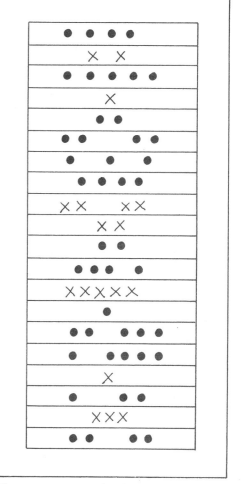

Forward and Backward

Four black and four white markers are used. Each player takes his four markers and tries to be the first to move all of them to the opposite end. If he lands on a space with dots, he moves his piece forward when his next turn comes. If he lands on a space with X's, he has to move the piece backward by that many steps. If a space is occupied, he skips it, thereby going farther either forward or backward.

The games presented so far are all parallel-role games. Tug O' War, which is described here, is a complementary-role game.

Tug O' War

The board is a long rectangle on which a rope is drawn as shown in Figure 3.13 and Photograph 3.13. In the middle is a white circle. On one side of the white circle are six red circles, and on the other side are six blue circles. Two players sit at each end of the rope. A marker is placed in the white circle to begin the game. The players take turns throwing a die and moving the marker toward their end of the rope. For example, if the player on the red end throws a 4, he moves the marker to the fourth red circle. If the player on the blue end then throws a 3, he moves the marker back three notches to the first red circle. The winner is the first player to move the marker to his end of the rope. (56 Games 1975)

Figure 3.12. *Forward and Backward.*

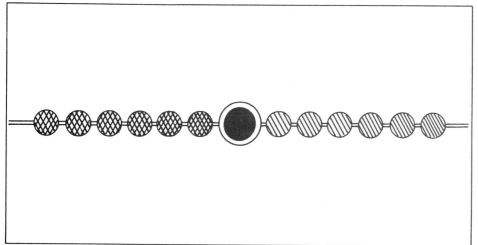

Figure 3.13. *Tug O' War board.*

[27] Credit goes to Isabelle Saucy, formerly a teacher in the Geneva Public Schools and now an Assistant at the University of Geneva.

Types of Group Games

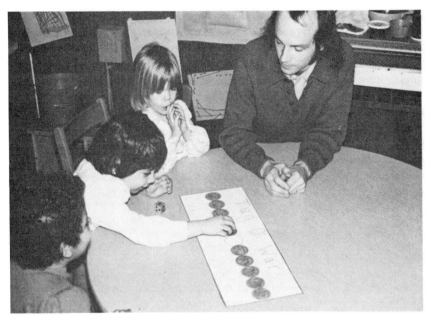

3.13. *Tug O' War.*

The cognitive value of the preceding board games

Like card games, board games generally depend partly on chance and partly on strategy. To the extent that the outcome of a game depends on strategy, the game serves as an incentive for children to think of alternatives and anticipate what the opponent might do. To the extent that a game depends on chance alone, it serves only as an opportunity to do what chance dictates.

Candy Land, Chutes and Ladders, Track Meet, and Tug O' War depend almost entirely on chance alone. This is why these games are appropriate for very young children. Candy Land is the easiest of these games because children do not even have to count the number of dots on a die.[28] Numbers are not involved in Candy Land because the cards only have one or two squares, and discrimination between one and two is possible *perceptually*. Small, perceptual numbers, according to Piaget, are different in nature from number in a logico-mathematical sense. The latter cannot be judged by perception.

Chutes and Ladders, Track Meet, and Tug O' War are good for learning how to count. What makes Chutes and Ladders particularly difficult is the zigzag involved in going through the number series. It is by reading the numerals and/or extending the direction shown by two or more arrows that the child can know if he should go to the left or to the right. This game is good for learning numerals up to 100 and for mentally transforming a matrix of 100 squares into a path.

Track Meet, like the card game War, provides an opportunity to compare two numbers. Modifying this game makes it more challenging. By using cards

Figure 3.14. *Going Shopping.*

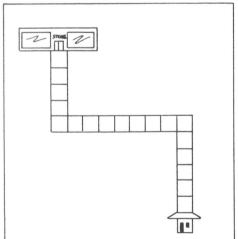

[28] When young children have difficulty knowing which way is forward in Candy Land, the teacher may want to consider making an even simpler, less "busy" game such as Going Shopping, which is shown in Figure 3.14. In this game, the children can easily see the house and store connected with a relatively straight and short road. In Candy Land, it is only by putting the local area into relationship with the entire winding road that the child can know which way is forward.

to draw, or dice that have six numbers starting with 5 or 9, the teacher can present numbers that are bigger than 6. Increasing the numbers may necessitate increasing the number of spaces in the track field.

While playing Tug O'War, children can see that the gain of one player is the loss of the other, and that when the first player's gain is small, the loss of the other is also small.

Parcheesi and Forward and Backward are the only board games presented so far that provide some room for minimal strategy. (These games are too difficult for very young children, and Parcheesi has particularly complicated rules.) In both of these games, each player has four markers. When a player can decide which one of four pieces to move, he has more alternatives than when he has only one piece to move. For example, in Parcheesi, a player may decide to move a piece that will send an opponent back to the starting line, or another piece that will land it in a safety area (when there is an opponent's piece trailing nearby).[29]

In Forward and Backward, the player can choose markers to maximize the possibility of skipping forward and minimize the possibility of landing in a space that has X's. This game also offers the possibility of figuring out how to make the opponent go backward. A player sometimes has to move from one space to another that has X's.

Putting markers on a surface

In this group of board games, the players place a number of markers on the board and leave them there rather than moving them. The object of some of these games (such as Lotto) is to cover up the surface. In others (such as Bingo), it is to produce a certain pattern. Each of these types is discussed in the paragraphs that follow.

Trying to cover a surface

In some Lotto games, children find identical pictures or numbers. In others they find pictures of things that "go together," such as a mailbox and letter carrier.

Lotto

The boards of Lotto games are divided into six, eight, or more squares, and all or some of the squares have different pictures (or numbers). Each player's board is different. A caller has a stack of small cards that are turned face down. As he turns them up one at a time, the player who has the picture that matches or "goes with" the one turned up claims it. (Chips are sometimes placed on each number when numbers are called.) The first to fill his card is the winner.

Snake Dice, which is described here, is similar to Lotto in that the object of the game is to cover a surface.

---

[29] When young children are given four pieces to play, they often deal with only one at a time. They take the first piece all the way to the finish line, and then deal with the second piece, and so on. We can see that the ability to take more than one piece at a time into consideration, thereby thinking of alternatives, is a reflection of ability to put objects into many relationships.

The game board is a sheet of paper on which the numerals from 2 to 12 are written, with a blank space for 7. Each player has his own sheet of paper. The players take turns rolling two dice and crossing out the number indicated by the sum of the two numbers which turned up. If he rolls a 7, he loses his turn and draws a wavy line on his paper (a snake). A player with seven snakes is out of the game. The winner is the one who has crossed out all of his numbers without being put out of the game. (56 Games 1975)

This game looks good on paper, especially for learning the different combinations that make certain totals. But children do not seem to like this game probably because the same number turns up too many times. When we see children's reaction to getting a total of six over and over, for example, we can appreciate Lotto, in which 6 turns up only once. Climb the Ladder, which is described below, is similar to Snake Dice but worse, because a player can cross out only the 2 first, then only the 3 next, etc., in sequence. After trying unsuccessfully a few times, young children seem to think that the desired number will never turn up. (Although the marker *moves* in Climb the Ladder, the principle of the game is the same as in Lotto, where the object of the game is to cover a surface.)

Climb the Ladder

The board is a ladder with 12 rungs. The first rung is labeled Start, and the remaining rungs are labeled with numerals 2 through 12. Each player places his marker on the first rung. Using one die to begin, the players in turn throw it. They must throw a 2 to move to the next rung, a 3 to move to the third rung, and so on until they reach the sixth rung. Then two dice are used, and a player must throw a total of 7 to move, etc. The winner is the first player to reach the top of the ladder. (56 Games 1975)

Trying to make a certain pattern

Bingo

Bingo boards are divided into 25 squares in a 5 × 5 arrangement. Each square contains a number, and the numbers are randomly arranged. Each player's card has a different set and arrangement of numbers. The word BINGO is spelled out across the top of each card, so that each letter heads a column of numbers. Each number is identified with its column heading, so that, for example, a 9 appearing in the N column is called N-9. On bits of cardboard, plastic, or wood is each letter-number combination. These are placed in a container and mixed. A caller takes these out one at a time, calls out the letter and number, and places the piece on a long master sheet on which all the numbers are listed under the five letter headings. When a letter-number combination is called and a player finds it on his card, he places a chip on that square. The winner is the first player to fill a row, a column, or diagonal. (Four corners is also a win in some games.) When a player wins, he calls out "Bingo!" His win is then verified by checking his numbers against the master sheet.

In Tic-Tac-Toe, the child usually draws on the board instead of placing markers. Since the child can place red or black checkers on the board just as well as he can draw them, this difference is of no consequence.

Tic-Tac-Toe

The Tic-Tac-Toe board is made by drawing two vertical lines and crossing them with two horizontal lines to create a 3×3 matrix. One player chooses to mark X's and the other, O's. In turn, each draws his mark in a space as shown in Figure 3.15. (Here, the first player made an X, the second player an O, and the first player, a second X. The second player now has to decide where to draw an O.) The object of the game is to get three marks in a line, vertically, horizontally, or diagonally.

Dot-to-Dot

The board is a square or rectangle in which parallel rows and columns of dots are printed as shown in Figure 3.16. The object of the game is to form squares by drawing a line from one dot to another. The players take turns connecting two dots. A player drawing the last line of the square puts his initial in it. The winner is the one who completed more squares than anybody else.

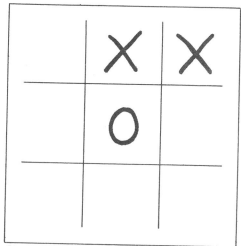

Figure 3.15. *Tic-Tac-Toe.*

The cognitive value of the preceding board games

Lotto and Bingo depend almost entirely on chance and are, therefore, appropriate for young children for whom simple tasks without strategy are challenging enough. These simple tasks include perceptual discrimination, establishing certain relationships in some cases (such as the relationship between a mailbox and letter carrier), and reading numerals and matrices. In addition, when a Lotto game consists of numbers up to 99 and each card is divided into columns, the first one being for "ones," the second for "tens," the third for "twenties," etc., the game requires the structuring of spatial, logico-arithmetical, and conventional relationships. (Number is a logico-arithmetical structure and not a conventional system. The decimal system and its representation in writing, in contrast, are examples of conventional systems.) The reading of a matrix in Bingo also requires the organization of what is observed. For example, to find N-9, the child is better off knowing that all he has to do is find a certain column and examine it.

Number Lottos are also excellent when the teacher substitutes addition and subtraction problems for numbers. When cards showing problems such as 7 + 8 and 15 − 7 are read, children compare their answers as they examine their cards. The possibility of challenging and verifying each other's answer is in itself high in educational value.[30]

Tic-Tac-Toe and Dot-to-Dot are complementary-role games which depend on strategies rather than chance. The attractiveness of Tic-Tac-Toe is attested by the fact that in schools that believe only in "serious lessons," children can be found playing this game on the chalkboard between lessons. By playing this game several times with the same five-year-old, the teacher can see the decentering that Tic-Tac-Toe encourages. Before they become able to aim at getting three marks in a diagonal line, young children can think only of vertical and horizontal lines.

Dot-to-Dot is good not only for decentering but also for spatial reasoning and perceptual-motor coordination. This game is much more fun than exer-

Figure 3.16. *Sheet used in Dot-to-Dot.*

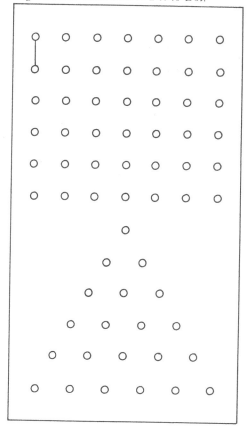

[30] Be careful with many commercial "teachy" games such as Color and Shape Lotto, Alphabet Lotto, and Initial Consonant Lotto. While the use of some games can be excellent, their overuse runs the risk of sugarcoating questionable exercises. The importance of colors and shapes seems greatly exaggerated in early childhood education.

cises such as those that can be found in Frostig's worksheets (Frostig 1966, a modified version of which is shown in Figure 3.17). Dot-to-Dot can be modified so that the object of the game is to make triangles (see Figure 3.16, p. 79).

Making collections of objects

Many of the first category of board games, moving a marker along a path, involve counting but in ways that differ from the present category. When the child moves a marker, he counts the units made up by dividing a length into many parts. This counting is not as good for the development of numerical notions as the making of collections with objects. In Hi-Ho! Cherry-O, children count objects. Unlike the counting of steps, the counting of objects permits the making of groups of objects.

Hi-Ho! Cherry-O

The box contains 40 plastic cherries, 4 plastic pails, and the board shown in Photograph 3.14. Up to four people can play this game. They each choose one of the pails and put ten cherries on their respective trees. They then take turns turning the spinner and pick as many cherries as indicated by it. The winner is the first one to put all ten of his cherries in his pail. (Western Publishing Co. 1975)[31]

---

[31] This game has the following shortcomings: The cherries keep falling off the tree, and children can hang more than one cherry from each of the ten holes in the tree. In addition, if children sit on the floor to play this game, they often cannot see the cherries on their own trees.

Figure 3.17. *Modified version of Frostig's worksheet (Frostig 1966).*

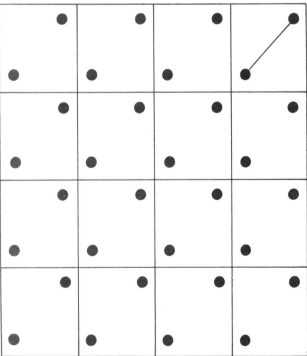

3.14. *Hi-Ho! Cherry-O.*

Chapter 3

The spinner for this game is divided into seven sections, four of which show one, two, three, and four cherries respectively. The other three pictures give ambiguous messages. One of them is the picture of 22 cherries spilled out of a pail, indicated by the arrow in the photograph. According to the instructions, this picture means that the player must put all his cherries back on his tree. The other two sections have pictures of animals—a dog and a bird. The instructions state that both of these pictures mean that the player has to put two cherries back on the tree.

The last three pictures discussed here are examples of arbitrary representation which must not be imposed on children. There is no reason why a dog (or a bird) should mean putting two cherries back on the tree. Telling children that this is what they must do is an imposition of one more arbitrary rule that makes no sense to them. The spilled pail, too, is an example of the author's imposition of *his* representation. To the author of the game, the spilled pail may mean "the cherries are lost, and this is like putting them back on the tree." To three- and four-year-olds, however, the picture of the spilled pail often means "a lot." "A lot" to some means four, while to others it means all ten. The nature of symbolization, according to Piaget, is such that whatever the child sees in the picture *is* what that picture means *to him*. In playing Hi-Ho! Cherry-O, adults must ask each group what they think these pictures mean, so that the children can come to an agreement, or a convention of their own. To the children we have worked with, the dog often means "take four" because it has four legs, and the bird means "take two" because it has two legs.[32]

Hi-Ho! Cherry-O encourages counting only up to four. The following game illustrated in Photograph 3.15 is appreciated by children who have outgrown Hi-Ho! Cherry-O.

All Gone

Bits of styrofoam packing, vegetable trays, and a die are used. Each child puts 20 pieces in his tray, and players take turns throwing the die and removing the corresponding number of pieces from their trays. The player who empties his tray first says "all gone," and is the winner.

---

[32]Sastre and Moreno (1977) found four levels in children's graphic representation of discrete quantities in the following experiment with pairs of children: They asked one of the children to step out of the room and wait until called. They then took out up to nine pieces of candy and gave the child a pencil and piece of paper, saying in effect, "I want you to use these, and when you have put something on the paper, I am going to hide the candy and ask the other child to come in. If he looks at your piece of paper and takes out the same number of pieces of candy as I will have hidden. both of you can have the candy."

At Level I, children made drawings of anything they pleased that had nothing to do with number or candy. For example, they drew mountains and a house with a road and a few trees (not the same number of trees as pieces of candy). At Level II, they drew objects that had the corresponding number of parts, such as a hand to show five (fingers) and an octopus to show eight (legs). Later at Level II, they drew the correct number of pieces of candy, or as many circles or lines as there were pieces of candy. At Level III, they wrote "1 2 3 4 5 6" to represent six pieces of candy. At Level IV, they wrote only "6" to represent the same quantity.

Seeing "four" in the picture of a dog and "two" in the picture of a bird in Hi-Ho! Cherry-O (because the animals have four and two legs respectively) is very similar to the thinking we see early at Level II in this research.

The cognitive value of Hi-Ho! Cherry-O

This is an easy game of chance alone. This is why it appeals to and is appropriate for very young children. It is good for children to learn how to count up to four objects meaningfully after "reading" the instruction given by the spinner. This ability to count differs from the ability to think numerically in a logico-mathematical sense. It is not by learning how to count that children construct the logico-mathematical notion of number. This notion grows out of more general coordination of mental actions that Piaget calls "reflective abstraction." [33] The ability to count as such is nevertheless useful for all children.

Moving many pieces along many different paths

Checkers

A checker board is a square divided into (8 × 8 =) 64 squares. Each player has 12 round pieces, all either red or black. To begin the game, the players place their pieces on the black squares in the three rows nearest them. This leaves two empty rows between them. The object of the game is to move one's checkers to the three rows on the opposite side and eliminate or block the opponent's pieces so that they cannot move. The players take turns moving. In the beginning all pieces can move only one space diagonally forward from one black square to an adjacent black square. They may not move backwards or to a red square. A piece can jump an opponent's piece if the square beyond is vacant. When a piece is jumped, it is eliminated from the board and kept by the person who captured it. A player cannot jump his own piece. Upon reaching the last row on the opposite side, a piece is "kinged" by placing a previously captured checker on top of it. A king can move or jump either forward or backward. (56 Games 1975)

---

[33] As can be seen in the Appendix, Piaget makes a distinction between reflective abstraction and empirical abstraction. In reflective abstraction, the child creates and introduces relationships between/among objects. In empirical abstraction, in contrast, the child abstracts information from objects. Number, according to Piaget, is constructed by each child by reflective abstraction—by a synthesis of two kinds of relationships, i.e., order and a hierarchical relationship of class inclusion. By ordering the objects, the child can count each one without skipping any or counting any more than once. By putting the objects in a hierarchical relationship, he mentally includes 1 in 2, 2 in 3, 3 in 4, etc., rather than considering each object only one at a time. For further detail about Piaget's theory of number, see Piaget and Szeminska (1941) and Kamii and DeVries (1976).

3.15.
All Gone.

The following game looked like a simpler version of Checkers for children who cannot yet play regular Checkers. When we tried it, however, we found out that the diagonal arrangement was so difficult for young children to imagine that they could not keep their objective in mind. It is presented here for an appreciation of the advantage of the horizontal arrangement of regular Checkers.

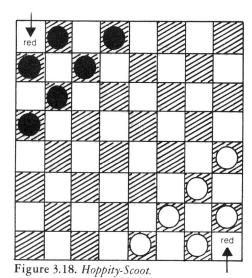

Figure 3.18. *Hoppity-Scoot.*

Hoppity-Scoot

Two players take six markers each, one taking red ones and the other, black ones. These move only on black squares of the board throughout the game. Each player lines up his checkers diagonally in a corner of the board that has a red square (see Figure 3.18). The players take turns moving one man at a time, in an attempt to win by being the first one to get all of them into the opposite corner. A man is moved only one space at a turn unless he can jump over one or more of his own men or his opponent's men. He may zigzag in any direction, as long as there is a vacant space beyond the man to be jumped. Men are not removed from the board when they are jumped. (56 Games 1975)

Some children who cannot yet play regular Checkers can play and like the following complementary-role game:

Fox and Geese

Four black markers (geese) are placed on black squares in one king row. A red marker (fox) is placed on any black square in the opposite king row. Taking turns, one player moves the geese and the opponent moves the fox. The geese try to corner the fox so that he cannot move. All markers move only on the black squares. Geese can move only forward, but the fox can move either forward or backward. Neither can jump over any marker. The game ends when the fox is cornered, or when he slips past the geese to the opposite king row. (56 Games 1975)

Foxes and geese mean very little to the children with whom we have worked. Cornering the Gingerbread Man makes much better sense to them.

The cognitive value of Checkers

Checkers is truly a game of strategy, as no move is dictated by chance. Each player has 12 pieces to move, and the path each piece travels is determined by the player's strategy. Out of many possibilities, the player chooses one move each time to get to the goal as quickly as possible while trying to capture the opponent's checker(s) and being careful not to have any of his captured. Because this is a game of strategy, each player must think on many fronts before making each move, and this coordination of one's own pieces with the opponent's pieces is excellent for becoming able to decenter and coordinate points of view.

Chinese Checkers (Warren Paper Products Co.) is similar to regular Checkers and is often played with great enthusiasm by five- and six-year-olds. The progress some children make in arranging their marbles to maximize their possibility of jumping highlights the importance of choosing appropriate games. Chinese Checkers provides opportunities for spatial reasoning, numerical reasoning, and planning strategies. This game is much richer in possibilities than games such as Chutes and Ladders that require no thinking beyond what was stated earlier in this chapter. Chutes and

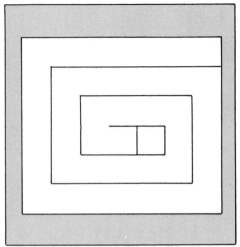

Figure 3.19. *Outline made on large posterboard.*

Ladders is limited to moving only one piece along one path as dictated by chance. Checkers and Chinese Checkers can be played at high levels by players who can put many possible moves into relationships and anticipate several turns in advance.

Board games made by children are especially high in educational value because (a) children have to think in order to make good games, and (b) their thinking cuts across many academic subjects when they make games. Some first-grade teachers use large posterboards with the outline shown in Figure 3.19 for groups of children to make their own games.[34] The children can then engage in spatial reasoning to figure out how to make the game. They usually decide to divide the long path into units and number all the squares from Start to Finish. They then write messages in various squares such as "Go bak to 6," "Skip a tern," or "Skip ahed to the mouse (when they land on the picture of a cat)." The thinking and discussion involved in making decisions are of great value, not to mention the obvious value of inventing, writing, and reading messages.

[34]Credit goes to Heidi Mounoud and Simone Bauer.

Part II

Examples

EACH CHAPTER in Part II is a detailed account of what happened with children playing a specific game. Although we selected each game from a different category presented in Chapter 3, our purpose in writing the chapter was not to show how to teach that particular type of game. Rather, our purpose was twofold: (1) to discuss the process of research that we went through to communicate the thinking we did in arriving at the principles of teaching discussed in Chapter 12, and (2) to show how difficult it is to reduce adult authority in the interest of promoting children's autonomy. In Chapters 4 and 8 (Block Race and Pin the Tail on the Donkey), we see examples of teachers who agreed intellectually that arbitrary adult power must not be exercised. Yet, in the details of their practice, without meaning to, they imposed their own ideas. The reader who finds these chapters too detailed may want to skip over to Part III after reading a few chapters in Part II.

The following steps preceded the writing of each chapter. We first selected and planned each game with the teacher who conducted the activity. This planning session turned out to serve two purposes: For the teacher, it was an ideal form of inservice training, as he or she could think through the activity with us and raise questions. For us, it was an invaluable occasion to learn about how the teacher made decisions with his knowledge and insights about the particular children in his classroom. When the teacher was willing to try a particular game, we knew that we passed the first test.

At the appointed time, the teacher tried the game, and the two of us usually took turns videotaping it. Afterwards, we discussed the tape with the teacher to evaluate the game and compare views about the way in which it went well or badly. After a general evaluation, we discussed how the game might be improved and whether or not it was worth further experimentation. We often asked teachers why they did what they did and thus found out about their perceptions and decision-making processes. With their intimate knowledge of each child, they almost always contributed interpretations which did not occur to us. We also discussed the mistakes they made.

After this discussion with the teacher, we sat down to write each chapter. We decided to begin with a detailed chronological account of how the teacher introduced the game, how the children reacted, what the teacher then decided to do, and so on.[1] Our comments appear from time to time as notes to point out why we think a particular intervention was good or bad in a particular situation or how a child's action can be interpreted in terms of Piaget's research. Following the detailed account of each activity is a section entitled Discussion. This part includes the ideas that came out of the videotape viewing session with the teacher who conducted the activity. The discussion includes an evaluation of the game and thoughts on how the activity might be followed up. We chose this format to enable the reader to look at the game from the teacher's point of view. We especially believe in pointing out the mistakes teachers made because it is often by understanding what *not* to do that one understands better what one *should* do.

We showed the first draft to teachers, especially the one who conducted the activity, to get their criticisms. In some cases the draft was modified several times. In doing this research, we became more convinced than ever that curriculum research must be done in close collaboration with teachers. Theorists do not have the insights and perspective of classroom teachers. In trying to use Piaget's theory to find better ways of teaching, theorists must work closely with teachers to build on their experience and vast amount of practical knowledge.

Just as children have to go through many levels of being "wrong" in reinventing knowledge to make it their own, teachers, too, must go through many levels in their development. The teachers who represent the first level can be found in Chapters 4 and 8 (Block Race and Pin the Tail on the Donkey). Although they consciously tried to reduce adult power, they imposed their ideas arbitrarily in spite of their intention. It is difficult to overcome the habit of "teaching" the "right" ways.

The teacher in Chapter 10 (Making Families) represents the second level of development. She modified the game well to fit the way the children were thinking and reduced her power almost "as much as possible." By continually telling the children whose turn it was, she made less than the maximum use of the game for the development of children's autonomy.

The teachers in Chapters 5, 6, and 7 (Tag, Back-to-Back, and Marbles) are at the third and highest level of development. They adapted well to children's ways of playing and reduced their power as much as possible while exercising as much of it as was necessary. They also intervened in ways that helped children to decenter, exchange ideas, and make decisions together under a variety of circumstances. We hope these chapters will communicate a way of thinking about games that can be generalized to many other situations.

---

[1]The children's names in Part II are pseudonyms that conserve only the sex and first letter of each child's name. However, the following three children are the same three: Anita in Chapters 4, 5, and 6; Jack in Chapters 4 and 5; and Jody in Chapters 5 and 6.

Chapter 4

Block Race

Constance Kamii

THE RACE described in this chapter was planned and experimented with by a teacher who did not believe that four-year-olds are not competitive in games. He kept thinking about a slide showing the response of a group of four-year-olds after a plain race to the question, "Who won?" As can be seen in Photograph 4.1, which was taken in a similar situation, almost all the children in the slide had their hands enthusiastically stretched up. The teacher knew that his group of three- and four-year-olds were at times competitive in the classroom, for example, when two children wanted the same toy. He decided to find out for himself whether his children were like those in the slide.

4.1. When asked "Who won?" after a race, almost all the children raised their hands.

BLOCKS

BOX

Figure 4.1. *A box placed at the finish line to make the order of arrival clearer to all players.*

The teacher remembered the statement that in a simple race it is not clear who crosses the finish line first, second, or third, since the event takes place quickly without a trace left of the order in which children finish. To make the order of arrival clearer to all players, he put a box at the finish line as shown in Figure 4.1. The children could then race to get their blocks and race back to put them in the box.

The teacher asked for volunteers by saying, "I am looking for four children who want to run a race. Who wants to come with me?" Since about ten children volunteered, he chose the following four, explaining that when they finished, he would be back to give the others a turn:

Jack (4;7)
Norbert (4;3)
Anita (3;7)
Semantha (3;9)

The teacher gave each of the children a block, saying, "This is your block," and, placing them in a line about 30 feet away as shown in Figure 4.1, he then said, "The winner of the race is going to be the one who puts his block in the box first." He walked to the starting line and continued, "We're going to start from this line." He made sure the children placed themselves directly opposite their blocks, and said, "When I say, 'Go,' you can cross this line and start running, but not before. And before I say, 'Go,' I'm going to say, 'On your mark, get set.'"

Race 1

Jack was fastest and, after dropping his block in the box, exclaimed, "I won!" jumping up and down. Norbert and Anita put their blocks in the box without saying anything. Semantha stood on the starting line watching the entire race. Norbert and Anita made no effort to run fast. Anita even took a leisurely skip as she picked up her block, and after reaching the box, waited for Norbert to finish putting his block in the box before putting hers in! Jack repeated, "I won," and Norbert and Anita echoed, "I won," "I won."

The teacher casually said, "Jack was first, Norbert was second, and Anita was third."

*Note: This was an appropriate response on the teacher's part. Rather than contradicting Norbert and Anita the teacher casually verbalized the order of arrival. Jack could interpret the teacher's remark in **his** way and Norbert and Anita, in **their** way.*

The teacher observed that Norbert and Anita were not competitive. They ran as if they were performing a ritual, and when they said, "I won," they seemed to mean, "I had fun doing what I was supposed to do." Since he felt the children were eager to continue playing, and he wanted Semantha to have a chance to participate, he asked, "Do you want to run another race?"

All the children responded, "Yeah."

Race 2

After the children replaced their blocks to get ready for the next race, they went back to the starting line, and at the signal everyone ran. Jack was first again, with Semantha, Norbert, and Anita following in that order. Anita slowed down markedly at the end and waited for her "turn" to put her block in the box. Jack said, "I won!" Everyone else echoed, "I won," "I won." Jack objected emphatically, "No, *I won*!" Semantha parroted, "*I* won."

The teacher noted that Jack was the only one who exerted all the effort he could to run fast, and he was also the only one who emphatically said, "*I won*!" The other three children showed a peculiar kind of "in-between" behavior. They ran rather than skipping or walking, but did not run as fast as possible.

Jack said, "Let's do it again," and the other children eagerly replied, "OK."

Race 3

The teacher said, "Everybody, please put your block back in its place." The children ran to put their blocks back at the other end of the room, but did not pay attention to the resulting irregular line, with Jack's block much closer than the others.

The teacher said, "Some of you are going to have a harder time because your blocks are farther."

Jack immediately knew what he should do and ran to align his block. The other children seemed completely unaware of the unevenness of the line or of the significance of the teacher's statement.

Note: The teacher's remark here seems appropriate. It made sense only to Jack, but did not hurt the other children (who viewed the situation not as "harder" but probably as "permitting a longer time to have the fun of running" if they even compared the distance).

As he gently pushed Jack back about four feet behind the starting line, the teacher said, "I think that this time Jack should start from back here because he's faster and he's been winning."

Jack looked unhappy and began to protest, "But I . . ."

The teacher interrupted him by asking, "Do you think you can win from back there?"

Jack pondered this possibility and, a bit mollified, nodded uncertainly as he answered, "I might."

Note: In a situation where losers are frustrated over one child's winning all the time, the teacher would be rightly concerned. In this situation, however, the other players did not even grasp the idea of winning by being first. Therefore, the problem here existed only for the teacher. Moreover, by pushing Jack, the teacher violated Jack's person. The teacher might have accomplished the same result by saying, "Jack, how about stepping back from the starting line a bit? I bet you can win even if you have a longer way to run." The difference in approaches is important for the development of children's autonomy. The latter approach gives to the child a choice and permits him to act on his own volition rather than having to yield to the teacher's power.

When the teacher began the starting call, only Jack was straining to run at the earliest possible moment. He shouted, "I'm going to be the winner!" Semantha was entertaining herself by jumping excitedly.

Anita, facing away from the starting line, said, "I'm two, three (probably meaning 'second, third')," and snuggled close to Semantha, holding her hand.

The teacher gently separated Anita from Semantha, saying, "We can't stand too close together."

Note: This move was again unnecessary, and bodily pushing children, even gently, should be avoided. The congestion was a problem for the teacher, but not for the children. The teacher was the only one who wanted to see a neat, evenly spaced arrangement which would give each player a fair chance to start at the same time.

When everyone was finally ready, the teacher said, "On your mark, get set, go!"

Everyone ran immediately except Anita, who stood looking at the teacher. When the others were halfway to the blocks, she started to run. Before reaching the box, Jack yelled, "I'm gonna win!" and comfortably won the race in spite of the handicap imposed. Far behind were Norbert, Semantha, and Anita. They all parroted, "I won," "I won," "I won."

The teacher decided the game needed variation to remain interesting. Inspired by Jack's placement of the block before Race 3, he thought of a new rule to introduce.

Race 4

The teacher said, "This time you can put your block anywhere you want." The children put the blocks in the same lineup as before. When the teacher repeated the new rule, Jack was the only one who seemed to understand something. He looked at the lineup and moved his block from its usual place at the extreme right to the extreme left. After holding it there momentarily, he moved it back to its usual place.

The teacher knew that Anita cried easily when things did not go her way, and he began to be concerned that she might get upset over losing all the time. Therefore, he took Anita's hand and gave her a head start of about four feet. To the other three who were on the starting line, he said, "I think Anita should start from here, since she got a slow start last time. Is that all right with you?"

Jack exclaimed, "Yeah," as he jumped up and down. Norbert and Semantha answered, "Yeah," without conviction, as if they did not understand the question but understood that they were expected to agree with the teacher.

Note: We appreciate the teacher's attempt to be considerate of Anita's feelings, but this move seemed unnecessary. Because Anita did not even realize that she was losing all the races, she felt no reason to cry. This

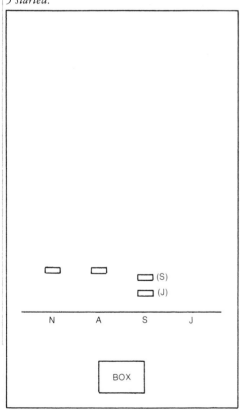

Figure 4.2. *Arrangement of blocks when Race 5 started.*

intervention did not benefit Anita and was not conducive to the development of Norbert and Semantha's autonomy.

This race had the same result as before, with Jack the triumphant winner.

Race 5

The teacher was surprised by the children's repetition of the same lineup after being told twice to put their blocks *anywhere* they liked. He said, "You don't have to put the blocks in the same place. This time, put it where you think you can get it very fast."

Jack put his block about four feet from the starting line, and Norbert and Anita imitated him by putting their blocks next to his. Semantha ran to place her block at the usual place about 30 feet away, set it down, looked up, and then realized the other children had put their blocks much closer! Meantime, Jack had moved his block even closer to the starting line, and no one objected. Semantha then put hers close to Jack's. When the race started, the blocks were arranged as shown in Figure 4.2. Of course, Jack won, but everybody claimed to be the winner as usual. Semantha did not run in a straight line but ran the long way around, as shown in Figure 4.3.

The teacher thought that we (Kamii and DeVries) wanted to continue videotaping, but he could not think of anything new to do. So he asked, "Where do you want your blocks for the next race?"

The children lined up the blocks inches away from the starting line!

Because this arrangement would not permit a race, the teacher thought he had to think of *something* to do. After a moment of desperation, he had an idea. He said, "This time, I'm going to put the box over here (where the blocks used to be lined up about 30 feet away from the starting line). When I say, 'Go,' I want you to pick up your block and put it in the box. Is your block where you want it? Do you want to move it?" (The teacher thought that the position of the block in this situation was irrelevant to winning, and he wanted to find out if the children realized this.) [1]

Note: It was unnecessary and unfortunate that the teacher moved the box. He was the only one who thought the children's arrangement of blocks would not permit a race. Solving problems for children that they do not even anticipate deprives them of a chance to learn. Besides, moving the box without consulting the children first amounted to unilaterally and arbitrarily changing the rule of the game that the children wanted to play.

Nobody felt any need to move their blocks, and all the children remained standing at the starting line.

The teacher turned to Norbert and then to Semantha, saying to each one, "Do you want to move yours?"

Note: The real message here was "I want you to move your block." Children usually respond to the real message rather than the words.

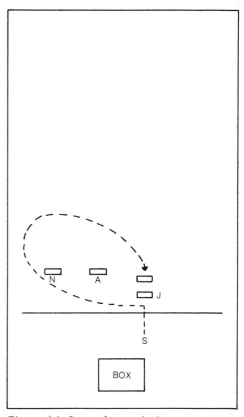

Figure 4.3. *Semantha ran the long way around.*

---

[1] Most of the children were not even thinking about winning. This is another example of adults viewing a situation differently than children do.

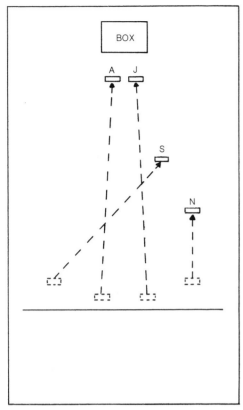

Figure 4.4. *How the children moved their blocks.*

Norbert and Semantha obliged by moving their blocks as shown in Figure 4.4. (Their only reason for doing this seemed to be to please the teacher.) Jack declared, "I want to move mine, too." Anita had been watching the other children and decided to put her block close to Jack's.

The teacher could not remember which block was whose, and felt that the children, too, might be confused; so he asked, "Whose block is this (pointing to the closest one)? Norbert's?"

Norbert responded, "It's not mine," and wandered over to examine the other blocks. Picking up Anita's, he said, "This is mine."

Anita protested, "That's *my* block."

Jack walked over to Norbert, took the block from him, and said, "No, that's mine."

Anita screamed, "It's mine," and started to cry.

Norbert turned to the teacher and quietly said, "It was mine."

The teacher asked himself whether the children could resolve this conflict without his intervention. He decided that they could not and suggested, "I'm all confused. Can we start over?" He gave each child a block and said, "You put it wherever you want, and let's all try to remember. . . ."

Jack leaned his block against the box, as if he felt that getting it as close to the box as possible was an advantage. Norbert imitated Jack and stood his block against the box, too. Semantha suddenly declared, "I'm tired."

The teacher responded, "OK, you can go rest and watch us."

Jack followed suit and said, "I'm tired, too."

Concluding that everybody had had enough of this activity, the teacher asked, "Shall we all quit and give a turn to the other children who wanted to come?"

Discussion

Children's play

The only one who ran races as adults usually understand this term was Jack, the oldest child of this group who was advanced for his age. The teacher could see not only from children's statements but also from their behavior (such as the effort they put into running fast and the placement of blocks) that young children are not competitive in group games. (The issue of competition is discussed in more detail in Chapter 11.)

The value of the game

The game showed the teacher that Jack was the only one who participated competitively. As an educational activity, however, the game lacks value, except that young children enjoy running, which gives them a sense of mastery.

The teacher's role

The teacher directed almost every move the children made, including telling them when to put the blocks down, where to stand, and when to start running. Although the children seemed to enjoy the game for a while, it was not surprising that they did not want to be regimented for a long time.

When we watched and discussed the videotape with the teacher, he was surprised that so many of his actions hindered the development of children's autonomy. Theoretically, his objective was to foster their autonomy, but it did not even occur to him to ask the group if anyone wanted to say, "Ready, set, go!"

The contradictions between what a teacher *intends* to do and what he actually *does* must not be viewed as his fault as an individual. This kind of contradiction can be found frequently and indicates to us the depth of the empiricist tradition in which we were all raised.[2] It is not easy for any individual to go beyond the centuries-old ideas of what it means to be a teacher.

[2]See the Appendix for a discussion of the empiricist tradition.

Block Race

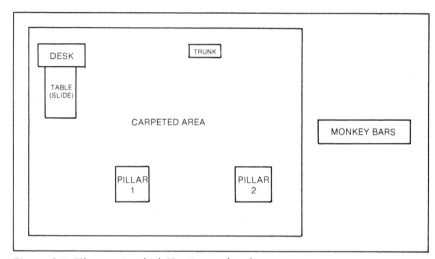

Figure 5.1. *The area in which Tag 1 was played.*

Figure 5.2. *Children could slide down an old table from which two legs had been removed.*

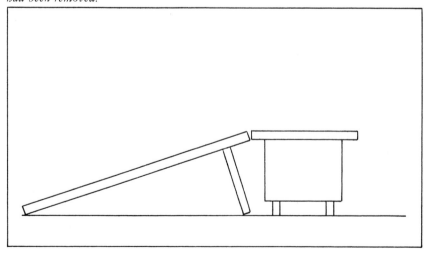

Chapter 5

Tag

Constance Kamii

Tag 1

TAG (p. 45) is a chasing game in which everyone runs away from "It," who tries to tag someone. When "It" catches someone, that person becomes "It." A safety zone may be designated where "It" cannot tag anyone.

When the teacher described in this chapter asked who wanted to play Tag, the following five children volunteered. Three of them had played Tag many times before and liked it very much. (The three were Jack, Richard, and Jody.)

Jack (4;3)
Richard (4;3)
Jody (4;2)
Pat (3;11)
Anita (3;2)

The area in which the game took place was about 20 feet by 40 feet and had the objects sketched in Figure 5.1. It was a large hallway in an old bank building, with two marble pillars. By climbing on the dilapidated desk, the children could slide down an old table from which two legs had been removed (see Figure 5.2). As usual, many children wanted to be "It," and the teacher suggested doing "One Potato" to decide who would be first. Anita got the first chance to be "It."

Because Anita had not played Tag before, the teacher said, "Anita, you are 'It.' That means you have to catch one of us."

Jack lost no time to say, "I bet she couldn't catch *me*!"

The teacher went on to say, "But we need a safety area, a place where Anita can't catch us."

"That!" said Richard, pointing to Pillar 1.

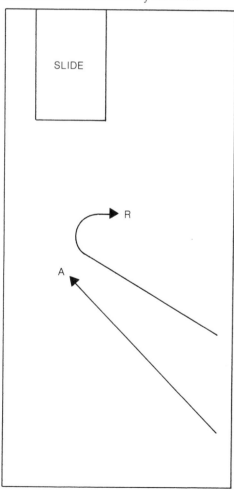

Figure 5.3. *Richard started jumping backward toward the center of the room.*

SLIDE

R

A

"Let's let Anita decide what safety area *she* wants," the teacher said. She said this because she felt that Anita might better understand the idea of a safety area if *she* chose it. Knowing that Anita was much younger than the other children and that she had never played Tag before, the teacher had hesitated to include her when she volunteered to play Tag. The teacher knew that Anita would have trouble but felt that she would do more harm to Anita's ego by excluding her under the circumstances than by letting her come and have difficulty playing with the other children. Besides, the teacher knew that the other children would not be mean or impatient with Anita.

Anita ran over to Pillar 1 and said, "Right there." She lay down, her body against the foot of the pillar.

The teacher noted that Anita must be confusing Tag with Hide and Seek. She felt the word *safety* must have triggered in Anita's mind the notion of "a safe place in which to hide." She realized that the introduction of a safety area was a mistake as far as Anita was concerned, but she also felt that eliminating it at this moment would only cause more confusion. Therefore, as she went over to the pillar to touch it, she said slowly and clearly, "If we touch this pillar, that means Anita can't get us because we are safe."

All the children except Richard followed the teacher and touched the pillar. Richard called out, "Anita!" hoping to be chased. Anita kept her face buried at the foot of the pillar, lying still as if she had no intention of moving.

"Anita can get Richard," the teacher said, suggestively. Anita still did not respond in any way.

The teacher said, "You can catch Richard, Anita, because he is not safe," urging her to run after Richard.

Anita finally looked up and started running after Richard in a babyish stumble which was her top speed. When Anita started chasing him, Richard ran to Pillar 2, thinking that it, too, was a safety area. Anita hugged Richard, saying, "I got you." Richard looked puzzled, his hand solidly planted on the post.

The teacher intervened, "*This* is the safety area (Pillar 1), not *that* pillar."

Accepting the teacher's point of view, Richard concluded that he had been caught. He pushed Anita away, and she ran toward Pillar 1 to join the rest of the group. Just before Anita got to the safety post, Richard started chasing her at full speed. He tackled her in grand football style, and both children rolled on the floor in great glee.

"Anita is 'It' again," the teacher announced, to make sure everybody knew. All the children left safety and moved away from Anita in every direction.

"I want to be 'It,'" Jack complained.

Richard challenged Anita to chase him by jumping past her and taunting, "Nyah-nyah-nya-nyah-nya."

Anita could have chased someone else who was equally close, but Richard got her attention, and she continued to chase him. Richard got close to the slide and then started jumping backward toward the center of the room as shown in Figure 5.3. At that moment, Anita could easily have caught him, but the slide caught her attention, and she lost interest in the chase. She crawled up the slide while Richard danced away toward the middle of the room.

Jack impatiently followed Anita up the slide and demanded, "You got to get me."

Anita obliged by coming down the slide and chasing him toward the trunk. As she passed the trunk, she noticed Richard climbing on it from the front and jumping with a great leap off the side as shown in Figure 5.4. She started after Richard, but instead of trying to catch him as he leaped off the trunk, she imitated him! She then followed Richard, but he reached the safety post. She stopped running and rolled on the floor, holding both feet up in a yoga-like position.

In an attempt to get Anita to get up and go on with the game, the teacher teased by pretending to tickle her in the stomach.

Laughing, Anita got up, ran to the other side of the slide, crawled under it, and stayed there as if to hide. Meanwhile, the other children were running all over the room, down the slide, around the posts, and to and from Anita. (The teacher observed that only Jack and Richard had been able to get Anita to chase them and that the other children were having fun running away even without being chased.)

After a while, because nobody seemed to be aware that "It" had stopped chasing anybody, the teacher asked, "Who is 'It' now?"

"Anita is," responded the others.

"Anita, you are 'It,'" the teacher said.

Everyone ran around Anita saying, "Come get me, Anita; come get me."

Anita grinned in delight over all this attention and began crawling slowly toward the children who started running away from her. Then, she got up and chased Pat and Richard across the room. They ran faster and got back to the safety post. Anita could then have turned to chase Jack or Jody, but instead she rolled on the floor again with gusto! Richard imitated, rolling on the floor right next to her! The other children ran toward Anita and then away, trying to tempt her into chasing them. Oblivious to all these approaches, Anita got up, ran behind the desk, lay down, and hid herself (not noticing that her legs were sticking out in plain view).

Seeing that Anita had once more stopped being "It," Richard ran up the slide onto the desk, stood just above her, and challenged, "Come get me, Anita."

Other children also stopped running away and came to plead, "Try and get me, Anita."

Anita finally responded and started to run. Richard then flew down the desk top and waited to see if Anita would chase him. Watching expectantly, he crouched, with both hands on his knees, ready to dash. Sure enough, Anita began to run toward Richard, who waited until she was within a foot and then took off. As Anita was slow, and Richard easily outdistanced her, he got bored, stopped, and waited to let Anita catch him. She caught him by hugging him again.

"Oh, Richard is 'It' now," the teacher said, standing in front of the slide.

Richard's becoming "It" rekindled excitement in the group, and everyone started running away from him as if in great jeopardy. Richard chased the teacher at full speed and caught her by cornering her behind the slide.

Seeing that the teacher had become "It," Jody ran to touch the safety post. Anita and Jack slid down the slide right in front of the teacher as if they considered themselves entirely safe because the teacher showed no intention of giving chase. Richard and Pat immediately got as far from the teacher as possible.

To heighten suspense and intensify children's interest, the teacher said, "Richard touched me, and I'm 'It.'" She started to move with deliberate and

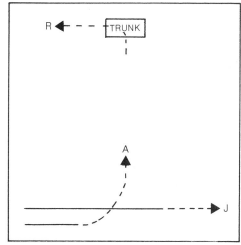

Figure 5.4. *Anita chased Richard toward the trunk.*

exaggerated giant steps.

All the children except Anita ran to the other end of the room as fast as they could, screaming excitedly. (Anita kept sliding on the slide.)

Rather than chasing the children right away, the teacher decided to guard the safety pillar and see what the children would do. She laughingly spread her arms wide as she kept herself between the post and the children. When they saw that she was not chasing them, they started moving toward her. Richard ran toward the pillar and then dodged away from the teacher as shown in Figure 5.5.

The teacher started after Richard, but when he dodged, she decided to catch Jody, who was following behind him. Easily tagging Jody, the teacher announced to the group, "Jody is 'It' because I tagged her."

Everyone stopped running to see what Jody would do. As they stood waiting for her to start chasing them, Jody in turn stood waiting for someone to start running.

Finally, after a few moments of suspended action, Richard taunted, "Nyah-nyah-nya-nyah-nya," and that was the signal for Jody to start chasing him.

After a long chase around the pillar, Jody's attention was caught by a fracas among the other children. Jack and Pat had somehow bumped and hurt one another, and the teacher took them to the safety area so she could take a look and comfort them.

As soon as Jody paused in her chase, Richard also stopped running. To get her attention again, he called out, "Nyah-nyah-nya-nyah-nya," and when Jody resumed her chase, Richard resumed running away. He outran Jody to the pillar. She looked wistfully at all the players on safety. Jack ventured out, but Jody did not notice him. Pat carelessly wandered a few steps off the pillar, still preoccupied with her bump and paying no attention to Jody. Jody ignored Pat as if she understood that Pat was out of the game for the moment.

Richard hopped away from the post, taunting, "Nyah-nyah-nya-nyah-nya." Teasingly, he crouched with his hands on his knees within six feet of Jody. Momentarily distracted by hearing the teacher, Richard failed to notice Jody approaching him. She hesitated for a moment when he failed to run away but then touched him quickly on both shoulders and instantly dashed off.

Figure 5.5.
Richard dodged away from the teacher.

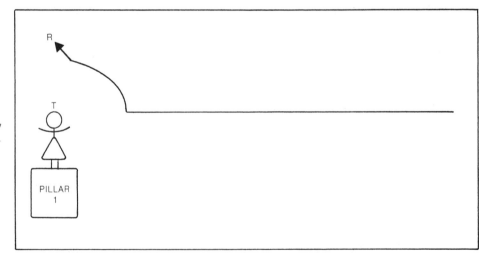

Richard ran after Jody, then saw Jack hiding behind Pillar 2. He tagged Jack and triumphantly shouted, "I got you!"

Jody and Richard rushed to safety where they joined the teacher, Anita, and Pat.

Jack followed them slowly and announced, "I'm 'It.'" Anita was sitting by the pillar without touching it, preoccupied with showing something to the teacher. Jack paid no attention to Anita. Because everybody else was on safety and showed no intention of moving, Jack went to the slide and slid down backward. Pat and Jody skipped to within three feet of Jack, hoping to catch his attention, but walked back to safety without daring any further. Jack saw the two girls but ignored them and continued sliding.

To get Jack interested in the game again, the teacher tiptoed sneakily toward the trunk. Richard walked with the teacher to challenge Jack, and Anita followed them.

Because Jack would not give chase, the teacher teased him by putting two fingers on top of her head like horns and wiggling them.

Jack could not resist this tease and came running down the slide. He was a little out of control and accidentally pushed Anita. He intended to circle around to tag Richard and seemed unaware of having touched Anita.

The teacher inquired, "You know what? You touched Anita. Does that mean she is 'It'?"

"Nope," answered Jack emphatically.

Richard and Jody danced around in circles near Jack, yelling, "Try and get me!"

Richard stopped and crouched in a you-can't-get-me stance and echoed, "Try and get me!"

Jack started after Richard, who took off, but Jack tagged him in no time.

"Richard is 'It,'" the teacher commented.

Seconds later, Richard tagged the teacher and shouted exuberantly, "She is 'It'!" Celebrating Tarzan-style, Richard jumped up on the trunk and leaped down, chanting, "Try to get me. Try to get me."

Jack was out of breath but kept running, imitating Richard's chant.

Creeping up too daringly close to the teacher, who was standing still, Richard got tagged.

"Richard is 'It,'" the teacher announced.

Richard started running, not in pursuit of anyone, but just for the fun of running once around Pillar 1. While Jack was distracted by watching the teacher fix the video machine plug at the foot of the pillar, Richard caught Jack by surprise. "I got him," said Richard with satisfaction.

"I'm 'It,'" Jack declared.

The teacher and Richard both leaned against the safety pillar, looking at Jack. Richard then dashed out, and Jack chased him toward the monkey bars.

The teacher asked, "What about Jody and Pat (who were swinging on the monkey bars)?"

As soon as Jack got to the monkey bars, he forgot the chase and started swinging by his hands. Jody, Pat, and Richard all casually jumped and hopped past Jack and ran slowly back to the safety post. Having satisfied his desire to swing on the monkey bars, Jack decided to join the group leaning against the safety post.

"Everybody is safe, but Anita is not safe," the teacher commented.

Jack looked over where Anita was lying under the slide. Richard hopped away from the pillar.

"And Richard is not safe," the teacher added.

Jack went over and pounced on Anita.

"Jack touched you, Anita. That means you are 'It,'" the teacher said.

Anita did not respond. As she lay passively under the slide, all the children crept up to entice her by saying, "Come get me, Anita, come get me." Richard and Jack amused themselves while waiting by sliding down the slide side by side.

Pat crawled on all fours to challenge Anita under the slide, begging, "Come get me, Anita."

Anita began to get up, and Pat ran away. When Anita started running full speed after Pat, Richard raced after Anita yelling, "Pick me, Anita, pick me!" Richard ran ahead of Anita and stopped in her path so that she would run into him. Sure enough, Anita bumped into Richard and touched him.

"Anita caught Richard," the teacher announced.

Anita ran toward the safety post, but the slide caught her attention as she approached the post. Without touching the post, she continued to run toward the slide.

Richard looked around and dashed toward the teacher, who was near the safety pillar. As he approached the pillar, he noticed Anita and decided to chase her, but he accidentally bumped into Pat, who was trying to grab the pillar. Not noticing Pat, Richard slapped Anita on the back. Anita turned around, walked to the pillar, and rubbed it as if she had no awareness of having been tagged.

Richard announced, "I touched Anita."

Jody and Jack approached Richard, challenging him by saying, "Come get me, Richard."

Richard protested, "I touched Anita."

Anita ran toward the slide and crawled under it. Jody slid down the slide, and Jack climbed on the desk.

Noting the general confusion, the teacher intervened by saying to Richard, "You better tell Anita that you touched her."

Note: This intervention was excellent because the teacher tried to get Richard to speak to Anita rather than regulating the game for the children. It would have been easier for the teacher to say, "Anita is 'It' because Richard tagged her," but that would not have helped Richard or Anita become able to play without the teacher.

Richard peered under the slide and told Anita, "I touched you, Anita."

Anita continued to roll around under the slide, showing no intention of coming out. Pat and Jody hopped across the room to play on the monkey bars.

Jack and Richard stood side by side and taunted Anita: "Try to get us. Try to get us."

Anita still showed no intention of coming out.

The teacher sat down by the slide, asked Richard to come over, and explained, "Anita doesn't know what that means. You have to tell her what that means."

Note: This intervention was again excellent. The teacher was trying to get

Richard to decenter and understand the situation from Anita's point of view.

Richard stuck his face under the slide and explained to Anita, "You have to come catch us 'cause I touched you."

Anita continued her yoga-like stretching as Richard ran away from her.

The teacher crawled under the slide and explained again to Anita that when Richard touched her, she became "It." She asked Anita if she wanted to continue playing or preferred to quit.

Anita slowly came out and began to run at top speed toward the monkey bars where all the other children were playing.

"Here comes Anita," the teacher warned.

As soon as Anita came close to the monkey bars, everybody except Pat fled, screaming in mock terror. Instead of tagging Pat, who continued to swing on the monkey bars, Anita began to swing on them herself, facing away from Pat and completely forgetting about chasing anybody!

Pat got down, ran past Anita, and joined the other children near the safety pillar.

Anita continued hanging on the bar and announced, "I'm a monkey."

The others crept up to Anita, chanting, "Come and get me, come and get me Anita."

Jody finally stood in front of Anita, thrust out her chest, and commanded, "Touch me, Anita."

Anita complied.

Seeing that Anita had no idea what touching Jody meant, the teacher squatted by the two girls and said, "Anita touched Jody. So, Anita, who is 'It' now?"

Both Anita and Jody pointed to themselves, saying, "Me."

Richard and Jack exclaimed, "It's Jody," and Pat looked puzzled.

The teacher said to the three girls who were remaining close by, "I don't understand, and Anita doesn't understand who is 'It.'"

Jody insisted, "I'm 'It.'"

"How come it's not Anita?" the teacher asked Jody.

"Because she touched me," Jody explained.

The teacher said, "Oh, I see (as if she finally understood)," and turned to Anita to explain slowly and clearly, "You were 'It,' and you touched Jody. When 'It' touches somebody, that person becomes the new 'It.' And you know what? There can be only one 'It' at a time."

Anita made no response, and the teacher was not at all sure what she understood.

Note: There are times when the teacher needs to modify the rule so that the game will make sense to children; there are other times instead when she needs to teach the rule to the child. This situation was one in which the teacher rightly decided to try to teach the rule to Anita because there was no other way for Anita to learn the convention of what tagging meant.

Richard challenged Jody, "Come get me."

Jody chased Richard around the safety pillar at full speed, but he got away. She tagged Pat, who happened to be standing around, halfway in and halfway out of the game.

Pat beamed and, instead of tagging Jack who was standing still right by

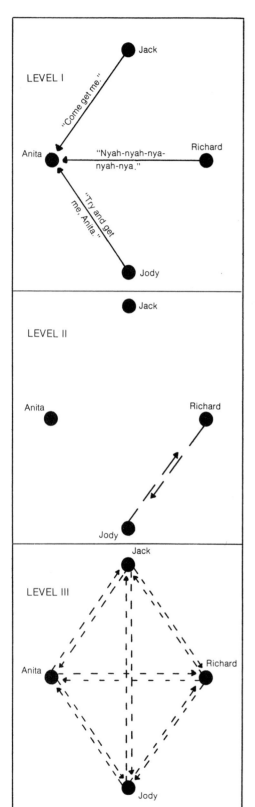

her, ran to the teacher to tell her with great pride, "Jody caught me; so I'm 'It' now."

At long last Pat had a chance to be "It."

Discussion

Children's play

The children played in ways that are very different from the usual game of Tag. The most striking feature of the play of three of the five children (Jack, Richard, and Jody) is that they usually did not tag the easiest person who happened to be close by and/or off guard. Rather, they began the chase after ascertaining each other's intentions that one would chase and the other would run away. Anita, in contrast, seemed not to know what was going on. The only reason why she participated in the game was that she was often "It," and the other players told her to try to catch them. Anita would then comply, but, while chasing someone, she frequently forgot all about the chase—until she was told again to catch "me."

All these behaviors were hard to make sense out of until the three levels of play shown in Chart 5.1 and Figure 5.6 were hypothesized. Level I, "no participation on one's initiative," is suggested by what Anita did. Level II, based on what Richard, Jack, and Jody did, is "part-time participation." Level III, "full-time participation," is the way older children play Tag. Pat can be classified at an intermediary level between Levels I and II.

The only solid "+" in the column for Level I is for "activities not relevant to Tag (such as engaging in a chase that does not involve 'It'; running alone, sliding, and rolling on the floor)." Anita had no idea what it meant to be tagged and did not do anything relevant to the game on her own initiative. She participated only because others tagged her and kept telling her to "come and catch me." The "+" for "running after someone" is in parentheses because Anita would never have chased anyone if they had not taunted her or told her

Chart 5.1.

	Level		
	I	II	III
Activities not relevant to Tag			
(e.g., engaging in a chase that does not involve "It," running alone, sliding, and rolling on the floor)	+	+	+
Actions relevant to Tag			
Understanding the significance of tagging and being tagged	—	+	+
As "It," running *after* someone	(+)	+	+
Running *away from* "It"	—	+	+
Coordinating complementary intentions			
By temporary agreement	—	+	—
By permanent agreement	—	—	+

Figure 5.6. *Three levels of playing Tag.*

to catch them. She did and saw a lot of running and fragments of interesting things but was completely blind to the rules of the game as can be seen in Figure 5.6. The arrows in this figure all come from others, and Anita chased only those who told her that they wanted her to chase them.

At Level II children know what it means to tag and be tagged, and all but the last "—" in the column for Level II in Chart 5.1 are "+'s." Children become able to run after or away from someone without being told to do so. The running unrelated to "It," sliding, swinging, and preoccupation with other interests persist, but the children return to the game continually on their own by ascertaining complementary intentions with "It." There is no pleasure in catching someone who does not try to avoid being caught. Hence the need to ascertain complementary intentions as shown by the two arrows in Figure 5.6. The broken arrows indicate that the coordination of intentions at Level II is not done through explicit language as it is done at Level I. Instead, the negotiation is done mostly by eye contact and body movements.

Their desire to become "It" keeps bringing Level II children back into the game. They want so much to become "It" that they even plant themselves in "It's" path as he comes chasing somebody else. Anita caught someone four times during this session, but three out of the four times were when Richard or Jody stood in her way openly demanding to be tagged.

At Level III, children tag those who are off guard, on the assumption that all players are vigilant at all times. The "+" and "—" at the bottom of the columns in Chart 5.1, therefore, become reversed when the child passes from Level II to Level III. There is no need for temporary agreements when a permanent one is in effect. As can be seen in Figure 5.6, every child at Level III pays attention to every other child at all times. The arrows are even more broken than at Level II to indicate that the coordination of intentions no longer involves verbal communication.

Once in a while, Jack, Richard, and Jody did tag someone without making an agreement first to begin a chase. However, these children cannot be said to belong to Level III because they only rarely tagged someone by surprise. Level II children thus engage in activities that characterize Level III as well as those that characterize Level I, but they are different from Level I children as can be seen in all the additional "+'s" in Chart 5.1, and the ascertaining of complementary intentions is a striking characteristic of Level II.

One is tempted to say that the children, rather than the teacher, regulated the game when Anita became "It." However, I do not think the children regulated the game. They each tried to get Anita to chase them by taunting her and saying, "Come and get *me*," which is not the same thing as saying, "Try to catch *somebody*." All these individual demands happened to have the effect of regulating the game with a minimum of intervention on the teacher's part.

The value of the game

Tag seemed good for this particular group of children in spite of all the problems created by Anita. The children played not only a long time but also with exuberance and investment in what they were doing. The great freedom afforded by this game probably explains its success. The children could decide what to do, when, and how. "It" could decide whom to chase, when to begin chasing, and whether or not to continue running after the same person. The other players could likewise decide whether to stay on safety or try to become "It." They could even go down the slide, swing on the monkey bars, and roll on the floor. In spite of all this freedom, the game remained loosely organized with a minimum of teacher intervention.

Tag seems particularly good for children's social development. As a complementary-role game, it encourages interindividual coordination but does not force it. Level II children interacted well among themselves as well as with Anita and Pat. Although Pat's participation was minimal, it was typical of her style, and she was comfortable in being herself throughout the game.

The teacher's role

Generally, the teacher's interventions were relaxed, low-keyed, infrequent, and excellent. She helped minimize her authority by joining the game as a player (although she would not have been authoritarian even if she had stayed out of the game). Remember the suggestion she made to Richard that he tell Anita that he had touched her. It would have been easier for her to take care of the situation by saying, "Anita, you are 'It' because Richard tagged you." By not stepping in here, she helped Richard learn how to communicate with others.

The teacher could have done two things better. First, as she realized later, introducing a safety area was a mistake. She could have suggested that the game be played without a safety area today because it is new to Anita, and it is easier to learn the game without safety. In this case, such a suggestion would probably not have made any difference to Anita's comprehension. However, it is desirable not to introduce exceptions from the beginning. Also, this teacher never communicated the rules of Tag explicitly to Anita, nor did she ask the others to explain to her how Tag is played. Discovery is often good, but young children should not be left to discover the rules of a game. This asks too much of young children (or adults), and they feel much more secure when the convention is communicated explicitly to them. Young children usually end up playing a different game, but this should not preclude letting them know how it is usually played. Again, with respect to Anita, not all the speeches in the world would have made any difference to her understanding. But it was not enough for the teacher to say at the beginning, "Anita, you are 'It.' That means you have to catch one of us."

Tag 2

Tag 2 is presented for two reasons. It will be recalled that the first of the three objectives for early education discussed in Chapter 2 is "in relation to adults, we would like children to develop their autonomy through relationships in which adult power is reduced as much as possible." But what does it mean to reduce adult authority "as much as possible"? In trying to foster children's development of autonomy, adults sometimes expect children to assume more responsibility than they can handle. When children cannot solve a problem, it is necessary for the teacher to step in. How to step in and when are questions that can best be answered with an example.

Tag 2 is presented also to show Richard playing at a much more sophisticated level in a group of more advanced children than in Tag 1.

The teacher asked if anyone wanted to play Tag, and the following four children jumped at the chance to play their favorite game:

Michael (5;2)

Theresa (4;6)

Richard (4;3)

Peggy (4;9)

The game took place in an area arranged as shown in Figure 5.7.

The two big boxes were parts of a kiosk which we disassembled and converted into climbing equipment. The monkey bars (a, b, c, and d) were long, heavy pipes which had once been part of a scaffold used for University maintenance. We laid them across the boxes to use as monkey bars.

Michael immediately asked, "Can this (the trash can) and the refrigerator be glue?"

The teacher was perplexed because she had never heard of *glue* and asked, "What's *glue?*"

"When you touch things, you're safe," Michael answered.

The teacher said, "It's OK with me. Let's ask all the kids." She called the rest of the children over and said, "Michael wants to know if you guys want to use the refrigerator and this for glue. Do you know what *glue* is?"

Note: Children naturally turn to adults for permission and rule making. It should be standard practice for the teacher to redirect such inquiries to peers.

The teacher hesitated about using the word *glue,* which she thought was probably a word or deformation of a word Michael had heard from older children.[1] She was concerned that other children would not recognize it and might be confused. However, she wanted to encourage Michael's initiative, and because the specific name of specific objects is only a matter of convention anyway (Piaget 1946), she decided to use Michael's word.

Richard responded vaguely, "Yeah, blue . . . glue," and the other children had a blank expression, saying nothing.

Urged by the teacher to explain what *glue* is, Michael answered, *"Glue* is when you touch things, you can't tag anybody."

The teacher noted Michael's difficulty with the passive voice. When he said "when you touch things, you can't tag anybody," he obviously meant "you can't *be* tagged by anybody." She recalled young children's difficulty in producing passive sentences (Sinclair, Sinclair, and de Marcellus 1971) and decided that it would be pointless to correct Michael at this moment. She needed to find a tactful way of making the rule clear to the other children. She therefore asked, "Do you mean that if *you're* touching that, I can't tag you?"

"Yeah, 'cause I'm safe," Michael replied.

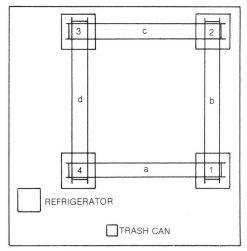

Figure 5.7. *The arrangement of the area in which Tag 2 was played.*

---

[1]We subsequently found that some people in their childhood used a word that sounds like "gool." However, they could not tell us how to spell the word. We would appreciate hearing from anyone who can furnish more information about the origin and meaning of this term.

The teacher turned to the other children and asked, "What do you think? Do you want to use the trash can and refrigerator for safety glue?"

Theresa emphatically said, "Yes!"

Richard loudly retorted, "No," and Theresa insisted, "Yes!"

Peggy, who had been listening from her perch atop Box 1, announced, "I don't want to use *anything*."

Michael argued, "We *have* to have glue because that's the way you play Tag."

The teacher was pleased to see the children express their opinions clearly. However, the impasse made her decide that this was a moment when she had to intervene as an adult. She felt it would be better to get the game started than to prolong the discussion and risk deterioration of interest. The best compromise she could think of was to play according to the rule proposed by Michael and offer Richard the privilege of being the first "It." In this way at least Theresa, Michael, and Richard would be satisfied, and she hoped Peggy would adapt. She therefore said, "Michael says that's how you play Tag. Would you like to be 'It,' Richard?"

Richard replied, "Yeah," with a bit of reluctance in his voice.

The teacher decisively announced, "OK, kids, the trash can and refrigerator are glue. Richard is 'It,' and he's going to try to catch you. And if you put your hand on this trash can or that refrigerator, then he can't catch you 'cause that means you're safe."

Peggy piped up, "Well, see, if I'm up here (on Box 1), then I'm glued on, and then I can't get up, and nobody can chase me 'cause I'm glued on."

The teacher asked, "Do you want that big box to be glue too?"

Theresa said, "Yes," and climbed up beside Peggy.

Peggy declared, "Theresa will stay up here, too."

The teacher recognized Peggy's declaration as a typical expression of her negativism when she does not get her way. In retrospect, she wished she had thought of promising to play by Peggy's rule (using no safety at all) later. This might have prevented Peggy's withdrawal. Under the circumstances, however, the teacher decided to suggest to the group, "How about the box, the trash can, *and* the refrigerator for glue?"

Michael objected, "Only the trash can and refrigerator!"

Then all the players talked at once, each repeating and insisting on his own preference.

The teacher sat down on the floor, folded her arms, and said with resignation, "Well, *you* guys have to decide."

Theresa suggested, "The whole monkey bars is glue!" (a, b, c, and d in Figure 5.7).

The teacher underlined this suggestion for the children to consider: "Theresa says the whole monkey bars is glue."

Michael reluctantly agreed but stipulated, "Yeah, but you can't stay up there all the time."

Peggy responded, "Well, we're just gonna play up here awhile."

The teacher supported Michael's concern by emphasizing, "Michael says it's all right, but he wishes we wouldn't stay on the monkey bars all the time."

Theresa said reassuringly, "Well, sometimes we can get off," and Peggy added with a tone of conspiracy, "Yeah, sometimes we'll sneak off. Right, Theresa?"

Michael, suspecting that Peggy and Theresa intended to stay glued onto the box, protested, "That's not how you play Tag. You either go inside (the classroom), or you got to run around so I can touch you."

Note: Michael was imitating the teacher, who often gave a choice between two alternatives. When children behave in ways that are not acceptable to the group and the teacher, giving a choice is much better than giving an order. For example, being asked either to go to the doll corner or stay with the group without bothering the others is much better than being ordered to go to the doll corner. In the former situation, the child is given at least some room to make a decision, even if it is a choice between two unpleasant alternatives. Being told to go to the doll corner leaves the child no room for participation in deciding what will happen to him. Participation in decision making, it will be recalled, is essential for the child's development of autonomy. When full participation is impractical, it is important for adults to give at least some room for the child to make a decision.

The teacher asked, "Shall we try it this way and see if it works or doesn't work? If it doesn't work, we'll think of something else to do, OK?"

Michael agreed but warned, "OK, but you can't sneak off."

The teacher got up, saying, "Richard's 'It.' Why don't you count to three, and we'll all run away."

Richard buried his face in Box 1 and started to count loudly. Peggy and the teacher ran past Box 2 toward the refrigerator. Michael hid on the other side of Box 1. Theresa stayed glued on the box.

Because Richard kept counting and did not seem about to stop, the teacher teased, "You can't get *me*, Richard."

Richard stopped counting, ran after the teacher in a clockwise direction, and caught her by Box 2.

"He caught me! *Now* what do I do?" the teacher asked. (She knew that the children knew the answer to her question. Her reason for asking this question was to try to get the group to be interrelated rather than psychologically dispersed.)

"You are 'It'," Peggy said as she climbed on Box 1 beside Theresa. Richard was touching the refrigerator, and Michael was on the monkey bars.

The teacher saw that everyone was on safety. To make the children aware of the situation from her point of view, she commented, "I can't get Theresa, and I can't get Peggy, and I can't get Richard, and I can't get Michael. I can't get *any*body!"

Michael took the hint and dashed away from the monkey bars, shouting, "Yes, you can!"

Peggy said defiantly, "You can't catch *me* because I'm on the safety zone."

"The only one I can catch is Michael?" the teacher asked, again trying to make the players conscious of her problem.

Richard ran toward Michael, and the two of them ran away from the teacher. The teacher finally caught Michael. Michael quickly took advantage of Richard's inattention and tagged him. Losing no time, Richard started to run toward the teacher.

Note: The game continued in this way for about ten minutes, with the two girls remaining on Box 1 and only the other three participating actively. The trouble with the game was that everybody stayed on safety most of the time, and "It" was constantly frustrated by having nobody to chase. As can be seen below, the game deteriorated, and the teacher kept hinting about the need for players to get off safety or reduce the number of safety areas. The children, however, simply could not see this necessity, and the teacher ended up proposing a drastic reform.

All players were on safety, and Michael had no one to chase. He complained, "That's not fair," and Peggy agreed, "Yeah!"

The teacher said quizzically, "That's not fair?" to encourage discussion.

Peggy replied, "There has to be somebody to catch."

"There has to be somebody to catch?" the teacher questioned as if she did not understand this remark.

Michael explained, "Yeah, there has to be somebody to catch, or the game stops."

"Michael said the game is stopped now," the teacher interpreted.

Theresa ran to the middle of the monkey bars (b in Figure 5.7) but took no chances, kept well away from Michael, and immediately returned to her safe spot on the box.

The teacher tried to get the children to figure out a solution. She asked, "What can we do to play the game some more?"

Theresa jumped down again and taunted Michael in a sing-song, "Dah-dah-da-dah-da."

Contemptuously, Michael ignored her as she was so close to the box that his effort would be pointless.

The teacher remarked, "Michael doesn't have anybody to chase because everybody is on safety."

Peggy cautiously climbed down from the box and took her hands just off the box, teasing, "Oh yes he does."

Michael ignored Peggy. As he expected, she immediately climbed back on the box without offering any real challenge. Disgusted, Michael sat on the monkey bars and whispered something to the teacher.

After getting Michael's consent to make his statement public, the teacher said, "Michael says that he's on safety, too, so now he can catch you guys."

Peggy objected, "But that's not the rule!"

"That's not the rule?" the teacher asked, to invite further discussion.

Peggy said, "Yeah, because that's not fair."

"Well, what do you think? What are we going to do? Do we need some new rules or what?" the teacher asked pointedly.

Peggy agreed, "Yeah, we need some new rules."

Richard yelled, "We have to run!"

Glad that someone finally offered a way to get the game going again, the teacher supported Richard's initiative. "OK," she said, and ran.

Everybody then got off safety, but Theresa and Peggy strayed away from their box only briefly. Michael caught the teacher, and everyone again took refuge on safety. The children began to tease the teacher, singing, "Nyah-nyah-nya-nyah-nya." Richard even sneaked up behind the teacher, thinking she did not see him.

The teacher suddenly turned and caught Richard by surprise. "Richard's 'It'," she laughed.

Richard was getting tired and only half-heartedly chased Michael, who easily got far away. Discouraged and angry, Richard picked up a cardboard tube and ran at top speed after Michael. Unable to catch Michael, Richard threw the tube at Michael but missed. Michael changed direction, and Richard tried once more to catch him, but Michael reached the safety of the refrigerator.

Richard complained, "He's too fast."

The teacher sympathetically repeated, "Richard says Michael's too fast."

Sitting down dejectedly, Richard nearly cried.

Theresa complained to the teacher that she hadn't been "It"!!!

The teacher suggested, "If you want to be 'It,' why don't you run around and give Richard a chance to chase you? He can't get you if you're on the glue."

Theresa dashed around the monkey bars at high speed with Richard in hot pursuit.

The teacher exclaimed, "Theresa's getting brave. Look at that!"

This inspired Peggy to jump down off the box, dance a few feet away, and chant, "I'm brave! I'm brave!"

Theresa beat Richard back to Box 1 and rejoined Peggy. Both began teasing Richard by moving only a few inches away from safety and chanting in a sing-song, "Richard-Richard-Rich-ard."

By this time, Richard's ego was bruised. He grabbed his tube and clunked Peggy on the head with full force. She was surprised but not really hurt.

To help Richard label his feeling and make the other children conscious of what they were doing to him, the teacher asked, "Richard, are you getting angry?"

Richard looked repentant but pouted, obviously not about to respond.

The teacher appealed to the other children: "I think Richard is feeling kind of bad. Let's ask him how come he's feeling bad. Richard, do you want to make us a new rule?"

Richard suddenly jumped at Michael, who started to run, chased him, and tagged him with huge satisfaction.

Seeing that the deteriorated state of the game required drastic intervention, the teacher took charge and firmly declared, "I have a new rule, and I want to know if you guys like my new rule. My new rule is *no more glue*, and if I tag you, you have to freeze and be very, very still."

Discussion

What does it really mean to reduce adult power "as much as possible?" As stated earlier, in trying to foster the development of children's autonomy, adults sometimes expect young children to assume more responsibility than they can handle. When children cannot solve a problem, it is necessary for the teacher to step in, even if this means exercising some power. The teacher in Tag 2 was excellent in sensing how far to go, and no further, in reducing her adult power and responsibility. Let us examine some of the things she did.

First, she encouraged the expression of wishes from all the children and asked the group to consider each idea. For example, before the game began, Theresa proposed the addition of monkey bars to safety when, in the teacher's opinion, there were already too many safety areas. Instead of expressing her opinion, the teacher asked the group what they wanted to do about this idea.

When the teacher felt, however, that there was an impasse that was too hard for the children to handle, she intervened with some authority. She did this once at the beginning of the game (by proposing to play according to Michael's rule and let Richard be the first "It") and once at the end (by proposing to play Freeze Tag). But even when she took charge, she still consulted the children and did not impose her ideas.

The teacher's first solution (to play according to Michael's rule and let Richard be the first "It") reinforced children's tendency to depend on adults to solve problems. After she suggested this solution, the children made one demand after another, assuming that it was up to the teacher to please everybody. When this happened, she simply sat down with her arms folded and said, "You guys have to decide." She gave responsibility back to the children.

When the children finally agreed on the rules with too many safety areas, the teacher knew that the game would break down, but she went along with the children's decision. She believed that they had to see the consequences of their decision to become able to construct a better rule in the future that would include what they will have learned from this mistake.

Once the game was under way, the teacher tried to point out that there was a problem, hoping that this would be sufficient for the children to come up with a new rule. She presented these problems not in abstract terms (by saying, "The game has stopped," for example) but in personal terms (by saying, "I have nobody to chase"). When pointing out a problem did not produce a new rule, the teacher hinted at the need for one, and when this was still not enough, she ended up proposing a new rule.

It is easy enough to say, "Reduce adult power as much as possible." It is difficult to translate this principle into practice.

Chapter 6

Back-to-Back [1]

Constance Kamii

BACK-TO-BACK (p. 57) is a game involving verbal commands. The players are in pairs, and each member of the pair must touch the other on the body part named by "It." Examples of commands given by "It" are "back to back" and "foot to foot." When "It" says, "Change," everybody including "It" must find a new partner. The player left without a partner becomes the new "It."

The following eight children volunteered when the teacher asked at the beginning of free play time who wanted to go to the game area to play a new game to be videotaped:

Jody (6;2)
Jasmine (5;0)
Jay (5;6)
Anita (5;2)
Richard (6;3)
Franka (5;2)
Jesse (6;3)
Ward (6;1)

Another child who later joined the group was Kanota (5;5).

The teacher wanted to introduce the game as everybody sat on the floor in a circle. She began by saying, "The game we want to play today is called Back-to-Back, and it's a game I don't think any of us have ever played before."

Several children responded, "I did. I played it before."

Note: It is very important for the development of children's intellectual and moral autonomy that they feel free to contradict the teacher. This statement by several children was a good sign indicating that the children were not afraid to tell the teacher that she was wrong.

[1] Credit goes to Colleen Blobaum for transcribing this session from the videotape.

The teacher thought about stopping to find out what the children had in mind, perhaps getting the children to describe the game to those who did not know it. However, knowing that we (Kamii and DeVries) were there with the video camera to observe the game that we had in mind, she decided to introduce it her way. She said, "Really? I never played it, never in my life . . . . The way you play it is you first pick a partner."

The children started to get up to pick partners. As she indicated with her hands that she wanted everybody to remain sitting on the floor, the teacher said, "Let's listen first, OK? And one person will be the leader."

Several children clamored to be the leader. Realizing this desire, the teacher said, "Just for the first time, let me be the leader, just to show you how it works. And then you guys can be the leaders, OK? . . . After you pick a partner, the leader will say something like 'back to back,' and then you have to turn back to back. Or the leader might say 'elbow to elbow,' and you have to go elbow to elbow (demonstrating by touching one of the children's elbows with her own). And then, when the leader says, 'Change,' you have to find a new partner. The person who doesn't have a new partner will be the new leader. All right? . . . Why don't you get a partner now."

The children paired off—Jody and Anita, Richard and Jay, Jesse and Ward, and Franka and Jasmine.

The teacher suggested, "Let's make sort of a circle (indicating with her hands what she meant). Just spread out a bit so you don't get in each other's way."

The children stood in pairs in a large circle. The teacher stood on the edge of the circle. When everyone was settled, she said, "Ready? Are you listening? . . . Back to back."

Each pair performed the appropriate action. Anita first faced Jody's back, but quickly turned around as she saw what the other children were doing. Most pairs linked arms, giggling.

The teacher then said "big toe to big toe," hoping that this might give the children the idea of thinking up other unusual, unexpected commands. Several children repeated the words as they performed the action.

The children continued with "elbow to elbow," and then "knees to knees." The children laughed as they bent their knees to meet their partners'. Richard and Jay fell on the floor laughing and saying, "Oh, I can't do it." Franka and Jasmine put their arms around each other.

Seing that the children were ready for a new command, the teacher said, "Very gently, head to head." After the children did this, the teacher said, "Change," and ran to be Jasmine's partner.

Franka announced that she was going to the bathroom. The other children looked for new partners, and everyone soon had paired off except Jody and Anita. Anita announced, "I'm the leader."

The teacher pointed out, "Jody needs a partner."

Anita retorted, "I'm the leader. I was her partner before."

"You were? Let's wait until Franka comes back," the teacher suggested.

Note: It was only while viewing the videotape afterwards that the teacher realized what Anita meant when she said, "I was her partner before." While playing the game, the teacher did not notice that all the other children, too, had in mind the rule that they could not have a partner they had before. (This is an example of a rule introduced and followed faithfully by all the children, without the teacher's thinking about it.) What Anita meant was, "I was Jody's partner before; so I cannot be her partner any more."

Franka returned shortly. The teacher said to Franka as soon as she was close enough to hear, "We said, 'Change,' so find a partner real fast."

Franka approached Jody, but Jody ran away from her. She then tried Anita, but Anita, too, refused, saying, "No—her (meaning, 'Choose Jody'). I'm the leader." Franka approached Jody again holding out her hand, but Jody backed away.

Jay pointed out, "It doesn't matter who's the leader. You all get a turn."
"Yeah," agreed Ward.

The teacher commented, "We can't play unless someone is her partner."

With her hands on her hips, Anita told Jody, "Jody, you have to have a partner."

Jody retorted, "I don't have to listen to you, Anita."

Franka folded her arms across her chest and walked to the other side of the circle. Some of the other children were getting impatient, saying, "Come on. Come on."

Richard offered a solution: "Jody, then you guys have to quit and she'll be the leader (pointing to Franka). How would you like that?"

Jay agreed, "You'll have to go back in the room."

Addressing Jody and Anita, the teacher said, "Did you hear what Richard said? He said he thinks that if you guys can't agree on being partners, then you two should quit, and Franka will be the leader . . . . Franka's waiting for someone to be her partner. He said that if one of you can't be her partner, then you should both quit."

"Yeah, that's right," Jay agreed.

"You think so, too, Jay?" the teacher asked.

Jay nodded his head.

After a moment of silence, Jody said to Richard, "Well, Richard, I didn't have a turn. Anita didn't have a turn. And Franka didn't have a turn."

The teacher interpreted Jody's argument to mean, "Franka shouldn't have any special privilege over the two of us because all three of us are in the same position." Although she was impressed with Jody's attempt at giving a logical argument, she decided not to deal with the point Jody had made and, instead, to try to communicate to her that the group was getting impatient. She therefore said with irritation, "But we're just starting the game, Jody. It's the beginning of the game. We just started. I sure would like to get going and play."

Jay said, "Why don't you pick somebody, Jody?" At this point, Anita walked over to Franka as if she were to become her partner, but at the last minute, she turned and walked away.

The teacher asked Anita, "Are you going to be Franka's partner?"

Anita shook her head to indicate no and said, "Then Jody's gonna be the leader."

The teacher said, "I know. Then when Jody says, 'Change,' we can change again."

Anita insisted, "I want to be the leader."

"So does everybody else," said the teacher.

Back-to-Back

Note: Here, the teacher could well have used her power to make Anita become Franka's partner. However, she purposely avoided imposing this solution to give room to the children to construct a resolution of their own.

Richard intervened again, "If you don't take Franka for a partner soon, then you guys will have to quit and she'll just be the leader."

Anita retorted, "No, we don't have to." Ward and Jesse had been clowning around with each other up to this point on one side of the circle. Now, they decided to sit up straight on the floor, observing the proceedings.

The teacher took this opportunity to draw Ward and Jesse into the discussion. "Ward, what should we do?" she asked.

Ward raised his hands slightly and shrugged.

The teacher continued and said to Ward, "Franka needs a partner."

Apparently thinking that the teacher meant she (the teacher) wanted him to be Franka's partner, Ward replied, "I got a partner." Jay in the meantime whispered something to the teacher.

The teacher announced to the group, "Jay has an idea. Let's listen to him."

Jay began his speech, "I think that all three should leave the room, and whoever wants to take a partner . . . ."

Interrupting Jay, Anita burst out, "No, that's not fair!"

Jay waited for Anita to finish and resumed, "Whoever wants to take a partner can come back."

Anita again protested, "That's not fair!"

The teacher pointed out, "Well, it's no fair for us, Anita. We just keep sitting here, waiting to play the game."

"We could start it all over," suggested Jody.

The teacher asked, "Would you like to start it all over?"

Jody nodded yes. Everyone else chorused, "No!"

Richard suggested, "Hey, let's have a secret vote."

"A secret vote? OK . . . . Everybody, close your eyes," the teacher said. Everyone complied.

"How many people want me to start all over? Raise your hand if you want to start all over," the teacher said.

Nobody raised a hand. Jody looked around and then walked out of sight behind a pillar with her head low.

The teacher continued, "OK. Nobody wants me to start all over. Keep your eyes closed. How many people want either Jody or Anita to pick a partner real fast? Raise your hand."

All the hands went up except Anita's. Jody was still out of sight behind the post.

The teacher asked again, "Jody, did you quit? You need to decide if you're gonna play. If you want to quit, you can go back in the room and do something different, OK? But you need to decide."

Note: It would have been much easier here for the teacher to have said, "I guess Jody doesn't want to play any more." However, out of the belief that children develop their autonomy by making clear decisions for themselves, she told Jody that she needed to decide what she wanted to do.

Jody came out, indicating that she wanted to continue playing.

"OK, then, you need to pick a partner," the teacher reminded her.

Ward asked, "Can we open our eyes now?"

The teacher replied, "Yes, you can open your eyes. Everybody wanted them to hurry and pick a partner."

Suddenly Ward announced, "I quit."

Surprised, the teacher responded, "You quit? OK, you go in the room then."

Jay asked, "Who's going to be Jesse's partner?"

The teacher suggested to Franka, "Why don't you become Jesse's partner?"

Franka went over to hold Jesse's hands. Jody asked, "What about me and Anita?"

The teacher answered, "I don't know. What about you and Anita?"

Anita exclaimed, "We can both be the leaders."

The teacher responded, "There's supposed to be only one leader."

Note: Here, the teacher could have said, "What do you think?" to get the entire group to decide. The children might have let the two girls be the co-leaders, and that could have been a solution acceptable to all concerned. Enforcing the rule here was not the best thing to do.

Jesse said, "I think one of them should go back in the room, or else . . . ."

Both Anita and Jay interrupted Jesse at the same time, Anita saying, "Then I won't have no partner!" and Jay, "Yeah, 'cause there's . . . ."

Richard spoke up forcefully here saying, "The one that's holding a partner will get automatic a leader."

Anita complained that there was no one left to be her partner (since Franka had become Jesse's partner).

The teacher offered, "Do you want to be Jasmine's partner, and I'll watch?"

Anita nodded and walked over to take Jasmine's hand. Jay remarked, pointing to Jody, "And she'll be the leader."

"OK, Jody, go ahead," the teacher said with great relief.

Kanota came from the room to join the game at this point and asked, "Can I play?"

The teacher replied, "When someone quits, you can."

Jay and Richard lost no time in reminding the teacher that Ward had quit.

"Oh, you're right. Ward quit. Well, we have to have a certain number . . . . All right, you can be my partner. How's that?" the teacher asked Kanota.

Kanota's answer was, "I want to be Jesse's partner."

The teacher said, "All right, Franka, do you want to be my partner?"

Franka agreed. Several people, anxious to get on with the game, said, "All right, finally . . . ," glad that the matter was at long last settled.

"Wait for Jody. She's going to tell us what to do," the teacher said to make sure everybody was ready.

Jody's first command was, "Elbow to elbow." Meanwhile, Jesse was explaining to Kanota that, "When she says, 'Back to back,' you go back to back." The two of them started clowning around and pushing each other.

Anita yelled to them, "Elbow to elbow! Jesse, elbow to elbow!" The rest of the group tried to get their attention, too.

Richard told them, "We're gonna be waiting for you (to do 'elbow to elbow')."

The teacher said, "Jesse and Kanota, everybody is trying to tell you something."

The others repeated, "Elbow to elbow!" Jesse and Kanota complied.

Jody's next command was, "Knee to knee." Several people repeated the words as they put their knees to their partner's knees. Jody then said, "Back to back," and everybody did this easily. The next command was, "Foot to foot." Almost everyone remained in the back-to-back position and stood with one foot behind the other in such a way that it touched the side of the other person's entire foot. One pair stood on one foot with the bottom of their feet together and arms locked.

Jasmine and Anita tried to do it facing each other but could not keep their balance. "We can't do it! We can't do it!" Anita complained.

"We can," the teacher said as she and Franka kept in the back-to-back position holding hands as they made the bottom of their feet touch, with their toes on the floor.

Anita watched them and then said to Jasmine, "OK, let's do it that way." They tried to imitate the teacher and Franka, but their feet did not manage to meet each other. Several other pairs of children giggled and shrieked in their efforts to maintain their balance. Some fell over. Finally, Anita said again, "We can't do it."

Jody tried to say something to everybody, but it was too noisy to hear her.

The teacher said, "I can't hear what Jody is saying."

The group quieted down a little. Jody repeated, "Head to head." Everyone did this. She then said, "Leg to leg." Most of the children repeated the words as they put one leg next to their partner's leg. Then Jody said, "Change partners." There was a mad scramble to find new partners. When the pairs reformed, they were all boy-girl combinations. Up to this point, the girls had chosen girls, and the boys had chosen boys as partners.

Anita managed to be the new leader. Her first command was, "Neck to neck." This caused a lot of giggling and shrieking as the children tried to do it. They came up with some very awkward positions. After several minutes, most of them were sprawled on the floor. Anita then said, "Sock to sock."

The teacher laughed and said, "OK, Anita, we'll try it." To Jay, her partner, she said, "Is that your sock?" as they tried to match up their socks.

Jody pointed out, "I don't got no socks."

Anita continued, "OK, pants to pants, then, no, shirt to shirt."

The teacher noted that after saying, "Pants to pants," Anita realized that not everybody had on pants.

"Shirt to shirt" was easily done for the most part, but Jesse and Jasmine fell down. Anita went on to say, "Ear to ear," and this was easy for everybody. The next command was, "Arm to arm."

As the children linked arms, Jesse asked the teacher, "When do we change?"

The teacher pointed to Anita and said, "Listen to her."

Note: This reply was good because it put the authority of decision making back in Anita's hands. Children naturally look to the teacher to make decisions, and it is easy to impose our adult authority in situations like this one.

Anita told them, "Nose to nose," which prompted lots of laughing and giggling. She then said, "Mouth to mouth," and this really broke them up. Several children put hands over their mouths. A great deal of laughing, pushing, running around, and yelling ensued.

Noticing that the game was falling apart, the teacher called over the noise, "I think we're getting too noisy. We're still inside."

Anita said, "Skip," and everyone skipped haphazardly around the area, repeating, "Skip, skip."

The teacher said, "You know what? I think it's time to go in and clean up." This idea was greeted with a chorus of protests. As they complained with "Aw's," the children skipped toward their room.

Discussion

Children's play

Older children and adults scramble to find a partner, trying not to be the one left alone. Anita and Jody viewed the role of "It" in exactly the opposite way and wanted to become "It." In Tag (p. 45), Duck, Duck, Goose (p. 46), Poison Seat (p. 43), Fourteen, Stand Still (p. 53), and many other games, too, we see young children's strong desire to become "It."

Except for this change in the object of the game, the game was played in the usual way as expected. Sometimes, children came up with more interesting commands than the conventional, routine commands that adults could think of.

The children took remarkable initiative in dealing with "discipline problems." When Franka came back from the bathroom and could not get Anita or Jody to be her partner, Richard, not the teacher, first proposed a solution. He said, ". . . you guys (Anita and Jody) have to quit and she (Franka)'ll be the leader," and Jay quickly agreed. When Jesse and Kanota were clowning around and pushing each other, too, the children took the initiative of correcting this behavior, first Anita and then the rest of the group, especially Richard. When the children's autonomy and initiative are cultivated over a long time, they do become able to govern themselves to a large extent.

The value of the game

Games involving partners must sometimes be avoided, for example, when there is a child whom nobody wants as a partner. In this situation, however, it served as an occasion for the group to deal with a social problem. At least some of the children could see that to satisfy a desire, one sometimes has to give it up for a short while. Anita conceded when she let Jody be "It," but by permitting the game to continue, she soon gave herself a chance to be "It."

The children thought at some level about numerical quantification when they observed that the game worked well as long as everybody except one had a partner. When there were three children, two of whom refused to take a partner, the game broke down. The children certainly did not think about the division of the group into subgroups of two, but these situations serve as a foundation for learning arithmetic later. They also argued that when one child leaves and another comes, the number remains the same.

The game gave to "It" an occasion to think up interesting commands to give. It also gave to the others opportunities to follow the same command in many different ways. "Foot to foot" was a particularly good task that elicited spatial reasoning around the physical problem of keeping balance.

The teacher's role

The teacher had a major part because more time was spent trying to resolve a conflict than in playing the game. When the teacher has a conviction about her objectives, she does not hestitate to give the children the time they need to engage in social experimentation. She had a remarkable amount of confidence, based on realistic knowledge, that the group could eventually construct a solution. Without this confidence, she could not have tolerated the long stress of cooperation. Without her conviction, the following techniques she used would not have had much effect either: She verbalized her own impatience and the other players' desire to go on with the game, and she picked up on children's suggestions to get the group to consider them ("Did you hear what Richard said? He said he thinks that if you guys can't agree on being partners, then you two should quit, and Franka will be the leader . . .").

As stated in Chapter 2, the fostering of children's autonomy helps their emotional development. Anita was not an emotionally strong child, and we were surprised that, in the end, she was big enough to give up wanting to be "It." The teacher could have solved the problem by suggesting that Anita would be "It" first (because she became upset and cried easily) and Jody would have a turn next (because she was emotionally a much stronger child). Such a solution would not have given either child the time and experience they needed to work out an acceptable resolution of their own.

This example demonstrates that children's development is inseparably social, cognitive, and emotional. The mutual respect we see in this chapter between the adult and children, and among the children, is inseparably social, cognitive, and affective at the same time.

Chapter 7

Marbles

Candace Arthur

THE CHILDREN had been playing Marbles since the beginning of the year. To extend their play further, I wanted the children to make up a game, with some help from the teacher. I suggested shooting the marble through an opening, which resulted in four long blocks placed in a square with spaces in three corners, as shown in Photograph 7.1.[1]

7.1. *Four long blocks placed in a square with space in three corners.*

[1] All photographs were taken later to clarify the points made in this chapter.

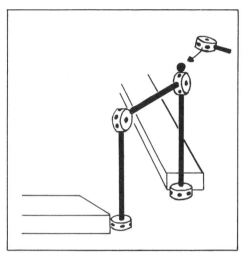

Figure 7.1. *Balancing a marble on top of the bridge.*

Three Tinker Toy bridges were set in each of the open corners. Other materials used were three mallets, ten blue marbles, ten orange marbles, ten white marbles, and a shooter (larger marble brought in during activity).

Only two children played because they needed time to experiment and to coordinate their ideas on making up their own game. This would be more difficult with more than two children. Also, in a small group, the teacher can respond better to the children's ideas. I presented the activity open-ended, asking, "How can we play a game with these things?"

Two avid marble players tried a new game: Rudy, age 5;4, and John, age 5;1. When we arrived at the play area, I said, "I put these things out here so we could play a new game." The children each chose their ten marbles, and played with the mallets. After they tried out the mallets and saw how they worked, John asked me how to play the game.

"I wonder if we could make up our own game. I've never played with this setup either," I replied.

John immediately had an idea, "I know! You put your marble up here, and hit it along here." He pointed to the top of one of the bridges.

To be sure I had understood him correctly, I asked, "You mean you balance the marble on top of the bridge (as shown in Photograph 7.2 and Figure 7.1), and hit it with the mallet so it will roll along the top of the bridge?"

John nodded, "Yeah!"

I could hardly believe he was serious about this preposterous idea, but he clearly was! However, I felt John would understand the physical impossibility of this idea far better by trying it out than by my telling him. "OK with me, how about you, Rudy?" I asked.

Rudy agreed and suggested, "Let's do Eeney Meeney."

"Let's start together," I added.

We said the verse in unison, and it landed on John. He took his turn, of course without success. The marble simply fell on the rug. Rudy seemed a little unsure, and looked to me, saying, "You go next."

7.2.
*John's idea:
Balance a marble on
top of the bridge and
then hit the marble
with the mallet.*

Chapter 7

I took my turn and naturally fared no better than had John. By the time Rudy took his turn, he saw that John's idea would not work. He then came up with a new idea, shown in Photograph 7.3 and Figure 7.2. "Let's try to hit it along the block instead," he suggested, indicating that he wanted to knock the marble from the top of the bridge as before, and on to the flat boards. We agreed to this, and all tried unsuccessfully. Then both children had new ideas simultaneously. Rudy suggested, "You hit it off the top of the bridge, and if it goes inside the square (enclosure) you get to keep it, but if it goes outside, you have to put it behind your back." This was the same game we had just tried, hitting the marble from the bridge along the block, except for the additional stipulation that if the marble happened to roll off the block and inside the enclosure, you keep it, but otherwise it was out of the game. John's idea was to "hit it from the top of the bridge and try to knock the pile of marbles, to knock one out of the pile," as shown in Photograph 7.4.

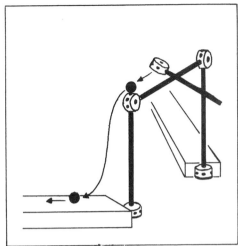

Figure 7.2. *Rudy's idea.*

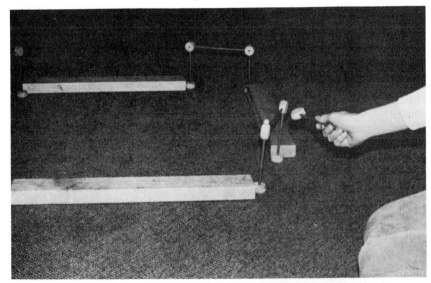

7.3. Rudy's idea:
Try to knock the marble from the top of the bridge onto the flat boards.

7.4.
John's idea:
Hit the marble from the top of the bridge and try to knock one of the marbles out of the pile.

Marbles

121

I asked Rudy, "John has a different idea from what we've tried; want to try it?"

Rudy agreed and John began to do Eeney Meeney. Rudy then suddenly noticed a different way of using the bridges, and exclaimed, "Hey, we could shoot the marbles through here!"

Since John did not respond to Rudy, I interrupted his reciting and asked, "Did you hear Rudy's idea of hitting the marbles through these bridges? . . . Want to try that?"

John shook his head.

Note: Looking at the videotape afterwards, I realized that I had responded to Rudy's idea and interrupted John because it matched my own notion of what would be an interesting game. A more constructive way to handle the situation would have been to acknowledge Rudy's idea, leaving it up to him to pursue it, or else suggest he bring it up again after trying John's idea.

I then said to Rudy, "Well, we already agreed to play John's way, and he doesn't want to change."

Rudy was disappointed and objected, "But I know it's not going to work." John finished Eeney Meeney, landing on himself, and took a turn, not hitting any of the marbles. He seemed surprised that his shooting marble bounced on the carpet and jumped over the pile of marbles. I took my turn and also missed.

Rudy balked, saying, "I don't like that way, and I'm not going to do it."

Note: Perhaps part of the reason Rudy was uncooperative was that I had conveyed the message that I liked Rudy's idea better than John's. When both John and I failed, Rudy's negative feelings about John's idea increased.

Turning to John, I suggested, "You know, this is still pretty hard. Shall we try a new way now?"

"OK," John agreed.

Rudy then instructed that one person should put all his marbles in the enclosure, as shown in Photograph 7.5. Using one as a shooter, he could shoot it from the hand to make it hit a marble out through an opening. "If you hit a marble out, you get to keep it," Rudy added. He further specified that after a

7.5.
Rudy's idea:
Put all the marbles
in the enclosure and
use one as a shooter.

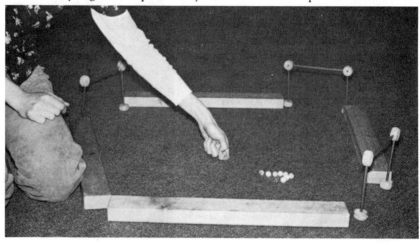

completed turn, the player should take out his marbles, and the next player should put his in. When John's turn came, he placed the shooter on top of the bridge, and used the mallet to hit it down at the pile of marbles below, continuing his previous game.

Note: I knew the children found it difficult to shoot a marble from their hand because their hands were too small to grip the marble firmly enough to shoot it forcefully, especially on the carpeted surface. We had been playing about fifteen minutes without any success, and I worried that the children might become frustrated and lose interest. I decided to model using the mallet to hit the shooter.

On my turn, I placed the shooter on the rug and got ready to hit it with my mallet. Rudy complained that this way was too easy.

"Why don't you try, Rudy? Maybe you'll get one out," I suggested.

Rudy tried it my way and hit a marble out. However, this seemed to convince him even more that this method was too easy. He protested, "That's like a dumb hockey game, Candy," and insisted, "use your *hand* to shoot the shooter, like I did."

Note: Rudy's persistence made me realize that my fears were unfounded. His statement also shows that when the children felt strongly, they were not afraid to refuse my suggestions.

After a few more turns, John became impatient and announced, "Teacher, I always have to play his game, and he won't pay attention to my game."

I asked, "Well, what was your game, John?"

He answered, "My game was to put *all* the marbles in the middle and try to knock out someone else's."

"Oh, you mean you thought of a *new* game to play, John?" I asked.

"Yeah," John responded.

Rudy spoke up, "Yeah, then I'll hit your marble."

"So then you get to keep it, Rudy," responded John.

I asked Rudy if he wanted to try that way.

"No, I don't want to do it."

I shrugged my shoulders and remarked, "Well, I don't see how we're going to be able to play at all if we can't agree on a way to play."

Angrily, Rudy said, "I want to do it my way."

"And John wants to do it his way," I added quietly.

Note: I think this was a good response because, rather than use adult authority to decide, or try to persuade Rudy, I merely stated the facts. Both wanted to play their way. By confronting Rudy with John's feelings, I hoped he would be moved to decenter and realize that John had desires just as he did and both were equally legitimate.

"You know what?" asked John. "He got lots of his turns and I didn't."

Rudy was indignant, and retorted, "I didn't get lots of my turns."

"You got two," John insisted.

I thought that neither Rudy nor I understood John's point, so I inquired, "Do you mean that Rudy had two ideas, John?"

John nodded, "He had two turns to play his way."

I didn't remember whether this was true and was confused about how to respond. I asked, "You want to say we finish Rudy's game, and then play your way?"

Note: I think I acted indecisively in the teacher's role. I should have stated that we would finish one game before starting another. It would have been more constructive to have acted in the player's role, saying, "I think we should finish one game, then start another. What do you think?" The teacher's stating a rule, as opposed to a player's expressing her opinion, is a subtle but important difference.

Rudy ignored my suggestion and voiced his own solution, "I know what we could do. Say Eeney Meeney, and whoever it lands on, we get to do it his way."

"What do you think about that, John?" I asked, turning to him.

John refused, saying, "No, 'cause maybe he'll say . . . (he started doing the verse silently).

Rudy stopped his hand, ordering, "Stop! John, don't do it yet!"

John was aware that Rudy knew where to start the verse to make it land on himself. However, John did not realize that Rudy could do this only with two people, not with three. I asked John if he were worried Rudy would make it land on himself. John didn't answer, but started to do the verse silently again. "John, it looks as though you're trying to figure out how to make it land on you. Maybe we should do something that nobody knows where it will land."

"Yeah," John agreed to this idea, but Rudy didn't.

"Rudy, I think John was afraid that you know how to make it land on you," I said to Rudy.

"Huh uh, I don't either," Rudy stated flatly.

By this time I was no longer sure what this conflict was about and I wondered whether or not they knew themselves. I expressed my frustration to get them back into the game. "Boy, we can't even agree on this!"

There was a moment of silence. John then volunteered to a compromise. "OK, let's finish his game."

"Whew," I said, much relieved. "Whose turn was it?"

"It's my turn," said John. He aimed the shooter, this time with his hand, but it only dribbled a few inches. He quickly took it back and tried again, with no complaints from Rudy. The shooter veered to the left this time, and missed the marbles again.

John looked frustrated, so I suggested, "How about having more than one try? This is real hard."

"OK," Rudy agreed, "three tries."

On my turn I shot the shooter forcefully. It missed the pile of marbles and shot right through the opening and out of the enclosure. Rudy laughed, "It went downtown! I'm going to shoot mine soooo hard, right out of that hole (the opening across from him), and it'll go clear to my house on 35th Street!"

While waiting for his turn, John had noticed that one of his marbles was slightly bigger than the others. He offered to share it as the shooter. He also suggested five tries each, to which we agreed.

I found it interesting that on each try the children regrouped the marbles into a pile, rather than leaving them where they had landed previously. Instead of trying to hit out a single marble nearest an opening, they aimed at the whole bunch. As Rudy bunched his marbles together for his second try, I asked, "How come you move them all together again? You had one pretty near the opening that time."

Seeming to think my question silly, Rudy replied, "'Cause I want to hit them *all* out, Teach."

On my next turn, they cautioned me to shoot "real hard," as if that were more important than aiming.

John suddenly announced, "I'm on Rudy's team."

Surprised, I asked, "We have teams? Whose team will I be on?"

Rudy answered, "You're on John and mine's team."

"We're all a team?" I asked him.

"No," laughed John, "'Cause who could we win?"

We continued to play this way for about ten minutes. Since no one yet had hit a single marble, I asked again to use the mallet to hit the shooter. This time they agreed. I hit one of my marbles, but not hard enough to make it go out.

Rudy used the mallet next, and he succeeded in knocking one through an opening. We all cheered. He then declared, "All you need is two marbles out to win." On his fourth try, he got another out, and won the game.

John lost no time in announcing the rules for the next game: "Everyone's marble's inside the square. You hit the shooter with the mallet, to knock out someone *else's* marbles, and you get to keep 'em." Again a conflict erupted over who would be first. Both wanted to start Eeney Meeney on themselves, which would make it land on themselves.

I complained, "I sure would like to get started."

Note: The fact that they had figured out how to make the verse land on themselves, or even realized that this is possible, shows an advanced level of thinking. However, it is also a sign that another method of determining who goes first is necessary. It would have been appropriate to have introduced a method based on chance, such as tossing a coin, rolling a die, or drawing straws.

John offered to do Bubblegum, another verse, but Rudy refused, and lay face down on the floor.

"Rudy," I said impatiently, "John and I agreed to do Bubblegum, and we're tired of waiting for you. Do you still want to play?"

Rudy sat up slowly, and John recited the verse. It landed on Rudy. I went to the classroom to get a real shooter (so that John would have all ten of his marbles), and the game finally began.

On John's turn, he attempted to make up a new rule, "Six tries each."

Rudy protested, "I didn't get six turns."

"When you told us the game, you didn't say that," I added.

Rudy declared, "And I'm sick of starting over and over."

John complied, "All right, one turn for all."

After two turns each, Rudy hit one out, and became very excited. "Whee! I got one out!"

John spoke up quickly, "Yeah, but it's your own! Remember I said to hit out someone else's?" He looked to me for support.

"What happens when you knock out your own, John?" I asked.

"You have to put it back," he replied, then he looked over to Rudy, who was crestfallen. "But you get another turn!" he added quickly.

Impressed with this solution, I looked to Rudy and inquired, "How does that sound?"

Rudy nodded, put his marble back, and said smugly, "I get another turn."

Two turns later, Rudy hit out *two* of his own marbles. "You win 'em!" shouted John. "If you hit out two, you get to keep 'em, but if you hit out just one, you have to put it back and shoot again."

"That sounds good to me," I responded, again impressed with John's improvisation. "I sure hope I get two out."

Rudy cheered and pretended his mallet was a lollipop. "Mmmm, mine's a good lollipop, how about yours, John?"

"Mmmm, good," answered John, pretending to lick his. Right before their turn though, each pretended to "lock" on the round connector to the stick because they sometimes came apart. They also adjusted the mallets, attaching the sticks to the side or the front of the connector, to compare which way worked best, as can be seen in Photograph 7.6. They also experimented with holding the mallet differently. They soon became skillful and after each turn counted their marbles to compare how many each of us had. Noticing that I was doing poorly, they offered encouragement and advice. Rudy ran excitedly around the room each time he went to fetch a marble that had rolled out.

After about fifteen minutes of smooth playing, Rudy began to jump and fall on a nearby mat, shouting, "Hey, John, come here!"

"Rudy," I asked, "are you still playing, or do you want to quit now?"

Rudy ran back to his place, saying, "Not me, I'm still in."

I noticed that when there were many marbles left to aim at, the children no longer regrouped the marbles after each shot as they had done previously, but left them as they had landed on the last turn. However, when few marbles were left, they again regrouped them. I think they thought that aiming at many would increase their chances of hitting one, which was better than hitting none, even if it didn't go out.

When there were only eight marbles remaining, John cautioned Rudy,

7.6. *Adjusting the mallets to compare which way worked best.*

Chapter 7

"Don't hit them *all* out, Rudy, 'cause then the game is over."

Rudy reassured John, "Well, I don't think I can get them all at once, John, 'cause there's (after counting them) eight left, and that's a lot."

The game ended when John hit the last marble out. Each of us counted our marbles. Rudy had 18, John had 8, and I had 4. "I'm the winner," exclaimed Rudy.

"And I'm next!" chimed John. "And you lost, Candy." Both seemed equally satisfied with the results.

"I guess I sure did. But that was a good game. Now it's time to go back to the room." The children protested at first but were satisfied when they found out they could take the materials into the room and play with them later.

Discussion

Children's play and the value of the game

The activity proved appropriate for these children. Despite the numerous conflicts and interventions, both children remained highly involved throughout the 45-minute activity. They sustained interest because they invented their own games, and therefore felt a personal investment and desire to complete them. The activity not only was enjoyable, but also fostered development in the following areas:

1. *Ability to come up with interesting ideas.* Both children when presented with an opportunity to think up their own games were prolific in their inventions. Below is the sequence of games they invented:

Place marble on bridge and hit it so that it rolls across the top of the bridge.

Place marble on top of bridge and hit it so that it rolls along the block.

Place marble on top of the bridge and hit it to a pile of marbles on the floor in the enclosure.

Place one's own marbles in the enclosure, and using a shooter, first by hand, then with the mallet, hit own marbles through openings.

Place everyone's marbles in the center and use mallet to hit the shooter and knock opponent's marbles through openings.

This sequence clearly shows how from the first impossible idea, each successive game built on elements from the preceding one and elaborated upon it, making each new game a little more playable and interesting than the last. The final game was remarkably similar to pool.

2. *Physical and logico-mathematical knowledge.* This game was an elaboration of a physical-knowledge activity. As can be seen in Kamii and DeVries (1978), one of the criteria of a good physical-knowledge activity is that the phenomenon be observable and producible by the child's own action. The child should also be able to vary his actions in order to change the effects he produces. This activity meets both criteria and also gives the child the possibility of constructing logico-mathematical knowledge as he elaborates his physical knowledge. For example, in figuring out where to place the marbles in order to hit them out, and in deciding which marble was in the easiest position to knock out, the child engaged in *spatial reasoning*.

The children also found out that shooting with the mallet was easier than shooting with the hand, that some ways to use the mallet were more effective than others, and that hitting just one marble produced a different result than hitting a bunch. These comparisons are examples of the types of *logical relationships* children construct as they observe the variations in their actions and the resultant movement of the objects. The children would not have invented increasingly playable games, dropping impossible ideas along the way, if they had not coordinated all the relationships in their minds.

The children also engaged in *numerical reasoning* when they counted and compared how many marbles they got, as well as when they kept track of the number of tries each player had taken.

I was amazed that the children conceived of the first impossible idea (to balance the marble along the top of the bridge and hit it across). Both thought this was a good idea, and tried it seriously. We also each took a turn at the second, equally implausible idea. Before trying these ideas, the children had no feeling for their impossibility. Even after trying, they were not convinced that the ideas were physically impossible, but instead, only felt that these ideas did not work this time.

Genuine caring for each other's feelings came through despite the conflicts. The most touching example occurred in the last game, when Rudy finally hit out the first marble which turned out to be his own. John reminded us of the rule (to hit out someone else's), but upon seeing Rudy's disappointment, quickly improvised a solution which saved face for both children.

Finally, although the children decided on the rules, they did not see them as being absolute. For example, in the last game, the rule was one try per turn, but if a player's shot clearly missed its mark, no one complained if the player took his turn over.

Reflections about my teaching

The activity was both challenging and enlightening for me as a teacher. Several unexpected developments created challenges, and the discrepancy between what I wanted to do, thought about, and ended up doing was enlightening.

My difficulties stemmed from my overconcern that the activity be a "success." Even though I asked the children to think up the game, it was hard to dissociate myself from the activity that I had thought up. As a result, I sometimes lost sight of my main intention to encourage autonomy and independent thinking. At times I intervened in ways opposed to my objectives. The most blatant example of this was interrupting John to call attention to Rudy's idea, which happened to coincide with my own.

Gradually, as I realized the children were actively involved in the games and capable of handling the conflicts with assistance, I balanced the roles of teacher, observer, and player. As I relaxed, the activity became enjoyable.

Another difficulty, built into the activity, was the initial groping and experimenting with the materials before the invention of the last, most viable game. This was difficult for the children, who had many ideas to try out and became impatient quickly. It was also frustrating for me because I could often tell before trying out an idea that it was not going to work. I handled the situation well by refraining from making judgments about the various ideas before we tried them.

This activity provided me with a greater feeling of trust in my ideas of what children might find interesting and their ability to invent activities conducive to their own development.

Follow-up

The final game could be played in the classroom anytime during free play. I might initially help set up the blocks and spaces, but the children could teach their game to the others in the room. For the other children, this would be like learning any other game with the object and rules predetermined. This would be an equally valuable, but different experience.

Although the bridges revealed useful information about the children's physical knowledge, I would not use them again. They tended to fall over, and leaving a space between the blocks would suffice.

Chapter 8

Pin the Tail on the Donkey

Rheta DeVries

A CHILDHOOD MEMORY of a friend's birthday party brought to mind the classical game of Pin the Tail on the Donkey (p. 39). In this game, blindfolded players try one at a time to pin a paper tail on a picture of a tailless donkey. The winner is the one who places the tail most accurately. In the game I remembered, the "store bought" donkey picture was a special novelty, and everyone was excited to learn there would be a prize for the winner.

I impatiently awaited my turn to be blindfolded. Most children ran off to do something else as soon as they finished their turns, but everyone appreciated the humor of seeing the donkey with a tail on his ear, nose, or other unlikely place. When my moment came, I groped toward the paper, attached the tail, and pulled off the blindfold. I remember a vague feeling of discomfort and disappointment upon seeing that I had lodged the tail on the donkey's midsection. I knew that I had not won the prize, and my enthusiasm for the game was over. Later, there was some conflict over who had won because two players had stuck the tail close together near the donkey's rear. My friend's mother judged the winner and awarded the prize.

The memory of this experience led to reflections about the educational possibilities of Pin the Tail on the Donkey. The game involves children's representation of spatial relationships of a special kind (having to do with body images), and inspires children to construct a visual image of the shape of a donkey. To aim when blindfolded, the child must imagine the donkey's tail in its spatial relationship to the rest of him. The suspense of the blindfolding and the often amusing results seemed potentially interesting for small groups of children. However, the classic materials offer children little possibility for using or elaborating their imagery to figure out where to aim. Blindfolded aiming at a flat drawing is primarily luck. Therefore we tried to figure out how to improve the materials, and found inspiration in Piaget and Inhelder's (1948) experiments with tactual perception.

As part of their study of the development of the representation of space, they examined how children imagine an unseen object or cardboard shape simply by exploring it tactually. After feeling a shape (such as a saw-toothed semicircle or trapezoid, irregular surfaces with one or two holes, open and closed rings, or intertwined or superimposed rings), children were asked to name, draw or point to it among a group of objects. The child had to translate his tactile perceptions and movements into a visual image.

The results showed that progress in constructing these visual images developed in correspondence with the development of children's perceptual activity. When a child touched a part of an object, he got a certain kind of information from this single tactual perception (which was a centration on the part contacted). The resultant visual image, however, is necessarily incomplete, and children with limited perceptual activity made many errors in identifying the shapes. Each tactile perception gives new information which can be coordinated with previous information. This new perceptual activity results in decentering from the previous more limited perception. Piaget and Inhelder comment, "The passage from one centration to another (or 'decentration') thus tends to the correction or regulation of centrations by each other, and the more numerous the decentrations, the more accurate becomes the resulting perception (p. 24)." Piaget and Inhelder emphasized that recognizing these shapes did not occur by touch alone (simply by tactile perception), but by the intellectual coordinations of a whole group of exploratory movements (by perceptual activity which goes beyond perception). This distinction between simple perception and the perceptual activity which is such a crucial part of the constructive process constitutes a basic difference between Piaget's views and empiricist or behaviorist views of knowing.

This research gave us the idea of using a cardboard cutout of an animal to permit children's tactual exploration of its contour. We hoped that the possibility for such exploration would lead children to construct their image by thinking about relationships among the parts of the whole. We also thought that using several detached parts would offer more possibilities for elaborating the image. Such a figure is already a representational object which occupies a position midway between reality and the mental image. It differs from reality by being a two-dimensional model of a larger three-dimensional object, having some characteristics of the real object. It differs from imagery by having physical properties lacking in mental images. The child can manipulate such a reduced model of reality in ways not possible either in reality or in imagery. By encouraging the use of tactile exploration (which in seeing children is far less developed than the visual and gives different information), we hoped that the game would provide abundant possibilities for children to translate tactile perceptions and movements into visual images. We expected that such experiences would contribute to children's representation of space and to their general development of symbolic instruments. Our first rather unsuccessful effort with the revised form of the game illustrates the kinds of difficulties children have with it and shows the importance of giving careful consideration to certain characteristics of the materials used.

An intrigued teacher who wanted to experiment with the preceding ideas cut an incomplete pig and four missing parts from bright yellow and blue cardboard (see Figure 8.1). She planned to put masking tape on the back of each piece after children had first looked them all over and assembled the pig on the floor. The following four-year-olds volunteered first:

Figure 8.1. *The incomplete pig and four missing parts.*

Linda
Pat
Jackie
Daphne

Figure 8.2. *How the children spontaneously assembled the pig.*

Spreading all the cutouts on the floor just outside the classroom, the teacher asked, "What parts of the pig do you see?"

Pat immediately picked up the curly tail and put it at the pig's rear, saying, "This is the tail. It goes here." Linda confidently arranged the leg under the stomach.

Jackie reached for the nose, saying, "This is the eyes." Placing this part on the pig's face, she pointed at the two holes (meant to represent nostrils) and explained that these were the eyes.

The teacher, surprised that Jackie saw the nose as eyes, wanted her to correct herself. She asked, "What else could it be?"

The children stared silently at the piece. The teacher decided she would have to suggest the answer, and asked, "Have you seen a pig's nose?" She thought they would take this hint and see immediately that the shape was a nose.

Instead, Daphne pointed to the protrusion at the bottom of the piece (marked D in Figure 8.2), and responded, "This is the pig's nose."

Jackie (perhaps thinking that Daphne meant the whole piece) disagreed hotly, "That's a big lie!"

Note: Jackie did not mean that Daphne was deliberately telling a falsehood. Typically young children use the word "lie" to refer to something which is not "true." For Jackie, the truth was that the part represented eyes, and Daphne was therefore wrong to call it a nose.[1]

By this time, the teacher was frustrated and felt that she had to tell the children what the piece was. She put it in front of her own nose, saying, "Let me show you on my face. Does this look like a pig's nose?" She pointed out her own nostrils and grunted like a pig.

Note: The teacher thought it was important for the children to see the parts the same way she did. However, this was not essential to the game, which could have been played just as well according to Jackie's interpretation of the piece, especially since the other children seemed to accept her idea. Although the teacher had made the materials with certain symbolic meanings in her mind, she should have realized that Jackie's interpretation was equally valid. The teacher should have accepted it instead of imposing her own view.

Daphne accepted the teacher's idea and agreed compliantly, "Yeah, it looks like a nose." Jackie said nothing, but stubbornly took the piece from the teacher and put it back where she had placed it before.

Note: Jackie's persistence illustrates how fruitless it is to try to change children's convictions merely by telling them they are wrong. In this situation, there was no objective way Jackie could see the part as the teacher did.

[1] This use of the word "lie" is an example of what Piaget (1932, pp. 139-162) found when he asked young children what a lie is. The youngest children said, "A lie is a bad word you shouldn't say (including a swear word)." At the next level, they said, "A lie is something that is not true (including 2 + 2 = 5)." Only much older children defined a lie as "something that is not true that you say on purpose to fool the other person."

Figure 8.3. *The pig finally assembled on the floor.*

Jackie's persistence shows that she already had developed a significant degree of autonomy. Moreover, her insistence on her own idea shows that her general relationship with the teacher was such that she could behave in this autonomous way.

The teacher commented, "Jackie thinks it's an eye," hoping for correction by other children.

Daphne pushed the piece down closer to where the teacher had intended it to go. Jackie started to protest, but was cut off by the teacher's next question, and sat unhappily.

The teacher was relieved to see the nose in the right place, and seemed unaware of Jackie's dissatisfaction. She picked up the ear and asked, "What about this one?"

Daphne lifted the head of the pig and put the ear underneath. Figure 8.3 shows how the pig looked at this point.

The teacher had an impulse to correct the arrangement of the two pieces which were not placed as she had intended.[2] However, after the difficulty with the nose, she decided this would take too much time, and that it was not worth delaying the game.

Note: The artistic pig pleased the teacher's aesthetic sense but caused the children unnecessary confusion. Only the tail and the leg were clearly recognizable, and children did not spontaneously "see" the other parts in the way the teacher intended.

The teacher then suggested the game by asking, "If I put the pig up on the wall, and put a blindfold on you, do you think you can put the parts on the pig?" She passed out the pieces, giving the leg to Linda, the nose to Pat, the ear to Jackie, and the tail to Daphne.

Daphne protested, "I don't want to! I want to watch!"

The teacher responded, "OK, you can watch how we put the parts on the pig."

Note: Daphne had an unusually low tolerance for frustration, and was always highly anxious about new experiences. The teacher knew that it was important to support her feeling of being in control of entering the game only insofar as she felt comfortable.

The teacher suggested that children could help her put the pig on the wall with tape, and began to put tape on the backs of the missing parts.

Everyone struggled with the problem of how to affix the tape. Jackie first attempted to stick a flat strip on the back of the ear. When she then tried to make it stick on the face, she saw that it would not stay. Next she tried to put the tape on, sticky side up, but then the tape did not stay on the ear. Finally, she watched carefully as the teacher made loops of tape, sticky side out, so that one side of the loop stuck to the part and one side was ready to stick to the pig. Awkwardly and with great effort, Jackie managed to get her piece ready for play.

Note: This was an excellent natural situation in which the teacher encouraged children's construction of knowledge of physical objects and their

---

[2] The detached ear was meant to be the left one, and the leg piece was meant to go to the right of the other three legs, directly under the tail.

spatial reasoning.

When everything was ready, the teacher asked for the first volunteer. "Who wants to try first?"

"I do," Linda quickly replied.

The teacher blindfolded her and turned her around three times, suspensefully chanting, "'Round and 'round and 'round she goes/And where she'll stop nobody knows." At the end of the chant, the teacher aimed Linda toward the pig to make sure she would walk in the right direction.

Figure 8.4. *Blindfolded placement of the leg by Linda.*

Note: Spinning rituals create disorientation and the problem of finding the wall itself. In this situation, the problem of sticking the piece on the pig was hard enough, and disorientation may even have interfered with visualizing the pig.

Linda groped forward, holding the leg in her right hand and reaching into space with her left. Her left hand encountered the wall just at the pig's head. She followed the contour of its back with the palm of her left hand and, without feeling for the other legs, she planted the leg as shown in Figure 8.4. She immediately removed the blindfold and beamed at the result.

The teacher saw the result as inaccurate because it conformed neither to her original idea nor to the model made by the children. While she did not want to crush Linda's feelings, she also wanted her to see a need for correction. This ambivalence led her to smile and exclaim, "Very close! How did you know to put it there?"

Linda answered with a shrug, "I don't know."

Persisting, the teacher probed, "Did you feel for it?"

Linda did not respond.

Note: It is often a good idea to encourage children to verbalize their techniques to help them become more conscious of their actions. It may also be a useful way to get children to become conscious of what others do. Here, however, the question, "How did you know to put it there?" seems inappropriate early in the game. Although Linda had felt the outline, it was too soon to expect her to be conscious of her technique. Such premature questioning can spoil children's pleasure and squelch their initiative. Throughout the first day of play, it is better just to encourage children's focus on the action of producing the desired effect.

Linda started to remove the leg from the pig. Stopping her, the teacher suggested, "Let's leave all the parts on so we can see what kind of pig we made." Noticing that Jackie seemed eagerly impatient, the teacher inquired, "Do you want to be next?"

Jackie nodded as Pat protested, "*I* want to be next."

The teacher consoled Pat by telling her she could be after Jackie, and then blindfolded Jackie.

Pat took the initiative to turn Jackie around while chanting "'Round and 'round . . . ," in perfect imitation of the teacher.

Thinking that Pat must have played with this ritual before, the teacher was pleased to see her cope in such a constructive way with her frustration over having to wait for a turn.

Holding the pig's ear in both hands, Jackie shuffled hesitantly toward the wall. Without any tactual exploration, she haphazardly stabbed the ear at the

Figure 8.5. *Jackie's blindfolded placement of the ear.*

Figure 8.6. *Pat's blindfolded placement of the nose.*

wall, with the result shown in Figure 8.5. Everyone burst into laughter.

After removing Jackie's blindfold, the teacher leaned down sympathetically to see if Jackie felt unhappy or embarrassed. As they looked together at the result, the teacher saw neither pleasure nor dissatisfaction on Jackie's face. She again resorted to her ambiguous comment, "Pretty close, wasn't it?"

Note: Since the teacher did not have a clue as to how Jackie felt about her result, she could have asked her if that was where she wanted it. This might have opened up the possibility of self-correction and, eventually, the issue of what rules are needed if someone wants to change his piece. It might also have been helpful to make a good-natured comment on Jackie's process of producing her result. For example, she might have said, "You just walked up and stuck it on without feeling where it was going! Did it turn out the way you wanted?"

Turning to Pat, the teacher asked, "Are you ready to try the nose? Why don't you look at the pig and get an idea about where it goes?"

Pat scrutinized the figure, looking back and forth at the nose piece in her hand. After she was blindfolded, Linda offered to turn her around with the chant. It came to an end with Pat facing in the direction opposite the pig. She naturally walked forward, going entirely in the wrong direction. The other children watched with fascination, not saying a word as she approached the refrigerator.

Since none of the children were trying to help, the teacher stood by the pig and called, "Pat, why don't you come over toward my voice, and you'll find the pig."

Pat turned around and bravely stumbled in the right direction. Taking a cue from the teacher's effort to help, Daphne yelled, "Go to the wall! Go to the wall!" Jackie joined in this cheering.

The teacher could hardly keep from laughing at the egocentric "help" which was no help at all to Pat who was blindfolded and could not *see* the wall!

Pat seemed unaware that the direction gave her no direction. She responded, "I am!" and seemed spurred on to greater energies by her friends' supportive attitude. Finally, she found the pig, and touched it with her flat palm in several places—the hind part, the back, and the head. Then with certainty, she stuck the nose on the wall about six inches to the left of the pig, as shown in Figure 8.6! Removing her blindfold, she grinned in surprise and amusement.

"The nose on the wall!" exclaimed the teacher. She was astounded that Pat could touch the contour and fail even to get the nose on the pig at all. Seeing that Pat made no move to change the piece, she turned to all the children and asked, "Do you want to put all the parts where they should go?"

Note: Pat surely knew that the nose was incorrect since it was not on the pig at all. The teacher should have encouraged her to correct it.

Daphne moved the nose to its appropriate place and added the tail she'd been holding since the beginning of the game. No one else showed any desire to make a correction. Linda then removed all the detachable pieces and suggested another game. Jackie began by choosing the tail. Again without any tactual exploration, she managed to get the tail in the right spot, but upside down. She pulled off the blindfold and regarded the result seriously, with an ambiguous expression.

The teacher could not figure out whether Jackie was really satisfied. She said, "Isn't that close? You put it where you wanted to, didn't you?" Jackie nodded in agreement.

Note: The teacher's comment was gratuitous. Since Jackie got the tail in the right place purely by luck, it would have been more helpful had the teacher tried to make her aware of the possibility of using a tactual strategy. She might have said something like, "How were you so lucky? You got it in the right place even without feeling the pig."

Linda took the ear. Carefully exploring the pig's back and head with her fingertips, she lifted the head, and put one end of the ear underneath. She pressed the whole thing against the wall, exactly as Daphne had done with the floor arrangement.

The teacher burst out laughing, "That's good. It's even underneath!"

Note: Again the teacher's comment is directed almost exclusively toward the result and not toward the process.

Next, Pat felt the hind part of the pig, then the back and ear. Again, her exploration was with the palm of her hand. Without feeling the bottom part of the figure, she slapped the leg on with almost the same result Linda got in the first game (Figure 8.4). Pat then turned to the teacher and suggested that she take a turn. The other children joined in, begging her to play.

The teacher gently refused and asked who else wanted another turn.

Note: The children's request was a positive and generous gesture to the teacher, indicating acceptance and willingness to share the fun with her. She should have welcomed the opportunity to join the game at their request. It would have been good to do so because of the general value of reducing adult authority (discussed in Chapter 2). It would also have been an excellent opportunity to demonstrate how to explore the pig tactually. She could have made a running commentary on her actions, saying something like, "You had a really good idea to feel the pig. I think I'll do that, too. Here's the nose. Let's see, which is the bottom? Oh, yes, here it sticks down. Now where's the chin? I think I'll use both hands. Here's the top of his head, and down here I feel the bottom where his nose should be."

The game petered out soon after the teacher's refusal to play, and everyone returned to the free play period in the classroom.

Discussion

In the example described here, the teaching was weak, and children's play was much less active than we had hoped. Nevertheless, certain results were encouraging regarding the game's potential value. The idea of assembling the parts of the pig immediately caught the children's interest, and later they were intrigued by the challenge to add the parts while blindfolded. Even the child who did not want to be blindfolded remained an interested observer. The cardboard cutouts did inspire some tactual exploration which suggested at least limited use of visual imagery. The following analysis led to a positive conclusion about the value of the game, and to improvements in materials and teaching.

Children's play

1. The children understood the basic idea of the game. Everyone saw the need to put the missing parts in place, and all except Daphne seemed to enjoy the challenge of doing it blindfolded. They also easily accepted the spinning ritual.

2. Since the teacher did not identify the detached parts or specify where they should go, the children were free in the beginning to impose their own ideas. Their interpretations sometimes differed from those of the teacher and one another in the following ways:

   a. Although everyone saw the leg piece as a leg, Linda and Pat put it in the space between front and back legs (as shown in Figures 8.2 and 8.4) instead of to the far right below the pig's tail as the teacher intended. Neither child saw anything wrong with having one leg shorter than the others.

   b. Jackie saw the nostrils of the artistic nose as the pig's two eyes. When the teacher suggested the idea of a nose, Daphne elaborated Jackie's idea by interpreting the protrusion below and between the "eyes" as the nose. Later, after the teacher's demonstration of the whole piece as a nose, Daphne accepted this idea and corrected Jackie when she continued to insist on putting the piece at the pig's eye level (Figure 8.2).

   c. Pat arranged the curly tail as the teacher intended, but no one seemed to notice later when Jackie put it upside down.

   d. Daphne identified the ear piece as an ear but made it the right one instead of the left as intended by the teacher. She stuck it partially behind the head as if it were on the other side of the head, and Linda later made the same arrangement while blindfolded. Jackie's blindfolded placement of the ear across the face (Figure 8.5) probably did not reflect a different interpretation, but simply resulted from her failure to explore the figure.

3. Without any suggestion from the teacher, Linda spontaneously used the strategy of tactually exploring the pig, to figure out where to put the leg. However, she explored only part of the contour globally, using the flat of her palm. This approach enabled her to recognize the distinctive head and back, and then she aimed the leg more or less intuitively, without feeling the lower part of the figure. Piaget and Inhelder (1948) also observed this relatively passive form of tactual exploration among children still in the early stages of abstracting shapes. Pat's first effort was even less active as she touched the figure in several places without any spatial continuity. This disconnected information apparently led her to imagine that the head part was, instead, part of the back, and she ended up placing the nose on the wall to the left of the figure. Her later placement of the leg was almost identical to Linda's global, intuitive approach. Jackie made no effort at tactual exploration. Only Linda later seemed to explore more actively and systematically (seemingly trying to analyze specific features) when she used her fingertips to find where to put the ear under the head in a copy of Daphne's original arrangement.

4. Four instances of children's attempts to regulate the game occurred:

a. Jackie disagreed with Daphne about how to identify the nose piece. Jackie saw it as "eyes" and objected when Daphne (who had accepted the teacher's idea) called part of it a nose. She even tried to insist on her own idea after the teacher showed how she meant for the piece to go.

b. Pat spontaneously took the initiative to do the spinning ritual for Jackie, and Linda subsequently did it for Pat.

c. Daphne and Jackie tried to help blindfolded Pat by yelling, "Go to the wall!"

d. Pat suggested that the teacher take a turn, and everyone then begged her to play, too.

Value of the game

1. This revised version of Pin the Tail on the Donkey seems to be of particular value for the transition from perceptual activities, based on already present knowledge, to mental representation. This transition involves the extension of perceptual knowledge through direct contact to the ability to evoke objects in the imagination when they are not actually present. In general, the type of activity described in this chapter may inspire children to exercise and develop symbolic instruments which play a supportive role in later conceptual development. The content of the activity is mainly spatial (although it also bears on knowledge that pigs have two ears, four legs, etc.) and inspires children to think about spatial relations. Children are challenged:

a. *To imagine parts missing from an incomplete figure.* In order to recognize that something is missing from a figure, the child must somehow represent mentally the object "represented" by the figure and must construct the part which is not there. The loose pieces must be given meaning and put into correspondence with missing parts of the figure. When blindfolded, the child must at least maintain a memory image of the figure and parts.

b. *To think about spatial relations among the parts of a whole.* Spatial reasoning is involved in both unblindfolded and blindfolded assembly of parts. In the effort to figure out where the leg goes, the child has to establish a point or points of reference with other aspects of the figure. When Linda and Pat felt the pig's back, they quickly deduced that the leg had to go below this point. They both also seemed to take into account the vertical orientation of the leg. In addition, it would have been possible for them to consider the relation of the leg's length or lowest point to that of the other legs. Being blindfolded can encourage children to think in a more conscious and detailed way about the spatial relations among various parts of a whole. The activity also involves problems of dimensions and proportion.

c. *To translate tactile perceptions and movements into visual images.* Children's difficulties in this game are essentially the same as those observed by Piaget and Inhelder in their research. It is one thing visually to perceive a figure but quite another to construct a visual image of it. At this age level, children's techniques for obtaining tactual information that can be used for the construction of a visual representation lag behind their already good techniques for visual exploration. Assembling the pig without blindfolds presented no problems for the children's representations of space (apart from individual differences in interpretations of certain parts, as discussed above). When knowledge can be drawn directly from visual perception, the construction of a detailed visual image is unnecessary. However, when children have to rely on tactile perception, the knowledge they obtain is very different. They are forced to try to translate this knowledge into visual imagery which makes possible the necessary spatial reasoning. The game provides a situation in which children can abstract relationships by coordinating their tactile activities. Piaget and Inhelder (1948) point out that "exploration by eye is much easier than exploration by touch, for the simple reason that a visual centration can embrace many more elements simultaneously than a tactile centration, and hence visual shapes are more rapidly constructed than tactile ones (pp. 24-25).''

In pinning the parts on the pig, children take turns, and there is little need for coordination with others. Those like Jackie who make no effort at tactual exploration can play well alongside children like Pat and Linda who use somewhat more advanced mental imagery. It is probably an advantage for children at different levels to play this game together. Jackie may eventually profit from observing Pat and Linda, and Pat and Linda may profit from figuring out how to give helpful suggestions.

The teaching

1. **Materials:**

   a. *Use lightweight material with a distinct texture.* The thin cardboard used had two disadvantages. First, its smooth surface was not easily distinguished from the wall, and children could not know at first whether they were generally on target. The problem of knowing whether they are touching the figure can distract children's focus from the more important imagery problems. The second disadvantage of the cardboard was that it was too heavy and sometimes fell down from the wall. (Stronger tape might prevent this, but the first disadvantage would remain.) Using corrugated paper (or perhaps styrofoam) avoids both these problems.

   b. *Choose figures familiar to children.* Children's knowledge of the object represented limits their possibilities for visual representation. In general, common animal features such as the head, tail, ears, eyes, and legs present few problems. However, distinctive parts of unfamiliar animals (or objects) can interfere with the representational activity. For example, the same teacher who made the pig also made a rooster. Children had no difficulty assembling the head, tail, and legs as shown in Figure 8.7. However, they had to ask what the wing was. When told that it was meant to be a wing (intended by the teacher to go on the side as indicated by the T in the dotted area in Figure 8.7), the children could not agree on where it should go. One child thought it should go on top (indicated by C1 in Figure 8.7), and another insisted that it fit under the bill (indicated by C2). This disagreement led to a heated argument ("Keep it there!" "No, I won't!") which ended in a temper tantrum. Part of this problem (and perhaps also the problem

Figure 8.7. *Figure with ambiguous wing part.*

with the pig's nose) was probably a result of lack of knowledge about the animal. Thus, it seems much better to choose figures such as a dog, cat, or classroom animals and commonly experienced objects. Geometrical shapes are probably not good choices for this kind of activity because there is no objective right or wrong way to assemble them. For example, if a teacher cuts a square into parts such as shown in Figure 8.8, what is wrong if the child visualizes something like Figure 8.9? Moreover, each child may visualize something different. Except for an arbitrary imposition by the teacher, there is no reason for a particular assembly of a cut up geometrical shape.

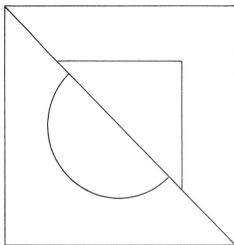

Figure 8.8. *One way in which a teacher might cut a square into parts.*

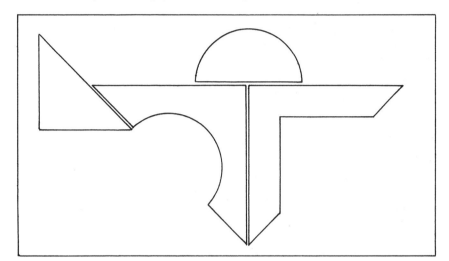

Figure 8.9. *Possible arrangement of parts of a square as divided in Figure 8.8.*

c. *Make figures and parts simple and distinctive.* As we saw in the preceding example, the pig's nose was not spontaneously recognized by children. It is unclear to what extent this resulted from lack of knowledge or the ambiguity of its artistic shape. In any case, the game did not begin with agreement as to what the part was and where it went. The figure would have made better sense to children if the two ears had been identical, the nose simpler, and the head full face, with two eyes instead of just one. These first experiments seemed to indicate that the simpler the materials, the better. The crude figure shown in Figure 8.10 was later used more successfully than the fancier figures.

Figure 8.10. *Example of figure with simple, distinct parts.*

d. *Divide the figure into parts according to children's knowledge and the way they think.* Once the teacher has chosen a figure familiar to children, it is important to give special consideration to how to cut the parts. Clues to children's knowledge and the way they think about the parts of objects, animals, and people can be found in their drawings. These suggest two basic ways to divide a figure:
1) according to parts having a specific function for children
2) according to parts that can be named
In the example of a human or animal figure, children spontaneously identify parts having a specific function, such as the mouth for eating and the legs for walking. These are also parts that children can name. However, some parts can be named that have no particular function as

far as children are concerned (for example, hair or forehead). In deciding how to cut a figure's parts, it may help the teacher to consider the most salient characteristics that children represent in their drawings. This consideration also suggests that schematic figures are probably better than more realistic ones.

e. *Prepare parts for attachment, or plan for children to prepare them, depending on objectives.* In the previous example, the teacher involved the children in the task of taping the pig on the wall and putting tape on the backs of the missing parts. This had at least two advantages. First, the problem of how to affix the tape was a challenging physical-knowledge activity which gave children the possibility of thinking about particular spatial relationships. The context of the game provided a natural situation in which children readily felt a personal need to solve the problem. Second, involving the children in preparing the materials increased their investment in the game and created a cooperative atmosphere. However, problems arising from the need to prepare the materials may for some groups be too much of a distraction from the game itself, especially before children find out that the game is worth the effort. If the taping is too difficult, children may become discouraged and disinterested. If too easy and especially if children already have well-established cooperative relationships, taping will unnecessarily delay the game. Therefore, whether or not the teacher prepared the materials ready for play depends on an assessment of the children to be involved and the objectives most important at the time.

2. **Introduction of the game**

a. *Begin by encouraging children to become familiar with the figure and its missing parts.* The basic idea of putting the missing parts on an incomplete figure may be presented in a variety of ways. In the situation described before, the teacher identified the figure as a pig and focused children immediately on what missing parts the four pieces might represent. She presented two representational aspects simultaneously. For the children, there were two basic questions: What is missing from the pig, and what parts of the pig could the pieces be? Then, the children had to make the parts correspond with the figure. It is unclear to what extent children's interpretation of the pieces was influenced by their interpretation of what was missing from the figure, or to what extent their notion of what was missing was influenced by their view of the pieces. It is interesting that no child suggested a missing part that he did not reconcile in some way with the detached parts given. For example, no child suggested that the pig's mouth, teeth, tongue, or whiskers were missing. This raises the possibility that giving the parts right away may unnecessarily limit children's visual imagery. An alternative approach is to present first only the incomplete figure and ask children what parts are missing. As parts prepared in advance by the teacher are mentioned, these can then be shown, to avoid initial disagreement or confusion over identification. If children are shown only the incomplete figure to begin with, the teacher may want to be ready with paper and scissors to cut new parts suggested by children. Or, the teacher may want to wait to show the prepared parts until after all the discussion is over, in order to permit children to decide what the parts should be. Whether to limit or open up possibilities for disagreement is a teaching decision that must be made on the basis of a variety of considerations. In presenting the game, the teacher should keep in mind that knowledge about the figure is less important than knowledge of the object represented by the figure. Discussion should therefore not be limited to the figure itself, but be extended to what a pig (or other figure) is.

b. *Keep the blindfolding ritual simple, and avoid disorienting children.* Some children feel insecure about or even afraid of being blindfolded. Even among the majority who easily accept blindfolding as part of the fun are some who become anxious when disoriented too much. The teacher should be sensitive to each child's feelings about being deprived of vision, and should never insist when a child resists. Children's mild anxieties can sometimes be handled by leaving the blindfold thin enough to see through or loose enough to permit seeing the feet. After a few experiences of this sort, most children overcome their anxiety and prefer not to see because the challenge is more fun that way. When a child is anxious about being blindfolded, the teacher can capitalize on this occasion to encourage other children's empathy and support. Frequently, too, there are children who protest the unfairness of letting someone else "peek," and this can provide a good occasion for helping children exchange points of view. As noted in the foregoing account, the ritual of spinning children created a disorientation which seemed to interfere with their focus on the pig and its missing part. It also added to the time children had to wait for a turn. Despite the positive value of the initiative children took in doing the ritual, it has too many disadvantages. For the objectives stated in the beginning of this chapter, the simple and faster the blindfolding procedure, the better.

3. Interventions

a. *Encourage tactual exploration.* In the activity described here, the teacher wanted to encourage children's tactual exploration, but she had little idea of how to go about it. She did well first to observe children's spontaneous efforts, but tried too soon to make the children verbalize what they did. She put the accent on conceptualization of the action rather than on its practical use. In studies of children's consciousness of their own actions, Piaget (1974a) and his collaborators found that practical know-how precedes conceptual knowledge. Children can *do* without realizing *how* they do something. For example, young children often managed quite well to swing a string with a ball on the end in a horizontal circular path, so that it landed in a box in front of them. To succeed, they had to let go of the string at a 9 o'clock position (if one thinks of the circular swing in terms of a clockface, when the swing is clockwise). However, successful children often did not describe accurately what they did. For example, many said they released the string from the 6 o'clock position, as they would if they were throwing it. Many experiments suggested that children are conscious of what they are trying to do (their goal) and whether they succeed (the results of their action) long before they are conscious of their actions toward the goal. For the development of visual imagery, it is important that children actively think about the spatial part-whole and part-part relationships. This can be fostered by encouraging tactual exploration if it is done in such a way that children feel the figure *in order to* know its parts, and not merely to follow directions. A variety of approaches to this rather delicate teaching problem may be used. The teacher may make casual comments which call attention to a child's exploration (for example, "Linda felt the pig's back and head," or "She's feeling all *over* the head, to figure out where to put the ear"). She might also wonder aloud in the beginning: "How will we know where to aim if we can't see?" or later, "I wonder how Linda knew to put the leg there?" After children have begun to feel the figure, the teacher may encourage more elaborate imagery by taking a turn and demonstrating more refined exploration, as described on p. 137. Teacher talk and demonstration should remain casual and not be overdone. Refined exploration should not be expected on the first day, and children should figure out the need for it in the course of their misplacements during many games over a period of time.

b. *Encourage self-evaluation and self-correction.* In the preceding game, the teacher wanted to avoid expressing disapproval but wanted children to be critical of what they did. The result was a half-hearted positive response that disguised a critical reaction. Avoid this kind of teaching dilemma by leaving evaluation to the children. Children see the result of what they do and are spontaneously pleased, displeased, surprised, or confirmed in their expectation. This natural evaluation by the child makes the teacher's opinion unnecessary and meaningless. If the child is pleased with what he has done and sees no need for correction, praise is superfluous and correction would be an arbitrary imposition. If the teacher communicates dissatisfaction, the child is likely to understand only that the teacher is dissatisfied. He is not likely to understand what is "wrong" with his result. However, if the child himself is spontaneously displeased with his result, the teacher should encourage self-correction. This activity itself requires thinking more precisely about the relationships involved. The teacher can ask, for example, "Is that just where you want it, or do you want to change it?" Children may quickly adjust their piece visually, or the teacher may have a chance to ask if they want another turn to be blindfolded. Correction while blindfolded was a spontaneous invention by one four-year-old in another game. When he saw that his placement was not what he wanted, he replaced the blindfold and made the change! This seemed to be both an excellent way to resolve a feeling of failure and to elaborate further his visual image. In addition, when children spontaneously offer opinions about one another's placements, it is an excellent occasion for the teacher to support discussion and mutual criticism.

Follow-up

1. *Vary the orientation of the figure.* When the pig is put at different angles, children must imagine the figure in its new orientation and think about spatial relations which are both the same as before and different. For example, the teacher might suggest that children try the game with the pig—
   (1) on its back;

(2) climbing (or coming down) a mountain;

(3) on a seesaw with another pig (perhaps different in size).

Children may eventually enjoy the idea of trying to trick one another by changing the orientation after someone is blindfolded.

2. *Use a variety of objects.* If children enjoy this kind of game, the teacher might ask if they want him or her to make different figures. Children usually have their own ideas about what to make, and can be involved in the preparation of materials. Familiar objects whose parts are well known are best (for example, a person or a house), and these can be made more elaborate and numerous over time if the game really takes root in children's interest. While the child's construction of the usual geometric shapes is an inevitable part of his general representation of space, these are easily incorporated into figures whose content is more interesting than squares, triangles, etc. Three-dimensional objects may be easier than two-dimensional and may offer a special advantage since children turn them around and spontaneously vary their orientation. Models involving perspective may eventually be introduced (for example, a scene with a small tree in the distance and a larger one in proportion to a house in the foreground. The teacher should remember that curved shapes seem to be more easily recognized by young children than shapes with straight lines and angles. Observation of the difficulties of particular children will help the teacher decide when to introduce more complex shapes and shapes having subtle differences.

3. *Suggest that children pick parts while blindfolded.* Another way to inspire children's imagery is to suggest that they choose their part from a pile while blindfolded. This gives them the challenge of figuring out what the part is. As children become more competent, they may even enjoy mixing parts from various figures.

4. *Encourage children to find objects from around the room for one another to guess while blindfolded.*

These follow-up suggestions are only a beginning. The game is open-ended and almost infinitely variable for the teacher who keeps in mind the theoretical basis and integrates this with observations of how children play.

A few final precautionary remarks need to be made on the theoretical significance of this kind of activity. Many psychologists think that the image derives directly from perception and is then directly used for thinking. However, for Piaget and Inhelder (1948, 1966a), the mental image (visual as well as that of other modalities) is the result of activities (actions on objects, including looking at them from different angles). This leads eventually to the use of the image (transformed into a more abstract representation) as a symbol in thinking. Images and other representations result from activities rather than activities or thoughts being dependent on previously-established images.

For Piaget and Inhelder, the role of mental imagery is subordinate to the general development of intelligence but, at the age considered here, is an important aid to thought. Piaget and Inhelder comment that imagery plays an important role "because it can act as a springboard for deduction, and because, through its symbolism, it enables one to outline in rough what the operations extend and bring to conclusion (1966, p. 379)." Later in the child's development, the function of imagery is far outdistanced by intelligence because images are inadequate for operational thinking.

Piaget and Inhelder also point out that imagery plays a more important role in relation to spatial reasoning than logico-mathematical reasoning. A member of a class (a dog, for example) may be visualized, but the mental image of the class will necessarily be incomplete since one cannot visualize all dogs. In contrast, the image of a particular spatial constellation is more comparable with the object represented (for example, the route from home to school). Moreover, the abstract framework into which operational thought will integrate particular instances (for example, a coordinate grid) is itself close in nature and structure to the particular spatial image. The evolution of imagery in its relationship to the evolution of intelligence in general and to spatial reasoning in particular is extremely complex. Experiences with games like Pin the Tail on the Donkey certainly contribute to the development of children's spatial reasoning, and also to their general intelligence.

Figure 9.1. *Spatial arrangement of bases and initial positions of players.*

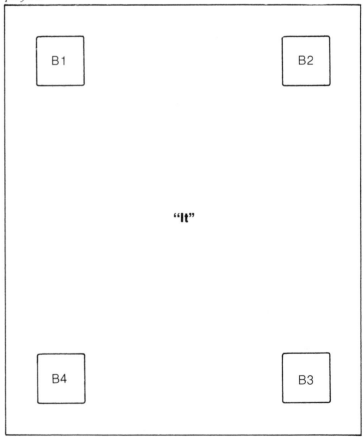

Chapter 9

Kitty Wants a Corner

Rheta DeVries

IN CHAPTER 4 we described a Block Race in which children played in parallel, feeling little need to consider the actions or intentions of others. Only one child saw the possibility of comparing his time of arrival at the goal with that of others. All the other children played the game as if they saw no necessary relation between what they did and what anyone else did. These observations led to the question as to whether different results might be found with a game like Kitty Wants a Corner.

In this game a nonparallel race offers the possibility of direct confrontation of opposed intentions and the possibility for strategies involving collaborative intentions. Four players occupy four bases at the corners of a square playing area, and a fifth player in the middle is "It." (Figure 9.1 shows this initial spatial arrangement.) As the four players run to change bases, "It" races to try to beat one of them to a vacant base. If "It" succeeds, the player without a base becomes the new "It." The basic goal is to avoid becoming "It," and if one becomes "It," to try to get a base again as quickly as possible.

It seemed that in this game, unlike the Block Race, children would be more likely to confront actions of others in ways that might inspire them to consider others' intentions. For example, when "It" and a runner race for the same base, the physical confrontation may lead to realization of opposed intentions and the need to decide who arrived first. Players wanting to change bases face the problem of finding an unoccupied one. If someone leaves his base but finds no other vacant, he might begin to see the need to consider whether another player intends to run. The teacher may then suggest the strategy of making an exchange agreement to have a vacant base. Further, by considering "It's" intentions to intercept a base, players might refine this strategy by making exchange agreements quietly when "It" is not looking, and timing exchanges at moments when "It" is too preoccupied or far away to beat them to a base. In Kitty Wants a Corner, "It" has the possibility of watching for cues to intended changes or exchanges to decide which base to race for and at which moment to run in the most unexpected way. It was generally recognized that in this game children might begin to recognize the intentions of others and coordinate these in action with their own intentions. Moreover, since there is no definite end with a single winner, it seemed especially appropriate for children to whom winning has only a vague meaning.[1]

Detailed accounts of this game in two different kindergarten classrooms are given here. The teaching in these two examples had many serious weaknesses. If we were to describe only good teaching in games that went well, we would be giving an unrealistic picture of classroom experience. Every teacher (and we) learns to overcome failures by trying to understand the negative as well as the positive results of imperfect efforts.

Game 1

At group time, the teacher asked if anyone wanted to learn how to play a new game, Kitty Wants a Corner. The following five-year-old children eagerly volunteered:

Cathy

Melinda

Ruth

Judy

Note: Fortunately for the teacher, only four children volunteered, since her participation as a player was then necessary to begin the game. This contrasts with Game 2 where five children wanted to play, and the teacher did not participate as a player to begin the game. This initial difference was a primary factor contributing to the greater overall success of Game 1. In retrospect, it would have been a good idea to limit the number of players to four.

Immediately after group time during free play, the teacher and children went into the hallway outside their classroom.

The teacher showed the children four large beanbags and said that the beanbags were "houses" for four kittens. She continued, "In this game, one kitty doesn't have a house."

Ruth immediately offered, "I'll be the kitty without a house."

The teacher agreed, saying, "OK, you be the kitty without a house. You go in the middle. I'm going to have a house here (dropping a beanbag on the

---

[1] This is one of the games we had in mind when we mentioned in Chapter 1 the absence of the possibility of winning in some group games. In Kitty Wants a Corner, there is a winner of each race to a base, but there is no single climax which marks the end of the game. No one is ever identified as the winner and the game continues until children are tired of playing. One *could*, however, devise rules by which to designate a winner. For example, players might agree that the goal of the game is to play as long as possible without becoming "It." Observers with stopwatches could be added for each player. Then, to prevent someone's winning by never leaving his base, players might decide that the winner is the one making the most exchanges and spending the least amount of time as "It." These modifications of Kitty Wants a Corner go far beyond the classic rules, and children who enjoy this game do not seem to miss the possibility of winning.

floor and standing on it), and you kitties put your houses there and there and there."

Cathy, Melinda, and Judy followed the teacher's instructions, and the square playing area was formed. (Figure 9.1 shows the designations of the bases used throughout this description.)

The teacher went on, "The kitty in the middle has to try to get a house. We go around visiting each other, and sometimes we're not in our houses." To Ruth she said, "You have to try to get into our houses when we're not there. We can change places anytime we want."

Note: This unclear instruction did not communicate the idea of moving to an unoccupied base. Children might conclude that more than one person could be visiting together in a house, in contradiction to the rule that only one player at a time can occupy a base.

The children simply sat in their places. Seeing that no one knew what to do, the teacher decided to demonstrate. She said, "I think I'll go visit Melinda." The teacher teasingly strutted from Base 1 (B1) over to Melinda's base (B2).

Ruth immediately saw her chance and dived for the vacant place. The teacher raced back to B1, but let herself be barely beaten by Ruth. She was glad to see that Ruth understood the rule that she was supposed to try to get an empty base.

To emphasize to everyone the idea of the race, she asked, "Did you get here first? OK, I'll be the kitty without a house." Smiling, she turned around, looking with a playful menacing air at each player.

Saying "uh, oh," in mock fear, the kitties began venturing away from their houses, teasing the teacher. The teacher saw that each of the children was playing an individual game with her, and that they were not playing with each other. She realized that she still needed to demonstrate basic rules to try to communicate the game's possibilities. She slowly moved toward B3 in an exaggerated tiptoe fashion.

Cathy hurriedly returned to her base, in excited mock terror at the teacher's "threat."

The teacher slowly turned to look intently at each player, and saw that Ruth had moved all the way from B1 to B4. Ruth simply stood beside Judy at B4, as if she did not know what to do next.

The teacher quickly ran to B1, saying matter-of-factly, "I got a house. Ruth's without a house." Ruth gazed around with a blank expression.

The teacher wondered whether Ruth had expected Judy to give up her place, and decided to demonstrate the possibility of exchanging places. With a conspiratorial air, she quietly ran up to Melinda at B2 and gestured for her to go to B1.

Melinda ran to B1, and Judy quickly imitated the teacher. She left B4 and ran up to Melinda, saying, "Let's change." However, when Melinda started running toward B4, instead of stepping on B1, Judy turned and ran with her to B4! Suddenly confronting one another at the base, both girls paused a moment in surprise. Then Judy reversed and ran back to B1. Neither child seemed to pay any attention to "It."

The teacher was amused to see how Judy had understood the ideas to exchange bases and race. She had not yet distinguished the role of "It" from that of players on the bases. She was unable to coordinate the ideas of exchanging and racing, and followed first one and then the other with the same person!

Kitty Wants a Corner

The teacher felt it unnecessary to make any comment because Judy had become conscious of a problem without help and had figured out her own solution.

Although Ruth had plenty of time to grab one of the bases during the foregoing exchange, she seemed unconcerned about this possibility. Instead, she became preoccupied with meowing, crawling on all fours, and pretending to be a cat.

The teacher tried to make Ruth aware of what was happening by saying, "Look, those kitties are changing."

Ruth turned and looked toward Judy and Melinda, but made no move to give chase. Cathy said to the teacher, "I want to change with you." Ruth responded by turning toward Cathy on B3 and crawling slowly toward this base as the two quickly changed places. "We got here!" exclaimed Cathy in relief.

Judy (B1) called to Melinda (B4) again, "Let's change." Meowing loudly, they started to rush toward each other. The teacher left B3 and ran to B4, easily arriving before Judy. Judy, seeing that the teacher had taken the base she was aiming for, reversed her direction and ran back to B1 before Melinda could get there.

In the meantime, Ruth saw that the teacher had left B3 vacant, and crawled there, without hurrying at all. Melinda thus became "It." She watchfully looked around, seeming to be looking for a chance to dash for a house. When she spied the teacher and Judy exchanging Bases 1 and 4, she ran toward B1 as fast as she could, but arrived too late. She returned to the center and began alertly looking around again.

When Melinda's back was turned, the teacher (B1) silently signaled Cathy (B2) to suggest an exchange, and waited to see her agreement. Seeing no vacant base (since the teacher was still standing on hers), Cathy responded to the teacher's signal by running to join Ruth on B3. Ruth protested that the house was hers and pushed Cathy away.

The teacher ran to B2, followed by Melinda. Melinda then noticed that B1 was empty and victoriously claimed it. Cathy said plaintively, "I don't have a house."

The teacher echoed, "You don't have a house, so you'll have to go in the middle." She wondered whether Cathy had expected Ruth to leave and give her the base. Cathy moved close to Melinda (B1), seeming to expect her to run.

The teacher meanwhile ran from B1 to B4 and playfully urged Judy to exchange with her. Cathy simply watched as Judy ran to B2 and the teacher took B4.

The teacher then ran toward B3, but Ruth did not move. This time, Cathy took advantage of the teacher's departure, and dived for B4.

The teacher exclaimed, "I don't have a house!" Then she saw that Ruth was not touching her beanbag, and stepped on B3, proclaiming, "I have a house now."

Ruth obligingly crawled to the center, meowing. The teacher teasingly strayed from her base. Ruth crawled slowly toward the empty base. However, her preoccupation with crawling and meowing gave the teacher plenty of time to jump back on the bag. Trying to make Ruth conscious of the disadvantage of crawling, she commented, "Ruth is a slow kitty, and I'm a walking kitty."

Mildred approached the teacher and asked if she could play. "Yes, you can have my house," responded the teacher as she withdrew to observe. The game began to gain momentum, and the children rapidly changed places.

As she watched, the teacher realized that she was continually reminding children not to take the beanbags with them when they ran. She made a mental note to chalk the bases on the floor next time to avoid this problem.

When Mildred became "It," she crawled teasingly first toward one base and then toward another, but made no real effort to take advantage of her many opportunities to get a place. She seemed more interested in pretending to be a cat. Meanwhile, the other players excitedly continued to change places for some time, seeming not to notice or care about Mildred's lack of effort.

The teacher observed that some changes occurred simply as children saw a chance to dive for an unoccupied base. Others were clearly planned mutual exchanges. Some, however, seemed to reflect uncertainty about the other's intention and uncertainty about how to communicate a desire to exchange. That is, players did not verbalize or gesture, but stood in taut readiness, leaning forward and watching each other expectantly. They would finally run at almost the same time (sometimes after a few false starts), as if by some tacit mutual understanding.

Note: Since the teacher was not playing, it would probably have disrupted the game to intervene with suggestions or demonstrations to help children figure out how to communicate. However, she might have followed up on her observation by mentioning at group time that she saw that some people had the problem of not knowing when someone else wanted to exchange bases. Asking for children's ideas about how to let someone know could lead them to figure out communication strategies to try the next time they played.

Finally, Ruth vacated B2 and called out to Mildred (in the middle), "There's a house for you." Mildred merely crawled toward it very slowly and Ruth raced back to the base ahead of her. Then followed a period in which the players ran or crawled rather randomly from one base to another. They even began exchanging places with "It"! Sometimes "It" reprovingly commanded a player to get back in his house.

At one point, Cathy asked to exchange bases with Melinda, but made no effort to hurry toward the vacated base. When Mildred, who was "It," paid no attention, Cathy tapped her on the shoulder and pointed to the empty base. When Mildred still made no move, Cathy stood in perplexity with her hands on her hips, and appealed to the teacher, complaining, "She won't go there."

Then Melinda and Judy decided to be "It," too, and began crawling and meowing in the middle with Mildred. Judy announced, "There are two people who don't have houses."

Melinda corrected her, saying, "There's three, because Mildred won't go to her house."

The teacher saw that the game had deteriorated. Children had begun simply to move from one place to another without paying much attention to each other, and then had become interested just in the fun of pretending to be cats. Except for Cathy, the children had completely lost sight of the rules. Trying to figure out how to get the children to become purposeful again, the teacher decided to reenter the game. Taking a base, she initiated rapid exchanges with Cathy and Ruth.

The children then began to try to get bases, and the game resumed, although no one seemed to notice that there were always two "Its." Then Mildred announced, "I hided my house. I still don't have a house. It's in there (pointing to the beanbag she had hidden behind the piano)." Ruth, who was "It," started to retrieve the beanbag for herself, and Mildred changed her mind, grabbing it just in time.

Then followed a period of excited exchanging, including frequent double occupancies, without any concern on the part of anyone. Players often also simply decided to evict someone by going to their place, expecting them to leave. They usually did!

Mildred and Judy then became preoccupied with pretending by meowing, growling, and clawing at each other. Melinda and Ruth continued to run from base to base, seeming to be oblivious to what Mildred and Judy were doing. Only Cathy (when "It") became unhappy about the situation and complained to the teacher.

The teacher had decided to let the play go as the children wished. However, when she saw Cathy's unhappiness, she took this opportunity to try to get the others to realize that the game had broken down. She said, "Cathy says you guys are not even trying to get a house."

When this comment seemed to have no effect, the teacher decided to model again. She strutted up to Cathy, playfully taunting in a sing-song voice, "Nyah-nyah-nya-nyah-nya," and hurried back to her base.

Cathy laughed and ran after the teacher, and so did Melinda who left her base to do so. Still, Mildred and Judy continued their pretending.

To try to stimulate interest in the bases, the teacher said, "Oh, the poor kittens without houses. It's raining and they're cold and wet and freezing, and they don't have a house."

Note: The teacher's effort to elicit interest in the game by elaborating on the symbolic play is commendable. However, by providing a reason to occupy a base in the context of their pretend game, she runs the risk of succeeding in manipulating behavior without affecting interest in the game. When the teacher has to artificially manipulate behavior, interest in the game is probably insufficient to continue. It would probably have been better to follow the deterioration of interest in the game. The teacher might have said (as she decided to do later) that people seemed tired of the game. Or, she might have tried to think of a way to follow the interest in pretending by suggesting acting out "The Three Little Kittens" or some other story about cats with which the children were familiar. Whether it was a good idea to try to resume the game is a debatable issue here, in light of subsequent play.

For a short time, the children resumed running with the teacher and one another for the bases. They sometimes raced one another rather than "It"! When Cathy and the teacher were both "It," Cathy suddenly realized that there were too many in the middle. She complained to the teacher that there should only be one "It."

The teacher withdrew from the game, announcing, "Cathy said I couldn't play because only five people can, and that there are too many cats."

After another short period of play, Mildred called out, "I'm starting to go to sleep." Immediately, the other children picked up on this idea and curled up on their beanbags, leaving Cathy standing unhappily in the middle.

The teacher tried to help by saying, "How can you get those kitties to leave their houses?"

Cathy answered mournfully, "I don't know."

Chapter 9

The teacher suggested, "Why don't you ask them to come out and play?"

Cathy went to B1 and yelled in a frustrated tone at Judy, "Wake up!"

Seeing that the game was over for everyone except Cathy, the teacher finally suggested that people were tired of the game and that it was almost closing group time. She felt that the game had completely failed.

Game 2

At opening group time in another classroom, the teacher announced that she had a new game and that anyone who was interested could meet her during free play in a large open area. When she put four large pieces of construction paper on the floor to define the square playing area, the following five children quickly gravitated to see what was happening:

Marvin
Carol
William
Jan
Bayley

The teacher began by saying, "The name of the game is Kitty Wants a Corner, and we're all going to be cats." She positioned four children on the bases and one in the middle.

Putting her arms around Marvin, who was in the middle, she continued, "Now this little cat over here, does he have a base? No, he doesn't have a base. You know what he's going to try to do? He's going to try to get a base! What you do is try to switch bases with somebody else. Carol, you and Bayley try to switch. Hurry!" As they changed places, the teacher gave Marvin a shove, saying, "Try to get one!"

After demonstrating similarly with other children, the game picked up momentum. As children ran from one base to another, and "It" tried to intercept, the teacher tried to make children more conscious of what was happening and what they needed to do by supplying running commentary and questions such as:

"Bayley, good!" (when he got a base).

"Try to get William to change places."

"Jan, did he get your base? Did he get their first? Are you in the middle now?"

"Who's 'It'? Is there a base left?" (when one base was overlooked and there were two "Its").

"There's somebody new in the middle now. Who's the new kitty in the middle?"

"Only one person can be on a base" (when two players occupied a single base).

Note: This was the teacher's first attempt to try such a group game. Like many teachers beginning to use games, her first preoccupation was with children's correct play. In giving instructions she put the emphasis on specific actions to perform and neglected intentions. She acted as a coach from the sidelines and ended up by regulating the children's behavior to such an extent that they were moving more in response to her instructions than on their own initiative. Generally, the teacher was accustomed to dealing with children in a friendly but directive way, and the children were well socialized to respond compliantly to the teacher's control.

After a short time, the teacher decided to withdraw. When there was a pause, she asked, "Do you think you know how to play? Do you need me to tell you when to change bases? Or, could you say something like, 'Hey, Kitty, do you think you can get my base?'"

As the teacher left to supervise other activities, Marvin immediately challenged Bayley (who was "It") by stepping off his base and yelling, "Do you think you can get my base?" When Bayley started toward him, Marvin quickly jumped back on his paper, stuck out his tongue, and wiggled his hips back and forth triumphantly. Everyone else then adopted the suggested taunt and imitated Marvin's tease. For several minutes, the game became a jeering ritual in which everyone taunted Bayley. After several attempts to race for bases, he saw that no one was giving him a real chance and that they were just antagonizing him. He stopped trying and simply stood looking unhappy and helpless.

Note: It is difficult verbally to convey the hostile affective tone of this period of the game, which differs from that of Game 1 when the teacher used a taunt. When she said, "Nyah-nyah-nya-nyah-nya" it was done with a smile, a playful attitude, and in the context of giving "It" a chance to catch her. In that situation, the function of the teasing was to model the fun of taking a risk and being chased. The children's affective response seemed to be one of amusement at the teacher's funny idea. In contrast, the taunt in this game went too far. The animosity became contagious, and with everyone taunting him, Bayley appeared to feel quite persecuted. Such a destructive dynamic is not an inevitable result of taunting behavior. In another group, we observed similar taunting which was accepted humorously and as a particularly difficult challenge to run especially fast toward a base. Here the teacher's emphasis on players' competition with "It" reduced the game to a form of keep-away and encouraged an unfortunate kind of rivalry without cooperative good will.

Bayley's lack of response seemed to take the fun out of teasing him, and William was the first to get tired of it. In a burst of energy, he ran to three different bases so quickly that no one even had time to protest a double occupany.

Players then began making exchanges in a free-for-all manner, without anyone trying to get anyone else's agreement to a trade. Players often left their bases and simply ran to one which was occupied, whereupon the occupant usually simply left without protest, as if obliged to do so! In the melee, the paper bases slid around. When a second one slid next to him, William then stood with one foot on one and one foot on another. He called to the teacher, "I've got two bases!"

The teacher returned from a nearby activity and responded, "You have two bases?" She then turned to the group and asked, "Can William have two bases?"

The children all chorused in unison, "No!"

"Why not?" asked the teacher.

"Because it's not fair," answered Carol.

"Why not?" asked the teacher again.

"Because we only need one kitty to get your place."

"So what happens if William takes two bases?"

"There'd be two kitties without bases. That would be too hard," said Carol. Jan became bored with all this conversation and told the teacher that she didn't want to play any more.

Turning to the group, the teacher said, "Jan says she's not playing any more. What should we do?"

"Take away a base," responded Marvin.

"OK." The teacher removed the base.

Mac, who had been observing, said he wanted to play and put the base back in place. William then suggested putting a base in the middle, and moved one paper to "It's" position.

"Why?" questioned the teacher. "Then where would the kitty stand?"

"Oh," said William, as he slid the base with his foot back next to two other bases.

"Is that OK where it is?" asked the teacher, hoping that William would see that the two were too close together.

"Yeah," answered William.

"Does everybody think that's OK to put it there?" queried the teacher.

"Yeah," responded everyone.

"Are you sure?" asked the teacher somewhat desperately, wondering what to do next.

Note: The teacher was extremely uncomfortatble trying to follow the principle of consulting children and turning over to them the regulation of the game. Her questions were oriented to "right" answers. She could accept only children's ideas which were in accord with the "right" way to play the game.

Not knowing what to do, the teacher reluctantly let the game continue. Some children teased "It" by jumping away from their bases without think-ing about needing to guard against its being stolen by other players. As children ran from one empty base to another without paying attention to "It" or anyone else, they sometimes took a base which was only temporarily vacant while its occupant was teasing "It." The dispossessed owner usually did not notice this short encroachment as the intruder quickly ran to another base. Base changing often occurred even when "It" was close by and could grab it easily. No one seemed concerned when three bases were close together and there was therefore no risk involved in moving from one to another. They seemed to have a marvelous time just giggling and jumping from one to the other.

The teacher was frustrated that the game was "going up for grabs." She tried to get the children's attention by calling, "Wait a minute. Who's not on a base?" "Why is Bayley's base so far away?" "Wait a second. Do you like it when the bases are so close together?"

No one paid any attention to the teacher. For William, the game became one of Tag when he started to chase a child who ran across the area from an-other activity. At this point, Audrey asked the teacher if she could play. The teacher gratefully stopped the game and tried to pull the group together. She announced, "Audrey wants to play. What do we need to do?"

Kitty Wants a Corner

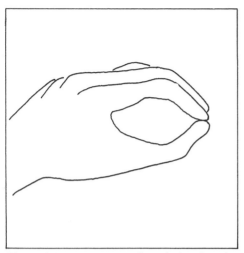

Figure 9.2. *Forming a circle with thumb and forefinger.*

William responded, "Add another base." He got another paper and put it on the floor.

The teacher then took the initiative and spaced the bases, saying, "This time we're going to try something a little harder because this is too easy." In a conspiratorial tone which mobilized everyone's attention, she said to Audrey, "This time, Carol is 'It.' She's going to try to get your base, and if she gets your base, then you're 'It.'"

William interrupted, "And if you've got a base, you're safe."

Nodding, the teacher continued, "What if you wanted to fool 'It' and change places real fast before he could get your base? What could you do to let each other know what you wanted to do?" When no one had an idea, she suggested, "Could you look at him? Could you point to him?"

Marvin nodded. Carol exclaimed, "I know. You could (she formed a circle with thumb and forefinger as shown in Figure 9.2, and gestured toward the teacher)."

"You go like this?" The teacher imitated. "OK, you could go like this to the person you want to switch with." She approached Audrey and asked, "If you wanted to change with William, what could you do?" Audrey gestured to William, in imitation of Carol.

"And, William, if you wanted to change with Audrey, what could you do?" William also imitated the gesture, looking expectantly at Audrey.

"It's sort of neat to signal one person so you'll make sure you have a base to go to. And you'll know where you're going." The teacher asked everyone to try the signal. When satisfied that everyone understood the new idea, she told the children to go ahead with the game.

Note: The teacher's way of beginning to introduce the idea of negotiating an exchange was a good combination of giving a rule concerning intention and consulting the children on how to communicate the intention. However, she then tended to focus too much on the correct action and not enough on the intention. Some of the children learned that they should signal to make someone move from a base, without considering their desire to do so. Instead of imposing Carol's idea and making everyone rehearse the action, it would probably have been better to ask children to focus on how to get someone's attention and make sure the person wanted to exchange.

At first, the children not only signaled but also called out to get the attention of the player with whom they wanted to exchange. This "clue" was usually unnoticed by "It," however. Genuine trade agreements frequently occurred, but players sometimes just signaled and ran, without seeing the need to wait for the other's agreement to an exchange. Occasionally, the children tried to help one another by pointing to an empty base.

In one case a real strategy appeared. Audrey said to Carol (who was "It"), "I'll help you get a base." Then she called to Marvin, "Let's trade." He ran toward her, but she stood firm! Carol thus succeeded in claiming his vacant base. Marvin seemed momentarily nonplussed at this deception, but then good-naturedly went on to be "It."

William's approach was to get the attention of another player by going directly up to him and making the signal just in front of his eyes. With high excitement, he pleaded wordlessly for them to give him the base, not noticing that his own base had usually by that time been taken. Most players resisted this advance and ignored him, but occasionally William was lucky enough to find someone who was ready to run or who responded to his enthusiastic plea by leaving. When Marvin and William got tired of playing and dropped out of the game, the other players continued to signal and run, oblivious that no one was "It" any longer.

Trying to get the children to realize what the situation was, the teacher asked, "Hey, is everybody still playing?"

Carol responded, "I'm not," and also left the game.

The teacher was surprised that her question did not have the intended effect. Seeing that there were not enough players, she decided to join the game, and asked, "Shall I take Carol's base?"

Audrey, Bayley, and Mac said yes.

Wanting the children themselves to realize that everyone had a base, and that there was, therefore, no "It," the teacher asked each player if he had a base.

Note: This was a time-consuming and boring procedure since the children had to wait for everyone's answers. It would have been better to pretend puzzlement and ask, "Who's 'It'?"

Finally, seeing the problem, Mac volunteered to be "It" and removed his base. Two more children decided to join the game, and the group decided that two more bases were needed.

After all was in order to start the game again, the teacher tried again to get the children to think about fooling "It." She loudly whispered, "Don't let Mac see you signal. If he sees you, then he'll know to try to get your place. Try to do it so quietly he won't even know."

In the short time remaining for free play, the children gleefully took up the idea of being more discreet. Although they often gave away their intentions by laughing while signaling, or signaling while "It" was looking at them, the children did act more deceptively and seemed to find their successful exchanges more exciting than before.

The teacher was relieved to see that children were finally playing the game as they were supposed to.

Note: It is unclear to what extent children understood the point of surreptitious exchanges, or to what extent they were once again behaving in compliance with the teacher's specific suggestion.

Discussion

Children's play

1. Generally, children followed the rules only partially. Children find it difficult to change bases while also trying to avoid losing a base to "It." Most focused at some time during the game on changing bases and on trying to keep a base from "It," but usually not on both these aspects at once. Even after demonstration, the following behaviors were observed which did not match the rules given by the teacher:

   a. Almost all players at some point had fun changing bases without paying any attention to "It." They even enjoyed changing bases when there was no "It"!

b. Many children played a keep-away game with "It," by straying away from their bases and then hurrying back, but without trying to move to a different base.

c. Players sometimes changed places with "It," and (in Game 2) even signaled in order to exchange with "It"

d. The rule permitting only one player to a base was not always seen as necessary, and children sometimes saw nothing unacceptable about having two players on the same base.

e. Similarly, the rule of one base per player was violated by a child who occupied two bases simultaneously.

f. Sometimes children played with more than one "It." (This occurred when children were conscious of the duplication, but more often when they were not.)

g. One player (Judy in Game 1) practiced the ideas of exchanging bases and racing by first initiating an exchange and then racing the same player back to her original base! Others at times also raced one another rather than "It."

2. Children introduced "rules" or ideas of how to play which went beyond or were completely different from those given by the teacher. For example—

a. Children often felt obliged to leave their base when another player ran up to them.

b. William wanted to give "It" a base in Game 2.

c. Children (in Game 1) subordinated the rules of the game to its symbolic theme. "It" sometimes just crawled and meowed without chasing anyone, or "raced" in a crawl. Pretending became so much fun for these players that at times they abandoned the rules completely.

d. Players in Game 2 saw no problem with having three bases very close together and enjoyed just jumping back and forth in single hops.

e. "It" (in Game 1) directed players to get back in their houses, without taking advantage of these chances to grab a base.

3. It is clear from the foregoing description that the two games were characterized more in terms of a lack of strategy than in terms of its presence. The first two examples that follow reflect children's unstrategic use of "strategies" suggested by the teacher. Only the last two are genuine strategies reflecting sophisticated knowledge of the game.

a. When the idea of an exchange was introduced, many children did negotiate trade agreements, but without considering "It." They often gave away their intention to exchange by loudly calling to one another! Exchanges also seemed fun even when there was no "It."

b. When signaling was introduced as an aid to making exchange agreements, some players then reduced the game to the fun of signaling without considering any necessity for another's response.

c. When Cathy (in Game 1) wanted to be "It," she called for an exchange with Melinda but made no effort to hurry to Melinda's base, clearly planning for "It" to take the base so that she herself could thereby become "It."

d. Audrey (in Game 2) helped Carol (who was "It") to get a base. She offered to trade with Marvin and then refused to leave her base while Carol took his. [2]

4. Very little regulation of the game by children occurred in these two instances. In Game 2, the teacher attempted to appeal to children for the resolution of certain problems, but no discussions followed, and one child's opinion was usually imposed on the rest. In Game 1, from time to time a player became aware of a problem and tried to enlist cooperation without the teacher's help. For example, when Ruth realized that Mildred was making no effort to get a base, she left hers and told Mildred there was a base for her. Similarly, Cathy deliberately slowed down to give Mildred time to take a base. When Mildred made no effort, Cathy tapped her on the shoulder and pointed to the empty base. These attempts at regulation failed because there was little shared understanding of how to play and no realization of the necessity for agreement.

The value of the game

1. By considering specific behaviors of children in Kitty Wants a Corner, one can infer that players can profit from the following challenges:

   a. *To differentiate the actions and intentions of the opposed roles of "It" and "Non-it."* The player who has as his goal to keep "It" from taking his base can follow this rule only if he has made an elementary differentiation between the actions and intentions of the two opposed roles. Players who teased "It" by straying from their bases and then running back clearly made this differentiation. This kind of play occurred in both games. However, the affective aspects of this differentiation were significantly different in the two games, and this gives rise to different evaluations. In Game 1, children spontaneously strayed off their bases when the teacher became "It."

   By stepping just a short distance away from their base, they could play with experiencing the "danger" of the teacher's "threat" while at the same time maintaining dominance over the teacher's power. The children's obvious pleasurable excitement had an overtone of humor which seemed to indicate that at some level they recognized an incongruity in the game's reversal of the usual adult-child power situation. They seemed aware that the teacher had voluntarily suspended her authority and would respect the rules of the game, thereby giving them the possibility of dominating her. The interplay of these kinds of dynamics resulted in a competition which combined a basic feeling of good will with individual assertiveness. Such an attitude was observed in other groups as well when a child was "It." It also seemed reflected in the pretending of Mildred and Judy when they pantomimed cats clawing at each other.

---

[2] Similarly, in other observations, players on the bases sometimes tricked one another by calling for an exchange and then refusing to budge! They then jumped up and down and laughed gleefully upon thus causing someone to become "It."

In contrast to this positive affective exchange, the differentiation of opposed roles in Game 2 was at times characterized by an entirely different dynamic. The teasing was not playful, but serious and nasty, more like the selfish possessiveness seen when children do not want to let somebody else have the use of a toy or take some privileged position. Clearly the value of children's differentiation of opposed roles must be considered in terms of the nature of its affective aspect.

As indicated in the preceding description, children frequently acted without this opposition in mind. Sometimes situations resulted which confronted players with a need to consider opposed intentions. For example, when they concentrated on exchanging without considering "It," they were sometimes surprised to find that "It" beat them to the base they were aiming for.

In addition to the elementary differentiation made by players who consider the opposed relation of "It" to a single player, Kitty Wants a Corner offers the possibility of differentiation of the entire system of opposed roles in the game. A player conscious that "It" is ready to grab *anyone's* base understands the opposition between "It" and all "Non-its." This system of relationships will be incorporated into the total system implied by sophisticated conceptualization of the game. The construction of this system of oppositions probably develops not in an isolated, but in a mixed, way with the construction of other relationships discussed hereafter.

b. *To coordinate the collaborative actions and intentions of "Non-its."* Taking the goal of making an exchange of bases following a mutual agreement with another is possible only for the player who coordinates the collaborative actions and intentions of himself and another "Non-it." This was manifested, for example, when a child signaled to another, waited for a sign of agreement, and then exchanged places. The affective aspect of this coordination involves, at a minimum, recognition of the need to communicate one's own desire and to interpret the desire of another. A pact necessarily involves the experience of reciprocity in mutual wishes. In addition to the possibility for coordinating collaborative actions and intentions with one other player, Kitty Wants a Corner offers the possibility of constructing the system of possible collaborative exchanges for himself and even for all players.

In both games, there were times when players succeeded in coordinating collaborative actions and intentions with another "Non-it." Many other instances occurred when even these same players were confronted with a failure at coordination. For example, in Game 1, Cathy went to Ruth's base and was pushed away. Many other instances were observed in these and other games when players were surprised to find that the base they ran for remained occupied. Such experiences can result in realization of the need to coordinate, and "failures" may be even more important than "successes" from the point of view of what children learn.

c. *To coordinate the opposed actions and intentions of "It" versus "Non-its" with the collaborative actions and intentions of "Non-its."* The simultaneous coordination of collaboration and opposition was shown when a player tried (success being irrelevant from the point of view of coordination) to negotiate a surreptitious exchange in which "It" would have little chance of winning the race. Further coordination is necessary for the player who considers not only the risk of losing his own base to "It," but also the risk of his partner in the collaboration. The goal can be a mutual exchange in which "It" will get neither base. One can imagine a network of all opposed and collaborative relationships which might be constructed by a sophisticated player who can conceptualize the entire system of actual and possible relationships.

Audrey's strategy in Game 2 reflected an unusually complicated system of coordinations. (She helped her friend Carol, who was "It," to get a base by negotiating an exchange with Marvin which she then refused to honor.) Her offer to exchange with Marvin reflected a coordination of "Non-it" roles. The idea of Carol's taking Marvin's base indicated her differentiation of the opposition between "It" and another "Non-it." The simultaneous consideration of these relationships was implicit in her suggestion of an exchange with Marvin so as to make his base available to Carol. Beyond these coordinations, Audrey went further to create a new opposition between "Non-its" and a new collaboration between "It" and a "Non-it." She not only operated with the idea of collaborating with Marvin, but also with the secret idea of taking an opposed role in relation to him. Further, she not only operated with the idea of the opposition between "It" and "Non-it," but also with the idea of a collaboration between "It" and "Non-it." This deceptive strategy reflected a complexity of thought unanticipated when the possible value of the game was first considered.

As indicated in the description of children's play, the coordination of collaboration and opposition was not possible for most players most of the time. Nevertheless, their failures often seemed valuable experiences for the comprehension of the desirability of coordinating with others.

The affective aspect of the coordination of collaboration and opposition involves a complex synthesis of the affective aspects discussed previously in a and b. This "simple" game situation provides a context in which children can practice the integration of many different feelings. In addition, one has only to mention that children also bring to the game previously developed feelings and attitudes toward one another to realize that the affective dynamic will be extremely complicated. For example, a child may be inclined to taunt when one person is "It," but not another. Players may feel that the risk in an exchange is diminished when the pact is with a trusted friend, but feel unwilling to run when no friend is on an adjacent base.

The intellectual challenge to make a collaborative exchange pact in opposition to "It" carries the danger of producing a possible destructive dynamic. One could conceive the possibility of children's ganging up on "It" in a hostile way which would negate the intellectual value of the coordinations exercised. The value of the intellectual exercise must always be weighed in conjunction with affective aspects. However, conflict-free play should not be expected. Conflicts are often good educational situations in which children are motivated to work out solutions to permit continuing the fun of the game.

d. *To reason spatiotemporally.* To consider the anticipated actions of "It" and "Non-its," children must construct spatiotemporal notions of potential movements. The idea of an exchange of bases, unlike a simple change, involves actions which are opposite and compensatory and which necessitate a kind of precursor "reversibility" in thought, at least at the level of practical intelligence. To assess the risk involved in a particular exchange, players can consider the trajectory of "It's" possible paths from a particular point and their intersection with the paths of exchanging players. Distance and time factors are also taken into account.

Kitty Wants a Corner may offer children a special spatial challenge in constructing the diagonal (the path between B1 and B3 or between B2 and B4). In only one instance of all observation of this game did children (four-year-olds) run to any base except one adjacent. This occurred when the teacher actively initiated such exchanges (and there were more than four bases in an arrangement more circular than square). While failure to run diagonally can result from factors having nothing to do with this spatial idea (for example, seeing the distance as longer than to other bases, or seeing "It" in the middle as an obstacle to the diagonal goal), somewhat older or more experienced children may be motivated to think about diagonal paths.

It is difficult to be specific about the affective aspects of spatiotemporal possibilities. It may sometimes be important to consider children's feelings of security and control (or lack thereof) about their movements through space and in relation to those of others (for example, feelings about collisions or anticipated collisions).

e. *To deal with numerical problems.* In Kitty Wants a Corner, many situations arise naturally which involve number. For example, children may confront the following questions:
1) How many bases are needed for five players if one person has no base?
2) What happens to the number of bases occupied when there are two "Its"?
3) What should be done if a new child wants to play and there would then be two "Its"?
4) What should be done when someone leaves the game and there are then enough bases for everyone?

The basic affective aspect of these possibilities involves feelings about the necessity for mutual regulation. When children want the fun of playing the game together, such problems confront them with the possibility to solve problems by consulting one another and reaching consensus.

2. Kitty Wants a Corner is especially good because children can play it in many ways. In both Games 1 and 2 children were able to play "together" even when they followed different rules or played with different degrees of sophistication. Children could simultaneously feel successful in the game when trying to become "It" or trying not to become "It," when changing bases or when exchanging with another player, when giving away inten-

tions to exchange or when trying to agree surreptitiously. Kitty Wants a Corner might even be played as a collaborative game in which "It" has a base. The game permits a certain divergence of views which allows each child to exercise his particular conception of how to play. These different conceptions sometimes lead to a breakdown in the game. However, play is not always dependent on complete commonality of ideas, and the existence of different views presents the possibility for children to become aware of others' ideas.

3. The foregoing analysis shows that Kitty Wants a Corner offers possibilities for children to exercise their intelligence and practice social reciprocity. Children often did take account of one another as they played. Situations did occur in which players were confronted with the need to consider the actions and intentions of others. Most children made exchanges based on mutual agreement at some point during the game, and there were moments when many players seemed to be taking account simultaneously of "It" and other players. However, much play was either individual and uncoordinated with anyone else, or coordinated with only one other player at a time. Moreover, many breakdowns of the game occurred, and its maintenance was heavily dependent on teachers. After observation of these two games, it was unclear whether children's failure to understand the game was a result of flaws in the way it was presented, or whether Kitty Wants a Corner was too difficult for these groups.

Because of the equivocal results of this initial research, further observations of the game were made with four-year-olds as well as with additional groups of five-year-olds. Other teachers (having the benefit of what was learned about what *not* to do) found that Kitty Wants a Corner was an excellent game when they were sensitive to certain principles of teaching (discussed later in the evaluation of teaching).

One group of five-year-olds who had considerable experience with each other in many other games especially liked the game. These children used the rules in all the same isolated ways noted in the accounts detailed previously, and they distorted the rules in most of the same ways. However, more children more often coordinated opposed and collaborative intentions, more strategies appeared, more arguments and confrontations occurred, and more regulation of the game by children was observed.

For example, Sam trickily tried to negotiate an exchange when he was "It" by asking, "Who wants to trade places?" When this failed to result in any immediate exchanges, he tried to attract Lucy's attention by excitedly pointing to Tim and screaming, "Look at him. Tim wants to trade places!" Then Sam yelled at Tim, "She wants to trade places with you!" Lucy looked expectantly at Tim, but he did not respond. Caught up in Sam's enthusiasm, Lucy then called to Terry, "Do you want to trade places?" When Terry replied, "Yes," Sam yelled, "Come over there!" Lucy then ran off toward Terry, and Sam gleefully jumped on Lucy's empty base, shouting, "I got this. I caught this one!" As Terry started to leave her place, she saw that she had no base to go to, and stayed in her place, instead. In chagrin, Lucy stopped short and jumped around with her hands on her hips in mock indignation, realizing that she had been tricked. After briefly demonstrating the game, the teacher only returned from time to time during more than half an hour of outdoor play.

Four-year-olds (who were completely inexperienced in playing games with one another at school) played in ways similar to five-year-olds, but with less frequent strategy and more need for the teacher's participation and help in becoming conscious of the possibilities for coordination and in resolving conflicts. With skillful active participation by teachers, most of the four-year-olds observed soon became able to play fairly autonomously, with little teacher regulation. However, one or two seemed unable to comprehend or accept the idea of changing bases (refusing to leave their base, or taking the cue of hearing someone's name called as a signal to run to that person). After observing the five-year-olds in the first two attempts, it was surprising to see so many four-year-olds making surreptitious exchanges, arguing with one another about the rules (with teacher support), and even using strategy in a few instances.[3] On the basis of this extended research, it was concluded that Kitty Wants a Corner can be an excellent game when well taught.

The teaching

1. Materials

Bases should be used which remain well in place. Beanbags were a problem because it was more natural for children to pick them up than to stand on them. Had they not had so many other difficulties in figuring out the game, this problem might have been a good one for group discussion about how the game was affected when someone carried a base with them. However, in this instance, the tendency to use the bases as things to carry only created more confusion. The paper bases were an even worse material because they slid around and became torn. In other situations, teachers found that rubber baseball bases work very well and facilitate the initial comprehension of children who are already accustomed to thinking of these objects as defining desirable places to be occupied by one person at a time.

Chairs also work well and may be especially good for young children who are inexperienced in using bases in games. Chairs are already understood as places to be, and they define well a piece of space to be occupied by one person. The problem of two players on a chair may still arise, but the sense of restricting a chair to one occupant is apparent even to young children. The use of chairs, however, leads to certain problems as a classroom has more chairs than are used in the game. Children tend to want a chair for "It," and if an observer gets a chair for himself and then leaves, this chair may then become assimilated into the game. Such problems may prove to be good for discussion, or they may create too much confusion for the children to deal with, especially if they are just learning the game. If chairs are used, it is a good idea to remove or put on tables all except the four used as bases.

---

[3] For example, Timothy signaled the teacher for an exchange but then refused to leave his base. When the teacher then became "It," he said, "Ha, ha, you're in the middle."

2. Introduction of the rules

   a. *The ideas of changing bases and racing "It" for a base should be presented before play begins, and the possibility of exchanging should be suggested soon after, but not as a hard-and-fast-rule.* These basic aspects make sense to most four- and five-year-olds, and the game can begin with content offering challenging possibilities. Isolated practice of rules will still occur, even when these ideas are well introduced. However, some children usually catch on and serve as models and teachers for others.

   The weakness in the teacher's introduction to Game 1 may be due to her tendency (otherwise a teaching strength) to give children freedom to construct their own ideas. She was so casual in presenting rules in the beginning that children understood little of the game. In this case, the teacher's problem was to clarify the difference between her role in introducing the game (where she should develop comfort as a rule-giver) and as a participant (where she should subordinate her adult authority).

   If the teacher has a group in which personal hostilities arise frequently and in which competitive attitudes might be expected to develop destructively, he or she may wish to omit the idea of exchange pacts in opposition to "It." It was only upon later reflection that the possible affective danger of this idea arose, and it is yet unclear to what extent the danger is a real one. From the cognitive perspective, the idea of exchanging seems a significant enrichment to the game's possibilities. However, teachers should be sensitive to the possibility of this value being negated on the affective plane.

   On the basis of many observations of Kitty Wants a Corner, it seems that early introduction of all three basic ideas avoids certain unfortunate results which occurred when rules were introduced in isolation. For example, when children began with only the idea of changing in mind, they tended to get caught up in this idea and to play in a parallel manner, with little awareness of any particular relation to anyone else. It was then difficult for the teacher to change this notion of the game. Early introduction of the idea of exchanging does not prevent all parallel play. However, it does prevent low-level play among children who *can* appreciate the idea of coordinating with another.

   When the idea of exchanging was presented unrelated to "It," children played a simple game of exchanging bases, and they had no reason to consider "It." Perhaps this explains why some children wanted a base for "It" and the tendency to exchange with "It."

   In both games, too, we can see the unfortunate effect of introducing the isolated idea of keeping a base from "It." When presented uncon-nected with the idea of changing or exchanging bases, children took up the game of vying with "It," with a particularly destructive result in Game 2. It may be that by putting the initial emphasis on the positive goal of "trying to get a base," the teacher can, from the beginning, help slant the game toward competition characterized by feelings of good will. In contrast to this idea, when the teacher in Game 2 emphasized the idea of "keeping one's base *from* 'It,'" she made the game into a selfish keep-away, and it degenerated into an exercise of raw power. It is important in the introduction to emphasize the fun of all roles without stigmatizing "It," and to promote reciprocity of attitudes by giving children the chance to see their role in relation to other players.

b. *The teacher should demonstrate the rules as a player.* Despite the weaknesses discussed before in the introductions to both Games 1 and 2, the teacher's participation in Game 1 made it easier for her to deal with the resultant problems. When she saw that children did not understand the idea of exchanging bases, she simply initiated an exchange between herself and a child. As an outside coach in Game 2, the teacher had to stop children's play to focus their attention on this idea, and her largely verbal explanation was still not well understood. Of course, some coaching from the sidelines may sometimes be effective, especially when children need only a little help in becoming conscious of the rules in a game. However, such coaching helps children only to the extent that it enables them to construct the rules themselves, or to become more conscious of their own actions and the actions and intentions of others.

3. Interventions by the teacher

a. *Participating as a player after introducing the game.* Clearly from the foregoing discussion the teacher's participation did not guarantee the game's success. However, by playing along with children, it was easier for the teacher in Game 1 to ameliorate the shortcomings of her introduction without creating a heteronomous situation. When she saw that children did not know what to do, she could easily model the actions, providing children with the possibility of spontaneous imitation and thereby protecting their autonomy. In Game 2, in contrast, the teacher resorted to sideline cheering and haranguing, thereby perpetuating children's heteronomous dependence on her. In Game 1, the teacher not only modeled actions, but also intentions and affective exchanges. For example, she showed her desire and pleasure over exchanges in which she awaited children's volition, and responded to their initiatives. When she won a race to a base, the pleasure she expressed at her success communicated a feeling of shared fun.

When she lost a race, she expressed good-natured acceptance of the result, with room for a certain chagrin and tacit acknowledgment of the child's superiority. In Game 2, the teacher relied on verbal direction of actions and did not communicate reciprocal intentions and affects. She not only failed to inspire positive affective exchanges, but activated taunting. (Such a result could occur, of course, if a teacher participated in a negatively competitive fashion.) Finally, in Game 1, the teacher as a participant created situations in which children confronted the unexpected and thus had the occasion to become aware of new possibilities. For example, the teacher stole a base when Judy and Melinda were exchanging, and Judy ran back to her base, leaving a surprised Melinda to become "It." Another example was the teacher's stepping on Ruth's base when Ruth was not touching it. In Game 2, when the teacher finally began to play with children, she first maintained her authoritarian role by questioning each player as to whether he had a base. She finally became effective only when she became a coconspirator by suggesting and showing quiet signaling.

Such intensive participation by the teacher may not be necessary if children are experienced game players. However, even when a game has been well introduced, children may understand the rules so differently that play by themselves is impossible. The teacher-player can then serve as an important mediator. In Game 1, the teacher took advantage of the opportunity to leave the game when a new child asked to play, but she reentered the game when it broke down and children wanted to continue to play but could not resolve their differences. To the extent that young children have difficulty coordinating with others, they need the teacher to help them begin to become aware of others' actions and intentions, and to feel a need to take account of these. For example, in one game with four-year-olds, when "It" was not trying to get a base, the teacher said teasingly, "Poor Robert. He's too tired in the middle. Now we can get our bases easily." She then made an exchange with exaggerated glee. Beginning to see the possible fun, Robert was then inspired to race for a base.

Other interventions discussed here should be considered in the context of this general guideline regarding the teacher's participation.

b. *Affirming the rules explicitly.* In both Games 1 and 2, the teachers followed up their introduction of rules by repeating them in certain situations. It has already been pointed out how in Game 2 this took the form of external coaching. In Game 1, the teacher affirmed the rules through her active play. However, she also did so verbally when Ruth refused to give up her base to Cathy and Cathy complained that she didn't have a house. In this situation, the teacher matter-of-factly told her that she would have to go in the middle. Such direction is sometimes necessary, especially in the beginning when what children often need is clarification of a rule. Telling the child what he must do can be experienced by the child as arbitrary external control. He may respond by doing what he is told without understanding the reason. However, it is likely that he will "hear" the rule as a helpful aid from someone equally involved in the activity. This is a subtle dynamic, and it is impossible to know how a particular child feels in a particular situation. Nevertheless, it is likely that even if the child sometimes responds to the heteronomous aspect of this dynamic, this effect will be compensated when in subsequent play the child knows what to do without having to depend on others.

c. *Commenting casually on what is happening.* Both teachers made comments about particular actions in their efforts to make children more aware of their relations to others in the game. However, these comments in Game 2 were generally aimed at correcting children's action. In Game 2, few comments were made which gave children the possibility of ignoring the teacher. In contrast, in Game 1, the teacher frequently made casual comments which children could easily ignore but which were designed to illuminate some aspect of the interaction of which a child seemed unaware. For example, when she took Ruth's vacated base in the beginning and Ruth seemed not to know what to do, the teacher said, "I got a house. Ruth's without a house." When Ruth did not try to get a base, but meowed and crawled, instead, the teacher tried to influence her attention toward the others by saying, "Look, those kitties are changing." Similarly, to try to make Ruth aware of the disadvantage of crawling, the teacher jumped back on her base and said, "Ruth is a slow kitty, and I'm a walking kitty." It might be argued that in these instances the teacher erred on the side of being too indirect and not communicating clearly enough the possibility she had in mind. However, it is probably better to err in this direction than to make children feel that the teacher is pushing them to play in ways they neither understand nor desire.

d. *Consulting the group.* More group consultation occurred in Game 2 than in Game 1. It occurred only once, ineffectively, in Game 1 when Cathy appealed to the teacher because Mildred and Judy were pretending instead of playing the game. The teacher tried to help by calling their attention to Cathy's feeling. She said, "Cathy says you guys are not even trying to get a house," but no one seemed to pay any attention. Sometimes, but not in this case, a teacher's group appeal may make children aware of the desirability of a common group concern.

In Game 2, some children responded individually to the teacher's appeals. For example, Carol became involved in the moral issue of William's possession of two bases. William responded to the problem of enabling Audrey to join the game by adding a base, and Mac later saw the need to remove a base when there was no "It." However, the consultation in Game 2 remained mostly a matter of teacher dominance.

As pointed out in several notes on this game, the teacher failed to follow up several good openings and stopped short of engaging children's awareness of the need for mutual agreement. For example, it would have been much more fruitful for the teacher to follow up Carol's idea about fairness in having only one base by repeating her idea to the group, asking what they thought should be done, and involving William in the decision rather than imposing Carol's decision on him. Similarly, the teacher might have consulted the group by asking how they thought it would work to have a base in the middle or three bases close together. If everyone thought that these were good ideas, she should have willingly agreed to try them and might have asked later if the children liked the way they work out.

Instead of genuinely consulting the group, the teacher quickly accepted "right" answers and subtly communicated the unacceptability of "wrong" answers. Instead of a real discussion among children, the conversation was always with the teacher. As a result, the children developed no strong investment in the issues raised by the teacher. (Jan's interest in the game completely disappeared.) They responded mainly to please the teacher and felt no necessity to convince anyone else about what to do. The way in which the teacher consulted the group was often so vague that children could not be expected to understand what the teacher had in mind.

Consultation of children as a group seems useful when there exists a basic desire for a common activity. In such a context, when a child's suggestion is not noticed by other children, the teacher can provide important support by focusing everyone's awareness on the need to make an agreement. For example, William's suggestion of a base for "It" might have been a situation on which the teacher could capitalize to mobilize group feeling.

Focusing the attention of the group together is also sometimes beneficial when no child is aware of a problem. For example, in another situation, when two four-year-olds were sitting on one chair, the teacher called the group's attention to the problem by saying, "Look, there are two on a chair. What can we do now? There's no one in the middle." One child suggested that a third player go in the middle, but she was unwilling. The teacher said regretfully, "We can't play anymore. What can we do?" Finally, a fourth child decided to go in the middle, and one of the two sitting together spontaneously moved to his empty chair. Here we see that children were inspired to respond helpfully to a fellow player who said in effect, "We have a mutual problem."

Finally, consulting the group is an excellent idea when conflicts arise. The teacher in Game 1 had a good idea in trying to appeal to the group on Cathy's behalf, even though this appeal did not work for reasons mentioned previously.

e. *Stopping the game and reorganizing it*. In Game 2, the teacher attempted the drastic intervention of stopping the game, belatedly to try to communicate the idea of an exchange. Audrey's desire to enter the game provided a natural basis for the interruption, and the teacher was somewhat successful in inspiring a higher level of subsequent play.

f. *Refraining from intervening*. Deciding when *not* to intervene is sometimes the hardest of all judgments for the teacher. It is clearly indicated, however, when children themselves take initiative in dealing with a problem. For example, in Game 1, when Judy raced Melinda back to the base she herself had just vacated, the surprising confrontation was enough to make her turn and run to Melinda's old base. Similarly, when Ruth protested Cathy's attempt to join her on the base, it was unnecessary for the teacher to intervene because Cathy herself then concluded that she had no house. Also, as long as Ruth and Cathy were trying on their own to get Mildred to try to get a base, teacher intervention might have discouraged their efforts to regulate the game.

In Game 2, the teacher reluctantly let children continue to play with three bases close together. She refrained from intervening further because she did not know what to do. Even more experienced teachers often find moments when they would like to intervene but cannot think of what is appropriate.

g. *Ending the game.* In Game 1, the teacher facilitated its termination only after several breakdowns. (The possible value of ending it earlier was discussed in the note on p. 152.) Had Cathy not been interested in continuing and frustrated with her friends' lack of cooperation, the teacher would not have been needed to end the game. It would have ended painlessly from lack of interest. Here, however, it was necessary to help Cathy adjust to the disappointment of the end by recognizing that the others were tired of playing and that little time was left. Game 2 came to a natural end when free-play time was over.

4. **Follow-up**

a. Because it was not clear from the results of either Game 1 or Game 2 whether Kitty Wants a Corner was a good game for these groups, each teacher may want to play again to decide whether it should be abandoned. The first teacher should try it again with a different group of children to find out whether a better introduction would interest the children more in the rules than in the symbolic content. If a second group also finds pretending more fun than the game, the teacher probably will conclude that Kitty Wants a Corner does not interest her group at that time. She might focus then on imitation, ritual, and physical-knowledge activities in which less coordination with others is necessary. The second teacher may also want to try the game with a different group of children. It might be important to try it again with the same children, to try to reverse the negative affective trends. (She can also work on this problem in other games.)

b. A group discussion seems important following Game 2, with the aim of bringing children to a more differentiated awareness of the possibilities of the game. How to do this cannot be specified exactly, as the approach will be different for different teachers and children. However, it may be useful to speculate on one kind of alternative. For example, the teacher might at group time mention that some people had tried a new game and that others may want to try it the next time. To help them decide, she can ask the players to explain how the game is played. The teacher should encourage discussion of specific events, perhaps by asking someone what he did when he wanted to exchange, by mentioning that some people thought there should be a base for "It" and asking what others think, by asking what might be done to avoid the problem of slipping and torn bases, and by getting Audrey to tell about her trick. The teacher should observe Marvin's reaction and try to reflect his feeling. If his reaction is an untroubled grin, the teacher may simply laugh with him and say that was a good joke or funny surprise. If he seems to have a negative feeling, recognition is especially important. The teacher may say that she thinks Marvin did not like that very much and ask him if that were the case. It is a delicate matter in such instances to give recognition to a negative feeling without disapproving the initiative of the child who invented the strategy. This might be handled simply by saying to Audrey that it was really a good trick but that Marvin didn't feel good about being tricked. Such discussion should remain casual and should not be overdone. If the teacher's attitude communicates a shared pleasure in positive aspects and shared concern over problems, children will begin the next game with more possibilities.

c. The teachers should participate as players in the game. The importance of this aspect has already been discussed. Both groups described in this chapter seem unable to take up the game on their own. It is necessary for the teacher to plan such a difficult game when she is free to concentrate on it.

In conclusion, Kitty Wants a Corner requires more skill on the part of the teacher than many other games. It should probably not be attempted by the inexperienced teacher, or with children inexperienced in games.

Chapter 10

Making Families (A Card Game)

Constance Kamii

MAKING FAMILIES (p. 64) is played as follows: All the cards are dealt. The first player begins by asking someone for a card, in an attempt to make a set of four of a kind. If the person asked has the card, he has to give it. As long as the first player gets cards he asked for, he can continue asking for more. If he fails to receive the card he requested, the turn passes to the person who said, "I don't have any." Play continues until all the cards have been put down in groups of four. The person who makes more families than anybody else is the winner.

The game described in this chapter took place in the Geneva public schools with kindergarten children. The teacher went to the classroom and said that she wanted to play the game of Making Families with Eron (6;4), Maurice (6;4), and Emanuel (6;6) as she had done the week before.[1] The three children were delighted to play.

As soon as the group sat down in a circle in front of the video equipment in the game room, the teacher spread out on the floor the same 20 cards she had selected the week before from a larger set.[2] The 20 cards consisted of the following five families, each of which came in four colors (red, blue, yellow, and white):

Duck (D)
Sheep (S)
Fish (F)
Cow (C)
Man (M)

[1] She explained that the videotape she thought she had made with them the previous week came out without any sound, and that she therefore needed to do the same thing over.

[2] A game room in the Geneva public schools is like a small gym—a huge room with a shiny floor and no furniture except for some benches and sometimes a piano.

The first question the teacher asked was: "Do you see any families that you can make with these cards?"[3]

Eron immediately answered, "I see a family of yellow cards." Maurice followed with "I see a family of blue ones," and Emanuel with "I see white ones."

"Can we make other families?" the teacher asked, hoping that this question might get the children to shift from grouping by color to grouping by object as they had done the week before.

Emanuel responded immediately, "Yes, I see a family of red ones."

As she pointed to an example of each color, the teacher said, "Yes, the red ones, the yellow ones, the blue ones, and the white ones." She felt that summarizing this grouping by color was the best way to get children to go beyond this criterion.

The children joined her in this description.

"But can't we make any other families?" the teacher continued.

"Yes, I will have to think," said Eron thoughtfully.

"What other families do you think we can make?" the teacher asked again. Emanuel began a sentence without knowing how to finish it, "We can put . . . mmmmm . . ."; he slowly picked up a white fish, looked at it, and finished the sentence, "all the fish together."

Eron immediately got the idea of saying, "Then *I* feel like picking up all the sheep."

Turning to Maurice, the teacher asked, "What do you feel like picking up?"

"Me? All the men," replied Maurice.

"Go ahead," the teacher encouraged.

Each player collected his own cards quickly. Eron then asked, as he picked up two cows, "Then who is going to take all the cows?"

"Me. I'll take them!" exclaimed Maurice as he picked up a third cow. Without a word, Emanuel took a cow, too, and added it to his collection.

Eron meanwhile objected to Maurice by saying, "Oh, no. It's me. It's mine." Maurice let Eron grab the cow from his hand and, seeing the four ducks, which were the only cards left on the floor, he announced, "I'll take all the ducks then."

The teacher asked Eron, "What families do you have?"

Eron answered, "Cows and sheep."

"Can you put them down so we can all look at them?" the teacher requested, knowing that Eron had only three cows.

Eron made a line of seven cards, separating the three cows from the four sheep and saying, "I have only three."

"Is that a family when you have only three?" the teacher inquired.

The other children also spread out their cards as shown in Figure 10.1. Eron did not say anything, but Maurice responded, "I have four," and Emanuel echoed, "Me, too. I have four."

Turning to Emanuel, the teacher asked, "Can you make a family with your cow all by itself?"

---

[3] The English in this chapter is at times unnatural. The conversation was translated from French, and it was sometimes not possible to find an exact equivalent in English. For example, the word "family" would probably not be used in English in this context.

Maurice answered, "No," for Emanuel.

"What are you going to do then?" the teacher continued.

Eron declared as he picked up Emanuel's cow, "I think you should give it to me." Emanuel did not protest.

The teacher pointed to each family, getting the children to name each one as she went around in a circle saying, "Then we have a family of?"

"Fish."

"And the family of?"

"Ducks."

"And the family of?"

"Men."

"And the family of?"

"Sheep."

"And the family of?"

"Cows."

Note: The teacher's purpose in going over the name of each family was not to teach words but to ascertain that the children would use the same words in playing the game. For example, a man could have been considered a boy by some children, in which case a child holding a man could have said he did not have any men when, in fact, he did.

Satisfied that the children were all using the same terms as the week before and that they remembered that each family consisted of four cards, the teacher said, "Now, we have to mix all the cards. . . . Let's make sure we all remember how to play this game. First, I'll distribute the cards, and the object of the game is to make families. For example, you can try to put together all the sheep, remember?" She said this as she picked up four cards showing sheep. She then arranged five cards as shown in Figure 10.2 and demonstrated, "If you get these cards, for example, you try to make a family of all the sheep . . . or all the . . . ?"

"Ducks."

"Yes, or all the . . . ?"

"Men."

"Yes. Do you all remember?"

Everybody nodded with certainty, saying yes.

As she held all the cards in her hand, the teacher asked, "Who wants to distribute them?"

All the players raised their hands enthusiastically exclaiming, "Me," "Me," "Me."

"How shall we decide, then?" the teacher asked.

Eron claimed, "I know," and went on to do the equivalent of "Eeney, meeney, miney, mo" in the order indicated in Figure 10.3. He ended up designating himself.

The teacher marveled and asked, "How did you manage to choose yourself?"

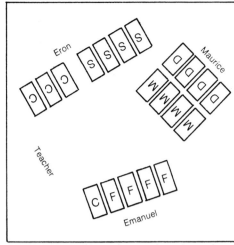

Figure 10.1. *The cards spread out by each player.*

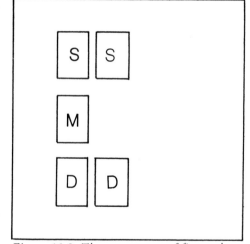

Figure 10.2. *The arrangement of five cards.*

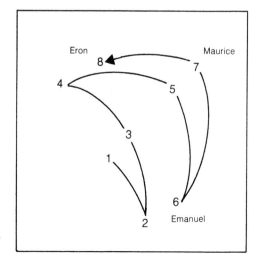

Figure 10.3.
Determining who distributes the cards.

Making Families

The answer was, "I thought."

The teacher remarked, "Oh, next time it will be somebody else's turn to distribute the cards."

Note: The teacher could not tell whether Eron had figured out that with three players the way to end up designating oneself in this ritual was to start with the person in Maurice's position. If Eron had figured out this regularity, the teacher would not have considered this "cheating" in the usual sense of the term. Instead, she would have considered this the result of thinking based on the discovery that there is a regular relationship between the number of players involved and the end of a patterned sequence. Most children of kindergarten age do not even notice this regularity.

Eron started dealing the cards, face up! No one objected, and no one seemed to be paying any attention to the specific cards anyone was getting.

Note: This face-up distribution can be attributed to the children's not knowing the rule about how the cards should be dealt. The teacher had dealt the cards the week before, and the children probably did not notice that she dealt them face down. (The fact that they did not notice the face-down distribution was indicative of their level of development. Those who notice the advantage of knowing other people's hand notice the necessity of distributing the cards face down.) The teacher made a mental note to give the rule explicitly next time. She also noted that the children's thought was limited to the present and did not extend far enough into the future to realize the desirability of studying other players' hands.

The cards each player received in this clockwise one-by-one distribution were the following:

Eron:	M C D D S
Maurice:	M F S D D
Emanuel:	C F C C M
Teacher:	M F F S S

"Do we all have the same number?" the teacher inquired.

All the children spread out their cards, still face up, and counted five in their respective rows. No one looked at anybody else's hand.

The teacher inquired, "Does everybody have five of them?"

The children replied in unison, "Yes."

"We can begin the game, then," the teacher ascertained.

"Yes."

She said, "We begin by asking someone for the card we want, don't we?"

Emanuel declared, "It's me that begin."

"It's you? OK, then, it's you who start," the teacher said.

Note: The teacher should have asked for the other children's opinions. Here, she put herself in the position of authority approving the child's request to be first. Even when an adult consciously tries to reduce her adult power to promote the development of the child's autonomy, it is still easy for her to slip back into the role of dispenser of privileges. Children have a natural tendency to look to adults to govern them. The teacher must counteract this tendency whenever circumstances permit.

All the players held their cards in a way that prevented others from looking.

Chapter 10

Emanuel began by asking, "Eron, do you have a duck?" (Emanuel did not have any ducks in his hand.)

Eron in turn asked, "A duck of what color?"

Emanuel hesitated and added, "Wait. Let me see if I have a duck." He looked through his cards and found none. Changing his mind, he went on, "No, the cow."

Eron inquired, "The cow of what color?"

Up to now, everybody had been looking only at his own cards, but now Maurice took a long, intent look at Emanuel's hand. Emanuel did not notice this inspection.

Note: The teacher viewed Maurice's behavior not as "cheating" but as an act of intelligence. Maurice was thinking about how Emanuel should answer Eron's question. He was ready to answer it if Emanuel could not. The teacher could still have introduced the rule that "in this game, we can't look at other people's cards, and we try not to let anybody else look at our cards either. The game is to GUESS who has the card we want, and if we take a look, we can't guess any more." In this kind of situation the rule must be communicated explicitly at least once. Children may or may not pay any attention to the rule, but it must be communicated clearly at least once. Otherwise, the teacher cannot know whether children look at other people's cards simply because they don't know the rule or because they heard it but did not accept it, as they have a different way of thinking about the game.

Emanuel was deep in thought. After a long moment, he replied, "The yellow cow (which he had in his hand)."

Eron said, "No."

Emanuel became unsure again and said, "Wait. What color do I want to say? Mmmmm . . . I have a blue, yellow, and red one. I don't know what to do." He reflected while everybody waited. Finally, he asked, "I know, Eron, do you have a red cow (which he was also holding in his hand)?"

Eron answered, "No."

The teacher wondered whether or not she should say that it was unnecessary to specify the color of the card one was looking for. Like the previous week, the children made their own rule that made the game much harder than the one she had in mind. She decided not to say anything because it seemed best not to interfere with the rule that all the children seemed to be accepting.

The teacher also considered Emanuel's tendency to ask for the cards he was holding in his hand, as if he did not know that there was only one of each. [By analyzing the videotape later, she observed that Emanuel had asked for "*a* duck," "*the* cow," and "*a* red cow," and that he had said, "I have *a* blue, yellow, and red one." The use of the indefinite article ("a" red cow rather than "the" red cow) indicates that he did not know or remember that there was only one red cow.] She decided not to say anything to Emanuel, recalling that correction by the entire group the week before did not do any good. [4]

[4] The week before, Emanuel had engaged in the same kind of behavior but in an even more extreme form. He kept asking for the red sheep which he already had in his hand. He asked the three other players, one by one, for the red sheep, and was told each time that that person did not have it. Finally, the entire group got into a discussion about where the red sheep was and ended up explaining with the teacher that nobody else could possibly have the red sheep because Emanuel had it. Emanuel listened to the explanation with a puzzled look, and when his next turn came, he again asked for the red sheep!

Turning to Eron, the teacher told him, "It's your turn to ask for a card."

Note: A better intervention here would have been "who is next?" The children would then have decided among themselves who should be next, probably by discussing how they decided on turns the week before. By declaring that it was now Eron's turn, the teacher parachuted an order, thereby taking away from the children a chance to learn to govern themselves.

Eron asked, "Maurice, do you have the duck that's yellow?"

Maurice gladly replied, "Yes," and gave the card to Eron.

Eron accepted the card saying, "Thank you."

The teacher explained, "You can go on asking for another card. As long as somebody gives you the card, you can continue asking for another one."

Making a row of three ducks in front of himself, Eron told everybody, "Look at what I've got."

The teacher asked, "Is that a family?"

Eron answered, "No, there has to be another one."

Continuing to address Eron, the teacher said, "Then you'll have to look for it." (She noticed that the children were now all looking only at their own cards, holding them like a fan so as not to let others see them.)

Instead of trying to complete the family of ducks, Eron turned to Emanuel saying, "Emanuel, do you have the sheep . . . ?"

Maurice interrupted Eron at this point, announcing, "I've got the blue duck."

Eron hesitated for a few seconds, smirking, and said sheepishly to Maurice, "Maurice, do you have the blue duck?"

Delighted, Maurice replied, "Yes," and threw the card on the row of three ducks.

"There, I've got four," Eron said beaming and straightening up the row of four ducks.

"Yes, you have a family. You can continue asking for a card because you got one again," the teacher explained.

The cards each player had at this point were the following:

Eron: M C S   (D D D D on the floor in front of him)
Maurice: M F S
Emanuel: C C C F M
Teacher: M F F S S

Eron asked, "Maurice, do you have the man . . . that's . . . white?"

Maurice gladly replied, "Yes," as he stuck the card in front of Eron's face.

"Oh, my!" the teacher marveled, beginning to think that Eron must have looked at Maurice's cards.

Eron put down two men, neatly arranging them in a row above his four ducks as shown in Figure 10.4.

"Is that a family?" the teacher asked.

Note: The teacher could have said, "Let's not put cards down until we have all four." This error would have been worth trying to correct, as (1) it could have been due simply to the child's not knowing the rule, (2) it was such a surface error that the child would not have been bewildered by the correction, and (3) it messed up the game for the entire group. It is sometimes

Figure 10.4. *The two men Eron put down above his four ducks.*

good to correct a child for the benefit of the group. This error differed from Maurice's announcing, "I've got the blue duck (p. 178)," when Eron was not even asking for a duck. The latter showed a lower level of development, and Maurice wanted to give his duck to Eron to help complete his family and to get rid of a card. This "error" was similar to the second level found by DeVries (1970, summarized on pp. 193-194 of this volume). It would have been harmful to correct Maurice at that point because he would have been unable to understand why he could not offer the card that made such good sense to give to Eron.

Eron replied, "No, I have to have two more."

Tactfully, the teacher said to Eron, "You can continue, since you are so lucky."

Laughing, Eron said, "I'll continue." He then turned serious all of a sudden as he studied his cards and said, "Emanuel, do you have the man that's yellow and the white man?"

"Wait, you have to . . . ," the teacher began to intervene about Eron's asking for two cards, but she was interrupted by Emanuel.

He replied apologetically, "I only have the yellow one."[5]

Eron demanded, "Then give it to me."

Emanuel threw the yellow man to Eron. (No one, including Eron, noticed that the white man Eron had asked for was on the floor, in front of him, in plain view!) Eron added the yellow man to his row of two men (see Figure 10.4). He continued, "Maurice, do have the man that's white?"

Maurice replied, "No," still not noticing that the white man was down in front of Eron.

The teacher reminded Maurice, "It's your turn to ask for a card."

Maurice was pleasantly surprised to get a turn and asked Eron, "Do you have a blue sheep?"

Eron answered, "Yes!" as he handed the card to Maurice with vigor. Eron now had only one card left in his hand. The four players now had these cards:

> Eron: C   (D D D D and M M M on the floor)
> Maurice: F S S
> Emanuel: F C C C
> Teacher: M F F S S

Beaming, Maurice added the new card to his hand that he was carefully holding away from other people's view. Emanuel meanwhile had been less careful about concealing his cards.[6]

The teacher said to Maurice, "You can continue. But I have cards, too."

Emanuel protested, "Yeah, but ask me first," addressing Maurice.

"OK, OK," the teacher retreated.

Maurice asked Emanuel, "Do you have the sheep that is white?"

Emanuel answered, "No, thank you."[7]

---

[5] This apologetic attitude is part of young children's conception of this kind of game. They are glad when somebody asks for a card they have, and they often feel sorry when they do not have a card somebody asked for.

[6] Emanuel's way of holding his cards reflected his developmental level—not outrightly showing his cards as four-year-olds tend to do but not concealing them successfully either.

[7] Emanuel could have meant "Thank you for asking *me*," or he could have meant "Thank you for asking me for a card I don't have because it is now *my* turn."

The teacher casually told Emanuel, "Then it's your turn."

Looking at his cards (F C C C), Emanuel asked, "Eron, do you have the yellow fish (the same card as the one on top of those he was holding)?"

Laughing, Eron pointed out, "No, you have it yourself. Look there." [8] Eron forcefully touched Emanuel's top card to show it to him. Emanuel looked serious, not embarrassed or amused. He continued to address Eron by saying, "Then a bl-red fish."

Eron replied, "No."

Emanuel went on asking Eron, "The blue fish."

Maurice piped up, "It's me that have it!"

The teacher said to everybody, "Wait, wait. We can continue only when we get a card. It's you (Eron) that said you didn't have a yellow fish; so it's your turn."

All the children accepted the teacher's intervention. Eron said, "Maurice, do you have the cow that's yellow?"

Maurice answered, "I don't have any cow. I have a sheep."

"Too bad," Eron muttered.

Since nobody seemed to be about to do anything, the teacher reminded Maurice, "It's your turn."

Note: The teacher has been telling the children much too often whose turn it was, instead of asking, "Who's next?" By telling children whose turn it was each time, she has made them dependent on her to regulate the game. If she had been asking, "Who's next?" the children might have been able by this time to run their own game.

Laughing, Maurice asked, "Emanuel, do you have the yellow fish?"

Seriously, Emanuel replied, "Of course," and handed the card to Maurice. [9] Maurice put down his two fish.

"Is that a family?" the teacher inquired.

"No, there has to be two more," answered Maurice. The 20 cards at this point were in the following places:

Eron:	C	(D D D D and M M M on the floor)
Maurice:	S S	(F F on the floor)
Emanuel:	C C C	
Teacher:	M F F S S	

Since Maurice was not about to make a move, the teacher reminded him, "You can continue and ask for a card."

Maurice readily said, "Eron, do you have the fish that's blue?"

Eron answered, "No, sir. No, thank you."

"Then it's your turn," the teacher said to Eron.

Stiffening his back, Eron turned to the teacher and asked, "Do you have the cow that's yellow?"

The teacher answered, "No," looking regretful and shaking her head.

Emanuel piped up, "It's me that have it."

[8] Eron had looked at Emanuel's cards to be able to make this statement. Because this was not considered "cheating" by the children in this situation, and because Emanuel made no effort to hide his cards, it was not stupid of Eron to make this statement that gave away the fact that he had peeked.

[9] Emanuel seemed to mean "Of course, I am glad I can give you a card you want."

Eron demanded, "Then give it to me!"

The teacher began to ask Maurice for a card by saying, "Do you . . . ?"

She was interrupted by Emanuel's response to Eron, "Oh, no." The teacher continued her attempt and asked Maurice, "Do you have the blue sheep?"

Maurice replied, "Yes," as he threw the card to the teacher with enthusiasm.

The teacher picked up the card and continued addressing him, "Do you have the red sheep?"

Saying, "Yes," Maurice threw the second sheep to the teacher. Then, with joy, he announced, "I don't have any more card."

"Oh, my!" the teacher remarked as she put down her family of four sheep. "I've got a family," she said with satisfaction.

The 20 cards at this point were distributed as follows:

Eron: C   (D D D D and M M M on the floor)
Maurice: (F F on the floor)
Emanuel: C C C
Teacher: M F F (S S S S on the floor)

Emanuel remarked to Maurice, "You can't play any more now."

The teacher said to Emanuel, "It's still my turn to ask. I'll ask you for something. Do you have the white fish?"

Note: The teacher could have picked up on Emanuel's statement to Maurice, "You can't play any more now." For example, she could have asked Maurice for one of the fish he had on the floor. However, she was too pre-occupied trying to decide which card to ask for next.

"No," answered Emanuel.

Maurice pointed to the white fish in front of himself, saying, "It's me that have it." He then turned his attention to Emanuel's cards and studied them intently.

The teacher said, "Ah, then, it's Emanuel's turn to ask for a card."

Holding his three cows (blue, yellow, and red), Emanuel asked, "Teacher, do you have the white cow?"

The teacher answered, "No . . . . Where is that white cow?"

Eron made a funny sound, "Hum."

Turning to Eron, the teacher asked, "Do you have the white cow?"[10]

Eron answered, "Yes," as he handed his last card to the teacher. He wiggled all over the place with joy, kicking up his feet as if he believed that he won the game.

"Wait, wait," the teacher said, looking at him and the three men on the floor alternately, as if to communicate something significant to Eron.

Eron looked on the floor and picked up his three men saying, "I still have these."

Maurice followed with "Me, too, I still have these," and picked up his two fish from the floor. The cards were now distributed as follows:

[10] This seemed to us like a question out of curiosity rather than a turn. The fact that Eron took it as a turn shows how eager he was to give the card to the teacher.

Eron:	M M M	(D D D D on the floor)
Maurice:	F F	
Emanuel:	C C C	
Teacher:	C M F F	(S S S S on the floor)

"Yes, of course," the teacher said approvingly. She went on to ask, "It's still my turn, isn't it? Maurice, do you have the white fish?"

Maurice replied, "Yes," as he threw the card across to the teacher. He said, "I have only one left."

Eron echoed, "I have three."

The teacher turned to Emanuel inquiring, "Do you have the fish that's yellow?"

Emanuel answered, "No, no thank you."

The teacher turned to Maurice, saying, "Then it's your turn."

"Mine?" Maurice asked with a puzzled look.[11]

"No, excuse me. I made a mistake. It's Emanuel's turn," the teacher corrected herself.

Emanuel asked, "Eron, do you have the yellow cow (which he was holding in his own hand)?"[12]

Eron replied, "No. No, thank you," and went on to ask, "Teacher, do you have the man who is . . . red?"

"Yes, sir," the teacher said emphatically as she gave this card to Eron.

Eron said, "Thank you," and put all four men in a row right above his four ducks. Eron now had nothing left in his hand and kicked up his feet in joy again.

Maurice complained, "He always gets good cards."

The teacher said, "We, too, have to try to find good cards." Turning to Eron, she asked, "To whom are you going to give your turn?"

Eron declared, "I'll give it to Emanuel. I won. I'm the champion." The players at this time had the following cards:

Eron:		(D D D D and M M M M on the floor)
Maurice:	F	
Emanuel:	C C C	
Teacher:	C F F F	(S S S S on the floor)

After looking at his three cows (blue, yellow, and red) again, Emanuel asked, "Maurice, do you have a white cow?"[13]

Maurice answered, "No, I have only one card."

Emanuel went on to say, "I'll ask the teacher then."

The teacher objected, "But it's Maurice's turn because he didn't have the card you asked for."

---

[11] Maurice's correction of the teacher at this point showed his knowledge of the rule about how the turn passes to the next person. The teacher did not realize that she could not stop telling children when to take a turn.

[12] The teacher marveled at Emanuel's lack of logic. Eron had just declared that he did not have any more cards and subsequently picked up three men from the floor. Yet Emanuel asked for the yellow cow (which he had in his own hand)!

[13] The teacher noticed that Emanuel was again not taking an obvious fact into account. Maurice had declared having no card left in his hand and subsequently picked up two fish from the floor. Yet Emanuel asked for a cow!

Maurice asked, "Teacher, do you have a white fish?"

"Yes," she said as she stuck it straight out to give it to him.

Maurice continued, "Emanuel, do you have a blue fish?"

Emanuel answered, "No." He laughed and did not seem about to make a move.

The teacher asked him, "What are you going to ask for?"

Emanuel said, "Teacher, do you have the white cow?"

"Yes, I have the white cow," the teacher said with gladness as she gave it to him.

Emanuel exclaimed, "Hurrah! I don't have any more cards," as he laid down his four cows.

The teacher asked, "To whom are you giving your turn?"

"To Maurice," answered Emanuel. The cards by this time were neatly sorted as can be seen in the list below:

Eron:		(D D D D and M M M M on the floor)
Maurice:	F F	
Emanuel:		(C C C C on the floor)
Teacher:	F F	(S S S S on the floor)

"What are you going to ask for?" the teacher asked Maurice as she clutched her cards teasingly.

"The blue fish," answered Maurice.

The teacher gave the blue fish to Maurice.

Maurice continued, "Then the red fish." Getting the card from the teacher (her last card), Maurice put down his family of four fish. With pride, he said, "I have a family."

"Who won?" the teacher asked the group.

"Me," replied Eron, and so did Emanuel.

Eron insisted, "No, it's me!"

The teacher asked him, "Why?"

Eron answered, "Because I was the first one to get eight cards."

"If we count the families, who has the most families?" the teacher asked.

Eron answered, "Me," as Maurice and Emanuel both said, "Him."

Note: It was good that the teacher did not explicitly ask Eron, "Did you win because you were the first, or because you made more families than anybody else?" The teacher encouraged the group to decide on the criterion (or criteria) to use by asking the question more indirectly: "If we count the families, who has the most families?" Competition is a delicate affair as can be seen in Chapter 11. It is often best to leave enough ambiguity in the situation to let each player think that he won. If children play the game meaningfully, the question of winning generally makes little difference to the way young children play.

"OK. Do you want to play another game?" the teacher asked casually.

All the children replied yes, and they went on to play the game of hiding one card for the others to guess which card was hidden.

Note: It was good that the teacher asked, "Who won?" but did not praise the winner. Instead, she simply went on to the next game.

Discussion

This session clearly demonstrated the value of card games in stimulating children's development of their logic. The material used resembles what is often found in "educational" materials made for sorting (by color and by shape) and for making matrices. Sorting for the sake of sorting and making matrices for the sake of making matrices are empty, pointless exercises because children do not develop their logic by sorting objects and making matrices. In card games, in contrast, children develop their logic by being required to use it in a social situation and by creating information beyond what they observe.

For example, to ask for a white cow, the child has to mentally group all the cows, put them into relationship with the four colors, and decide which color to ask for. The child mentally sorts the cards, makes a matrix, and does more than these when he asks for a card. He also does these for a social reason, and not as an empty exercise. For instance, when Emanuel asked for the yellow cow (which he had in his hand) and later said, "Wait. What color do I want to say? Mmmm . . . I have a blue, yellow, and red one. I don't know what to do," he was thinking very hard in a highly meaningful situation, thereby developing his logic.

Let us look more closely at how children played this particular game of Making Families and the value of this game for this particular group of children.

Children's play

Two aspects are worth noting. One is the fascinating mixture of competitive and noncompetitive thinking, and the other is the way in which all four children introduced common rules that were not given by the teacher. The mixture of competitive and noncompetitive play can be seen in the following three areas:

1. The criteria of "winning"
In each child's mind, *a* criterion of "winning" was to be the one to make the greatest number of families. But there was another criterion in each child's head—to be the first to get rid of one's cards. All three children were *very* glad when they got rid of all their cards and thought they had won. At the very end of the game, however, when both Eron and Emanuel claimed to have won, Eron explained that *he* (Eron) was the winner "because I was the first one to get eight cards." The others ended up agreeing with the criterion of the greatest number.

2. The children's attitude toward giving cards to others
The children had a tendency to be delighted, rather than disappointed, when they were asked for cards they had. Emanuel was even apologetic when he told Eron he had the yellow man but not the white one. Furthermore, all three children, especially Maurice, tended to take the initiative of announcing the possession of a card when someone was looking for it. This attitude is consistent with the second criterion of "winning" that existed in their minds—to be the first one to get rid of one's cards.

3. Their attitude toward looking at each other's cards
At the beginning of the game, Eron dealt the cards face up, and no one tried

to hide his hand or study the cards that others were receiving. Once the game got started, however, most of the children tried to hide their hand most of the time. Maurice, however, openly and frequently studied Emanuel's hand for a long time, and Emanuel did not notice or care about this. Eron, the most advanced child, in contrast, seemed to feel that it was necessary to take a quick look at other people's cards. Even the teacher did not know when Eron looked at his neighbors' cards.

Concerning the practice of rules, the teacher told the group the week before that the winner is the one who makes the greatest number of families. However, the children immediately introduced the second criterion and continued to play to achieve one objective some of the time and the other at other times. The two criteria are not in conflict, as the first one to get rid of his cards is often the one to make the greatest number of families.

Another rule not given by the teacher that the children introduced concerned specifying the color of the card. The teacher told the group the week before that each person was to ask for *a* card to make *a* family of four. The children immediately assumed that they had to specify the color of the card and continued to play in the same way the second time, thereby making the game much harder than what the teacher meant.

The value of the game

The game seems excellent because, in addition to motivating children to sort cards and decide which one to ask for, it stimulated them to think in the following ways:

1. Making sure everybody got the same number

By counting their own cards, the children compared the number they received. This comparison did not seem too easy for this particular group of children, and it was useful for them to go through this process. This is elementary division.

2. Making numerical comparisons to decide *which set* to try to make

Every child seemed able to determine which kind in his hand he had the most of. However, this ability did not automatically enable the child to know which set to try to make. For example, Emanuel asked for a duck without having any in his hand. (Eron asked for a sheep when he had three ducks and only one sheep, but he may have had a good reason for making this request.)

The children's logic was fairly good when they decided *which card* to try to get. Their logic was often surprisingly weak, however, when deciding *whom* to ask for a card. They decided whom to ask (1) by taking a random guess and then sometimes using the process of elimination or (2) by taking a look at a neighbor's hand. For example, Eron asked Maurice for a yellow cow and then the teacher for the same thing, when Emanuel had been asking for cows for a long time and had even said that he had a blue, yellow, and red cow. When he had three cows in his hand, Emanuel asked for a white cow from the teacher and Maurice, after being asked by Eron for a yellow cow. Subsequently, Emanuel even asked Eron for the yellow cow (which he was holding in his own hand) after seeing Eron give the white cow to the teacher! Maurice, too, asked Eron for a blue fish right after Eron had asked him for a yellow cow, holding only one card in his hand.

Making Families

The children thus played this game considerably below its possibilities. The game nevertheless seems appropriate for this group of children because they each thought hard at their own level and had an opportunity to grow. The game allowed each child to function at his own level, and no one called Emanuel, the least advanced child, "stupid." Note again that various aspects of development go together. Emanuel was the least advanced both in his logic and his language (such as the use of the indefinite article to designate a specific card). He also let Maurice study his hand, revealing his lack of awareness that the information Maurice was getting gave Maurice a huge advantage. Eron, by contrast, was the most advanced in his logic, never used the indefinite article to designate a specific card, and never let anyone peek at his cards. Maurice was at an in-between level. He often took a peek at Emanuel's cards and sometimes used the indefinite article.

The teacher's role

The teacher used these cards the week before because she happened to have them, and the pictures seemed unusually clear and simple. She assumed that if she told the children clearly that the object of the game was to make families of ducks, fish, etc., they would not pay attention to the four colors. However, they continued to specify the color of each card they asked for, making the game harder for themselves than the way the teacher meant. Using cards that lend themselves to grouping by color was a mistake, especially because young children strongly tend to group objects by color.

The teacher's general attitude was good because she respected the children and tried to participate as a player like any other player. In spite of this intention, however, the teacher had a tendency to say, "Now, it's so-and-so's turn" instead of asking "Who is next?" This question would have encouraged the children to become able to govern themselves. By telling children whose turn it was, the teacher unwittingly reinforced their tendency to depend on adults to control the group.

Out of the desire not to impose too many minute rules, the teacher did not specify many of them. By reviewing this session, we saw the desirability of communicating the rules more explicitly at the beginning of the game. Children can know conventional rules only by being told them. Children may or may not accept the rules, but they need to be informed of them explicitly at least once, rather than being left to flounder and "discover" them. They have no other way of knowing, for example, how Making Families is different from Lotto. In Lotto, the cards are distributed face up, and everybody inspects other people's cards throughout the came. In Old Maid they put pairs down, while in Rummy they can put down either three or four cards. All these conventions must be clearly communicated to children so that they will have the information necessary to play the game. What they do with this information and what the teacher should then do belong to a completely different set of considerations.

Follow-up of this game for this group would be more of the same game with cards that cannot be sorted by color. When the game becomes too easy with sets of four identical cards, it may then be good to try it with the cards used in this chapter. It would be helpful to give the following conventional rules at beginning of the game next time:

1. Distribute the cards face down so that no one will know which cards other people get.
2. Don't let other people look at your cards, and don't look at other people's cards.
3. Don't put down your cards until you have four of the same.

Part III

Chapter 11

The Issue of Competition

Constance Kamii

THE GAMES presented in Chapter 3 are all competitive games. The word *competition* is loaded with negative connotations, and teachers are rightfully concerned about the kind of competition that breeds rivalry and feelings of failure and rejection. While we share this concern, we do not believe that the negative effects that often result from poorly handled competition should blind us to the positive effects competitive games *can* have. The purpose of this chapter is to show that competition in games is inevitable and that the teacher should deal with it positively rather than avoid it.

Because many educators object to competition in group games, we wanted to devote a chapter to this issue before discussing general principles of teaching in the next chapter. The issue of competition will be discussed by considering the following three aspects:

1. educators' reasons for objecting to competition in group games
2. ways in which competitive games can contribute to children's development
3. principles of teaching with respect to competition in group games

Educators' Reasons for Objecting to Competition in Group Games

Teachers of young children frequently make the following statements: (1) Children are already too competitive, and we must not put them in situations that will make them even more competitive; (2) there is already too much competition in our society, and children will be exposed to it soon enough in school; (3) games are upsetting to the losers; and (4) children should compete with themselves and not with each other.

Authors of early education texts also oppose competition as the following example shows:

> Nursery school children are usually not ready for organized games, and only very simple games are appropriate for the kindergarten. Games suggested for use in the kindergarten include those that require little group cooperation, have few rules or directions, and *do not include the competitive element* or refined coordinated movements not yet developed by the child. Choose games in which many children can participate at the same time rather than those in which most children are inactive while only a few are active. Tag, Looby Loo, Here We Go Round the Mulberry Bush, and Musical Chairs are examples of games that involve all children and are loosely organized. (Leeper et al. 1974, p. 342, italics mine)

After saying that the competitive element should be excluded, the authors recommend the competitive game Musical Chairs. Tag is a competitive but complementary-role game, and the other two are not games according to the definition given in Chapter 1. The contradiction about competitive games may be indicative of the mixed feelings educators have about this subject.

Following is an example from another early education text. While Leeper et al. did not explicitly state their reason for opposing competition, Hildebrand explains that competition is too complicated for young children:

> Some of the group games used with older children must be adapted if they are to be used with kindergarten children. Many are totally unsuited to nursery-age children. *Too many rules, too many specific directions, and competition make them too complicated.* Even the traditional manner of playing "The Farmer in the Dell" . . . is too complicated. . . .
>
> The game of musical chairs is popular with elementary school children but is not recommended for younger children because a child cannot understand being left out. In this game sufficient chairs are available minus one. The group marches around until the music stops, then everyone runs for a chair. However, if at this point the child who is left out gets to choose a rhythm instrument and becomes part of the band, his concern about not having a chair is somewhat removed. (Hildebrand 1976, pp. 350-351, italics mine)

In both texts, one senses the belief that kindergarten children are considered different both from those who are younger and those who are older. The authors seem to say that kindergarten children *can* play certain games (which younger children cannot), but they *cannot* play competitive games (which older children can). I agree that a dramatic change often occurs in the kindergarten year, but I believe that the reason for this change has to be understood for the teacher to know what to do at various ages.

While Leeper et al. recommend Musical Chairs for kindergarten children, Hildebrand is against it. The two texts also differ in that the former speaks dichotomously of either playing or not playing certain games. The latter, in contrast, speaks of adapting certain games such as Musical Chairs. We think that Hildebrand does not go far enough in adapting the game to children's developmental level, but this point will be deferred until the next chapter.

There are differences among educators in early education, but none of those cited says that the competitive element *can* have positive effects. Before discussing the positive side, I would like to discuss each of the four objections mentioned earlier.

Objection 1. Children are already too competitive, and we must not put them in situations that will make them even more competitive

I agree that some people are more competitive than others, and that we can speak of competitiveness as a personality trait. Competition in the context of young children's games, however, differs from a personality trait. Most four-year-olds can fight for a toy, but they cannot compete in games such as the two which will be discussed shortly and others we have studied. When children fight for a toy, they fight for something that has intrinsic, immediate value to them. Other examples are adult attention and the pleasure of being the one at the table to pour juice. In games, in contrast, such intrinsically attractive objects or privileges are not involved. For example, nothing is gained by finishing a race first. There is likewise nothing to get by dropping more clothespins in a bottle than anybody else.

In games, competition is not for some "thing." It concerns the comparison of one's performance with that of others. As stated in Chapter 2, young children are too egocentric to be interested in what others are doing. They can care only about what *they* are doing as we saw in Block Race (Chapter 4). The ability to compare performances and compete in games usually begins to show itself between ages five and six (the year in kindergarten). In Pin the Tail on the Donkey (Chapter 8), the four-year-olds showed no interest in comparing how well the players were doing. For older children, such juxtaposed actions without competition would not have been a game.

There is a difference between comparing performances and competing. The former is a necessary but not a sufficient condition for the latter. Competition is a comparison plus something else—trying to outdo or outwit others. The teacher has an important role in educating children to handle this. Some children become boastful, aggressive, and obnoxious. Some adults reinforce children's feeling of superiority by giving prizes, saying "bravo!" and generally making a big deal out of winning. Adults must handle competition more casually so that children will also view winning as nothing more than winning. Its glorification crowns the winner with a sense of superiority and the loser with feelings of failure. When adults poorly handle competition, it becomes highly objectionable.

More systematic research shows that young children's ability to compete in games is a developmental attainment and not a personality trait. Two studies will be discussed—one by Piaget (1932) on the game of Marbles, which was already presented in Chapter 2, and the other by DeVries (1970) on the game of hiding a penny in one hand for the opponent to guess in which hand the penny is.

Marbles

The many versions of the game of Marbles are all variations on the basic theme of putting marbles in the middle of a square and shooting from a line outside the square to knock as many out of it as possible. The marbles knocked out become the property of the player who hit them. The winner is the one who gets the most.

By observing children's play and posing questions to them, it will be recalled, Piaget found the following four levels of play:

1. motor and individual play
2. egocentric play (ages 2-5)
3. incipient cooperation (appears between 7 and 8 years of age)
4. codification of rules (appears between 11 and 12 years of age)

Chapter 2 elaborates on these levels. Remember that until about five years of age young children cannot compete in games. This is why at the second level, egocentric play, the child plays alone without bothering to find a playmate or with others but without trying to win. When many players are involved, everybody can win at this level, since winning means "having a good time doing what one was supposed to do." The rules of a game have meaning only as a ritual to be followed. Egocentric play represents an intermediary level between purely individual and socialized play.[1]

The third level, incipient cooperation, is characterized by the players' trying to win. As long as no one is trying to win, there is no need for rules to make people's performance comparable. When competition appears, however, children have to cooperate to agree on rules. This is why the level at which competition appears is called incipient cooperation. As Chapter 2 showed, the term *cooperation* here does not have the same meaning as in common parlance. In common parlance, "to cooperate" means "to comply" with a request as can be seen in expressions such as "Your cooperation will be appreciated." In this context, the word means "to cooperate," or "to operate together and negotiate rules that seem right to everybody."

Piaget thus accounts for the development of ability to compete in games in terms of increasing ability to decenter and coordinate points of view. As stated in Chapter 2, the development of ability to decenter and coordinate points of view can be seen in every other area studied by him including children's language, scientific thinking, classification, seriation, conservation, and the construction of spatial and temporal relationships. The development of young children's ability to compete in games is thus part of a much larger developmental picture.

Guess Which Hand the Penny Is In

In this game, DeVries (1970) began by putting her hands behind her back, and each time she brought out her clenched fists, the child guessed which hand the penny was in. After about 15 or 20 guesses, which were always followed by a look at the open palm of the hand guessed, the two players

---

[1] The ability of very young children to compete in games manifests itself also in the games they invent. Here is an example of a game invented by a group of four-year-olds: After playing Marbles as described by Piaget, the teacher asked the group if they could make up a game with the marbles. The first volunteer said, "Sure, I'll show you," dumped the marbles in the middle of the square, and proceeded to roll all of them back into the container (a one-pound cottage cheese container), one by one. When she finished, the second player solemnly took the container and did exactly the same ritual. The third child then said it was her turn and repeated the same pointless action in all seriousness. To adults, this was a nonsensical non-game. To the children, however, this was a sensible game. Each one took his turn without any discussion or disagreement, and everyone watched the others with great interest.

reversed roles, and the child became the hider. While Marbles is a parallel-role game, the one presented now is a complementary-role game. The findings show exactly the same development from egocentrism to increasing decentration and coordination of points of view.

Adults and older children view this game as one in which the hider tries to get the guesser to select the empty fist, and the guesser tries to outwit his opponent by figuring out which hand the penny is in. To achieve their respective objectives, both players try to figure out what the other is thinking in order to do the opposite of what the opponent expects. One way to prevent the opponent from making the correct prediction is to change irregularly between right and left.

Young children played this game in an astonishingly different way. DeVries found five levels among children three to seven years of age.

At around age three, when the child tried to guess which hand the penny was in, he viewed the hider not as opponent, but as a partner who wanted him to find the penny. Since the point of the game was to find the penny, he assumed that the hider wanted him to find it! The idea of outwitting the opponent did not even occur to him.

To study the child's pattern of guessing without the contaminating effect of irregular success, DeVries put a penny in each hand while leading the child to believe that there was only one penny. For a series of consecutive guesses, the Level I child always found the penny by guessing the same hand. She then put both pennies on the chair behind her, again in a way that led the child to believe that there was one penny in one of her hands. The child thus had a series of unsuccessful guesses. When this happened, some children began using a regular alternation pattern. Others continued to guess the same hand or guessed the other hand over and over.

When asked to be the hider, many children at the first level said, "I don't know how." Others held out one hand with the penny in the open palm (Photograph 11.1). If they did make a fist, they extended only the one with

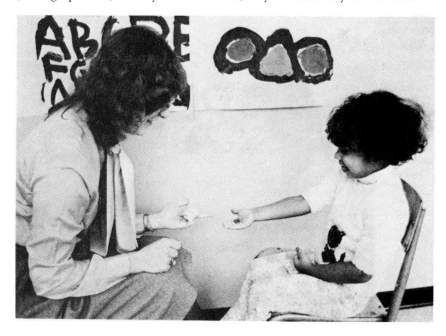

11.1. *One typical three-year-old child's notion of how to play Hide the Penny.*

the penny in it, or showed the other, empty hand (Photograph 11.2). At this level, the hider soon got bored with the game, because there was nothing interesting for him to think about.

At the second level (around age four), the child's understanding of the rules was that both the hider and guesser must act according to a regular alternation pattern (right, left, right, left, etc.). When he was the guesser, he tended to follow this rule faithfully, whether or not he found the penny. When he was the hider, he likewise tended to follow the same predictable pattern and was not at all bothered if the guesser found the penny. In fact, he was bothered if the guesser did not find it! When the guesser pointed to the empty fist, the hider at this level was even likely to correct him by insisting, "No, pick this one (the one with the penny)." He often extended suggestively forward the fist containing the penny, obviously wanting the guesser to be successful (Photograph 11.3). The children at this level were still unaware that the game could be played competitively. They did not decenter enough to think that the guesser and hider could have opposed intentions.

11.2. *Another typical way to hide the penny!*

11.3.
"No! Guess this one!" Many children insist that the guesser pick the fist with the penny.

At the third level (around age five), the child's behavior did not change, but he began to show a competitive *attitude*. He decenters enough to recognize the opposed goals of the players. When he was the hider, he showed strong disappointment when the guesser found the penny and glee when the guesser failed to find it. In spite of this attitude, the child at this level did not recognize a need to be unpredictable. He still hid the penny in a regularly alternating pattern, without thinking about what the guesser might be thinking so as to put the penny in the opposite hand. Most of the children at this level quickly brought their fists out instead of taking a long time to decide in which hand to put the penny.

At the fourth level (around age six) the child as hider used an irregularly shifting pattern. He usually kept his hands behind his back a long time while he squinted thoughtfully at the opponent before bringing his fists out. He took a long time thinking because he tried to take the guesser's perspective and figure out what the unpredictable might be from the guesser's point of view. Although the child could hide the penny deceptively at this fourth level, when he was the guesser, he continued to use the transparent, alternation pattern.

At the fifth and final level (around age seven) the child played competitively both as guesser and hider. Since he knew that the opponent-hider was trying to fool him, he modified his guessing pattern according to what he thought the opponent expected. As guesser, he took a long time to decide which hand to choose, and he frequently verbalized his recognition of the opponent's intent by saying, "You tricked me that time," or "I thought you would have it in this hand because I thought you thought I'd pick that hand."

Complementary-role games elicit behavior that looks different on the surface but is the same in meaning as what can be seen in Marbles and Block Race. Competition in parallel-role games takes the form of trying to *outdo* the opponent. In complementary-role games, it takes the form of *outwitting* the other. The uncompetitive behavior of young children is therefore a manifestation not of the child's innocence but of his inability to decenter and coordinate points of view. The peculiar behaviors we saw in complementary-role games such as Kitty Wants a Corner (Chapter 9), Tag 1 (Chapter 5), and Making Families (Chapter 10) can be understood as reflections of young children's development from egocentricity to increased decentering and coordination of points of view.

Objection 2. There is already too much competition in our society, and children will become competitive soon enough in school

This objection to competitive games is based on two erroneous assumptions. One is that competition is learned only from the environment. The other is that competition in games is the same thing as competition in a socioeconomic system and in an educational system. Because it has already been shown that young children do not learn to compete in games simply by being exposed to them, I will react here only to the second assumption.

Some of the ways in which competition in a socioeconomic system differs from that in games are that in a socioeconomic system (1) the objective is material gain, (2) competitors try to eliminate each other permanently, and

(3) competitors do not agree on rules before entering into competition. In a race for natural resources, for example, competitors do not agree beforehand to start at the same time, from the same place, and cover the same distance. In a game, there are no material gains or accumulation of wealth, and elimination and winning are in effect only during certain intervals. In games, those who do not play fairly are often rejected by the group and do not even get a chance to compete. [2]

Competition in school differs from that in games in that (1) school attendance is compulsory, and (2) at school adults set all the rules and standards and have the advantage of knowing all the answers. During the years of compulsory education, children have nothing to say about whether or not they want to join "the game." In games, in contrast, children are (or should be) free to join or not to join the activity. The making and enforcing of rules are (or should be) also up to the players. The teacher's role in games is (or should be) only to keep the activity organized, protect the weak from the bullies, and maintain an environment conducive to exchange of points of view among the players.

While I advocate competitive games because they can contribute to children's development, I am strongly opposed to the competition schools use to get children to work. Awards, prizes, and grades are often used in school to motivate children to learn, and many pupils end up pursuing these extrinsic rewards rather than the intrinsic pleasure and fascination of learning. [3]

Competitive people are often competitive in all three situations—in games, in school, and in the socioeconomic system. This observation, however, should not lead us to believe that all competitive situations are the same and that all the evils of a competitive society must necessarily exist in competitive games. There are similarities but also significant differences to which educators are often blind.

Objection 3. Games are upsetting to the losers

Losing is upsetting when it is a putdown. The teacher has an important role in developing the attitude that winning a game is nothing more than winning a game. It does not mean that the loser is inferior, incompetent, and worthy only of rejection.

In spite of all his efforts to take winning and losing casually, the teacher sometimes finds children who are crushed when they lose a game. When this happens, he might suggest to the child that he either consider the possibility of losing or just watch the game. The teacher might also ask the entire group, before the beginning of the game, "Do you want to play for winning, or do you just want to play?" Some children reply that they do not want to play for winning, "'cause I don't always win." Nothing can be gained by pushing

[2] The respective role of the socioeconomic system and the child's development could be better understood if there were comparative data from research on young children's development in group games in competitive and noncompetitive societies. My hypothesis is that competitiveness emerges around five to six years of age even in noncompetitive societies, and that adults react in ways that discourage competitive play.

[3] Whoever invented the term *Head Start* seems to have thought of education as a race.

children (or adults for that matter) into situations that they cannot cope with emotionally.

Objection 4. Children should compete with themselves and not with each other

This euphemistic twist of the term reflects a strange compromise between supporting and opposing competition. Competition, according to my dictionary (Barnhart 1963), is by definition between at least two individuals. Even if the definition included intra-individual struggle, this would not prevent children from developing their ability to compete in games. Development is so natural and powerful that when it occurs, it is impossible to suppress it. It is no easier to suppress children's ability to play competitive games than it is to prevent them from beginning to walk, talk, and have opinions and sexual experiences. The teacher's task is not to avoid competitive games but to guide children in this development so that they will become fair players who can govern themselves.

Ways in Which Competitive Games Can Contribute to Children's Development

Since the value of group games in general has already been discussed in Chapter 2, this section will focus only on the competitive aspect. The competitive aspect of games can contribute to children's development because games necessitate making rules and abiding by them. Competitive games also motivate children to think in particularly active ways, as can be seen in strategies. Each one of these points is elaborated in the following paragraphs.

Making rules and abiding by them

As was seen in Chapter 2 in a quote from Piaget (1932, p. 42), the fact of getting more marbles than anybody else is not important to players who have reached a high enough developmental level to want to win. For them, getting more marbles is significant only if the players observe common rules. Since competitive games require rules, they offer special opportunities for children to engage in the making of rules.

Teachers who use Piaget's theory make the most of these opportunities. In Tag 2 (Chapter 5), for example, the teacher encouraged children to agree on whether or not they wanted to play with areas of safety. She also got them to agree on which objects to designate as safety. She knew before the game began that the children's rules would not work, but the rules were theirs, and it was up to them to change the rules if they saw a need for a change. Teachers who believe in constructivism encourage children to make each new rule in a way that contains what they learned from previous experiences. This constructive process is of fundamental importance to children's becoming able to make fair and workable rules for themselves.

The making of rules stimulates development both socially and intellectually. In Tag 2, for example, the two girls were too egocentric to view the game from any point of view except their own pleasure. The boys' thinking did not go far enough to see a need to modify the rules. Throughout the game, the teacher intervened to call the players' attention to "It's" point of view and to hint that a new rule might be in order. She made these suggestions indirectly to get children to decide for themselves to modify the rules. On this day, she did not succeed in achieving this objective, but by going through this kind of session over and over, children do become able to govern themselves to a surprising extent. As stated in Chapter 2, this ability of a group to govern itself has social, political, and moral, as well as intellectual and emotional aspects.

Competitive games require not only making rules but also abiding by them. When players do not abide by the rules, the children can see that the game breaks down. In Spoon Race (p. 41), for example, if some players go back to the starting line after dropping the ball and others do not, the game breaks down. When children can see the necessity of abiding by the rules, they can accept the constraint voluntarily. They also can see the need to enforce the rules. As stated in Chapter 2, this learning to abide by the rules of one's free will involves social, moral, emotional, and cognitive development all at the same time. The fact that the rules were made by them, and that they are free to change the rules, makes a world of difference in learning to abide by them. Obeying rules that one participated in making contributes to the development of autonomy. Obeying rules made by somebody else is only surface compliance, unless the child has had an opportunity to question them and adopt them voluntarily.

Thinking motivated by the desire to win

The goal of outdoing or outwitting an opponent provides a focal point around which the child is motivated to think very hard. In Marbles, for example, the child is not devoid of thought when he plays alone. When he competes with others, however, he is more motivated to figure out how to knock out the maximum number possible. In Guess Which Hand the Penny Is In, too, each player has a reason for trying hard to imagine how the other is thinking. Even a simple card game like Snap (p. 62) that requires little more than perceptual discrimination motivates the child to do his best at top speed. In an individual exercise of perceptual discrimination, by contrast, the child does not have reason to mobilize the same effort.

In addition, certain games provide opportunities to plan strategies over time. In Checkers and Chinese Checkers, for example, A can think about all the possible moves, try to imagine what B might do in response to each possible move, and plan what to do on the second, third, and fourth turn. Some children of kindergarten age do not anticipate anything at the beginning of the year, but make spectacular progress in a few months, especially in Chinese Checkers, which allows jumping one's own marbles. Some children arrange marbles in ways that allow them four or more jumps most of the time. In competitive games, children are highly motivated to decenter and plan such strategies. Dami's (1975) research showed more systematically that children's strategies differ according to their general level of cognitive development. In the realm of strategies, too, games let each child avail himself at his level of the possibilities offered by them.

Although some principles of teaching were mentioned in this chapter, I conclude by conceptualizing them explicitly in the following section.

Principles of Teaching with Respect to Competition in Group Games

The following four principles can be delineated.

1. Handle winning in a casual way

Winning is objectionable only when children do objectionable things with the fact of winning. They sometimes boast about their victory and radiate contempt for those who lost. It is best to agree casually, in a matter-of-fact way, with the child who says he won, and quickly go on to ask, "What would you like to play next?" Adults too often fan children's boastfulness or the importance they attach to winning by making a big deal even to the extent of introducing prizes. Rather than glorifying victory, it is best to minimize the importance of winning from the very beginning.

The philsophy we advocate is that of a football coach of a small college who says, "Go out and have fun," rather than saying, "Go out to win."

2. Verbalize that it is OK to lose

The following anecdote shows how well young children can learn to handle the pain of losing a game if the teacher communicates a certain attitude about winning and losing. The mother of a six-year-old at Circle Children's Center reported that when she played Checkers with her son the evening before, her son beat her, and she was honestly upset. Noticing that his mother looked unhappy, the six-year-old consoled her by saying, "Mom, it's OK to lose 'cause in a game you can't always win. In a game, there *has to be* a loser."

3. Allow children to avoid competition if they want to

Some children cannot face competition emotionally. The principle to follow for these children is to let them avoid competition. Competition should be entered into voluntarily. Besides, there is no absolute necessity for children to play any of these games anyway, as our objective is not to teach children how to play games. There are many other ways for children to reach objectives such as autonomy, decentering, negotiation, and the development of initiative. Children construct their knowledge and personality in their own way. Pushing them into situations they cannot cope with will only block the constructive process.

As stated earlier, the teacher can allow a child to avoid competitive games by suggesting that he just watch if he cannot accept the possibility of losing. The teacher can also ask the entire group, before beginning the game, to decide if they will play for winning or just play without any winners.

4. Play games of chance

In some games such as races and Checkers, winning depends entirely on skill, physical prowess, or ability to think. In others such as Picture Cards (p. 61) and Chutes and Ladders (p. 73), winning depends almost completely on luck.

In the first type of game, the same children tend to win or lose consistently. One way of handling this problem is by playing games in which winning depends mostly on luck.

Whether a game belongs to the first or second category depends in part on the way children play it. For example, in Chutes and Ladders young children often figure out that they need a 5, and throw the die several times until they get the desired number. The role of chance can thus be minimized by the players. The teacher needs to observe the children's play to determine the extent to which chance plays a role in a particular situation. [4]

The reader may object that games of chance waste the more advanced pupils' time for the sake of the slow learners. But Piaget and Inhelder (1951) pointed out that even advanced young children do not understand chance any better than they can quantify a class within a larger class. (Probability is a refinement and a more precise quantification of the part-whole relationship we see in the hierarchical structure of classification.) By playing games of chance, children can learn something about probability at an elementary level.

In conclusion, both the harm and benefit of competitive games lie not in winning itself but in what people do with winning. Books such as Opie and Opie (1969) have shown that competitive games are natural activities that most children will eventually engage in on streets and playgrounds. Piaget's theory shows that competition in games is part of a bigger developmental picture from egocentricity to increasing ability to decenter and coordinate points of view. This developmental process can be seen not only in games but also in moral judgment, language, classification, conservation, the construction of a spatiotemporal framework, and causality. The way to handle competition in group games is to foster a healthy attitude toward winning and losing from the very beginning, rather than avoiding competitive games until children become "ready" for them in some mysterious way.

---

[4] Even results on achievement tests can depend entirely on chance. For example, when I was a junior high school counselor, I found out that many low achievers marked the answer sheet randomly without bothering to read the questions. The score they thus obtained was about the same as what they would have gotten by trying their intellectual best.

Chapter 12

Principles of Teaching

Constance Kamii

IN CHAPTER 2, I stated that although group games have unique possibilities for children's social, emotional, and cognitive development, they can be used in useless ways. Some teachers are so intent on having children play a game correctly that they even push, shove, and order children around, thereby bewildering them and reinforcing their heteronomy. In this final chapter, I would like to discuss some principles of teaching that make it possible for children to play games in ways that maximize their potential.

The two most basic principles of teaching that we derive from Piaget's theory are that games must be modified to fit the way young children think, and that adult authority must be reduced as much as possible. After a discussion of these principles, I will turn to some questions often asked by teachers concerning group games. The chapter will conclude with pointers on each of the eight types of games presented in Chapter 3. Because principles of teaching concerning competition have already been discussed in Chapter 11, they will not be repeated here.

Principles of Teaching That Apply to All Games

Principles of teaching are based on objectives. It will be recalled from Chapter 2 that we derive from Piaget's theory the following broad objectives for early education:

1. *In relation to adults,* we would like children to develop their autonomy through secure relationships in which adult power is reduced as much as possible.

2. *In relation to peers,* we would like children to develop their ability to decenter and coordinate different points of view.

3. *In relation to learning,* we would like children to be alert, curious, critical, and confident in their ability to figure things out, and say what they honestly think. We would also like them to have initiative, come up with interesting ideas, problems, and questions, and put things into relationships.

The first principle of teaching group games that we conceptualize in light of these objectives follows.

Modify the game so that it will be in harmony with the way young children think

As we saw in the preceding chapters, young children think differently from older children and adults in group games, just as they do in conservation, class-inclusion, seriation, and many other tasks. When four-year-olds run a race, everybody can win. When they play Hide and Seek, a hider often yells, "Here I am! Come and find me!" In a guessing game, a player often gives the answer away, and the others do not object to this. In Duck, Duck, Goose, the goose can run without making any effort to catch "It."

Adults naturally want to correct a child when he does not play a game "correctly." If our objective were to teach young children how to play group games, it might make sense to correct them when they make a "mistake." If, however, our objectives are the ones summarized earlier, we must help children construct rules and think in ways that make sense to *them.* The surest way to defeat our objectives for children to become autonomous, exchange views with peers, and be mentally active is to make them play in the "correct" way. Development takes place through the child's construction of something new with what he already has—not through the imposition of the "right" way from the outside.

The principle of modifying the game to fit the way young children think was important in all the games we have tried, including the seven presented in Part II. In Block Race (Chapter 4), Jack was the only child trying to win, and the race was essentially a ritual for the others.

The first way in which the teacher modifies rules is by not doing anything and simply going along with the way children play. When all or most of the children make a ritual out of a competitive game, there is no need to call a legislative session to change the rules. The teacher in Block Race modified the rules by not correcting the children when they did not start at the same time, skipped in a leisurely way, and misused the word *winning.* While it was good that he changed the game to the way the children thought, he also changed the rule arbitrarily to fit the way *he* thought! For example, he imposed a handicap on Jack and a head start on Anita, when the children had no idea why he was doing all this.[1] He also separated Anita from Semantha, gently but bodily, saying, "We can't stand too close together." The teacher was the only

---

[1] Giving a handicap to a fast runner and a head start to a slow child is an example of what Piaget calls equity (as opposed to equality). Equity can be defined as making allowances for attenuating circumstances, and Piaget (1932) showed that this kind of thinking does not develop before the end of childhood. Children need to construct a belief in the necessity of equality (starting at the same time from the same distance in this case) before they can think about equity.

one who wanted to see a neat starting line, when there was no rule in any of the children's heads that prohibited them from standing close together.

In Tag 1 (Chapter 5), too, the teacher modified rules by not making the children play the game "correctly." For example, when they started a chase only after agreeing to begin the chase, the teacher went along with the children, thereby encouraging them to think actively in their own way. In Back-to-Back (Chapter 6) likewise the teacher did not correct the children who wanted to be "It." Making Families (Chapter 10) was also full of situations in which the teacher modified rules by not correcting the children. For example, when a player looked at another child's cards, she did not say that this was against the rule or that this was cheating. When a player offered a card instead of waiting to be asked for it, she did not correct him either.

The second way to modify the game is by introducing it in a noncompetitive form from the beginning. Pin the Tail on the Donkey (Chapter 8) is an example of this kind of adaptation. The teacher in this chapter knew that these children would not play competitively anyway. Besides, for them the task of putting a part on an animal while blindfolded was challenging enough to occupy their undivided attention.

In Marbles (Chapter 7), we find *constant modification of the game by children.* This is a third way of modifying the game to fit the way young children think. The teacher in this chapter encouraged the children's initiative by asking them to invent a game and supporting the process of cooperation as the children argued about whose game to play. She had a game in mind which she could have introduced, but decided to ask the children to invent their own.

The children tried five different games, beginning with one that was not even physically possible and ending with a sophisticated game that resembled pool. Each successive game was built on previous experiences, and each one was a little more playable and interesting than the previous one. When young children are encouraged to modify the game to make it more sensible to them, they come up with increasingly challenging ones that are appropriate to their growing intelligence. They like to be mentally active and do not choose to continue playing games that have become too easy or unworkable.

Our belief in modifying the game does not imply that we think children should never be corrected. We feel that when children are still unfamiliar with a game or when they are distracted, correction is appropriate. In Tag 1, for example, Anita played the game for the first time, and the teacher corrected her by saying, "You were 'It' and you touched Jody. When 'It' touches somebody, that person becomes the new 'It.' And you know what? There can be only one 'It' at a time."

Correction is more often necessary in complementary-role games than in parallel-role games because a game like Tag otherwise breaks down. In a parallel-role game, each child can often play in his own way without upsetting the game. For example, in Block Race (Race 3) Anita started to run long after the others, but this did not disrupt the game. In Tag, however, she stopped the game when she became "It" but did not chase anyone. The teacher first tried to get the other children to explain the rules to Anita, but when this proved inadequate, she stepped in directly. The correction did not help this particular situation, but this does not change my reasons for thinking that the correction was appropriate under the circumstances. The only way a teacher can find out that a correction does not help is by trying to correct the child.

Principles of Teaching

The challenge for the teacher is that early education covers the age range when children change drastically in the way they play. Within a group of children of the same age, we find some who play competitively and others who make rituals out of competitive games. Within the same child, too, we find a mixture of competitive and noncompetitive elements. The same child can also play differently in different groups as illustrated by Richard in Tag 1 and Tag 2. The teacher, therefore, cannot anticipate what will happen in each game, and it is not easy to decide from moment to moment what is the best thing to do.

Let us turn to the second general principle of teaching group games. It is related closely to the first one but must be conceptualized separately.

Reduce adult power as much as possible and encourage cooperation among children

If a major reason for playing group games is to foster the development of children's autonomy, both intellectually and socially, it is essential that adult power be reduced as much as possible to allow children to make decisions. The best way for the teacher to teach in games is as a player, who submits to rules like any other player. In Tag (Chapter 5), Back-to-Back (Chapter 6), Marbles (Chapter 7), and Making Families (Chapter 10), the teacher taught as a player. In Pin the Tail on the Donkey (Chapter 8), in contrast, the teacher maintained her adult status by even declining the children's invitation for her to take a turn.

Although we believe that adult power should be reduced as much as possible, the adult still has to play a major role when children are four and five. The reader can see in most of Part II that there would have been no game without the teacher to keep the group organized. As players, the teachers in Tag, Back-to-Back, and Marbles especially tried to develop in children the ability to enforce rules and/or make new ones without depending on them. Although teacher intervention is often necessary, the teacher can intervene in ways that maximize children's chances of developing their autonomy.

Let us see a few examples of the different ways in which children can be taught to enforce rules. In a race among seven-year-olds, if some children start running before the signal and others start after it, the teacher might hypothesize carelessness or desire to win. (At age four, when most children do not even compare themselves with others at the end of the race, it is pointless to even think about enforcing the rule of simultaneous departure.) The teacher might ask the seven-year-olds what they think of this uneven start. (Merely correcting the surface behavior is useless because we only get surface compliance from children.) An even better way is for the teacher not to say anything but to wait for one of the players to point out that it is unfair when some people start before the signal. The discussion that follows will encourage children to enforce the rule if this exchange of views enables them to see the necessity of the rule.

In Back-to-Back (Chapter 6), we saw a way of fostering children's ability to cope with a game that had clearly broken down. (The rule was that there could be only one "It.") The teacher asked the children what should be done about the problem, refrained from giving a solution, and supported a long and painful search for a solution. The specific suggestions made are different in different situations, but the principle is always the same—reduce adult power, give time to children to encourage cooperation among them, and help them come to their own decisions. When the objective in playing games is children's development of autonomy, the teacher does not hesitate to spend a great deal of time discussing what to do about a conflict, even if this results in little time left for playing the game.

A rule is sometimes not enforceable, and the problem has to be redefined in terms of changing the rule, rather than trying to enforce it. In Tag 2, for example, the children made so many safety areas that there was no one for "It" to chase. It does not easily occur to young children, however, that the rule must be changed. In such a situation, the teacher can drop hints in hopes of getting the children to redefine the problem. In Tag 2, she repeatedly hinted that a new rule might be necessary. It was only because no one picked up on this idea that she ended up suggesting the elimination of all safety areas. But she made this suggestion as a player, so that the children did not have to accept her idea if they did not want to.

Children naturally look to adults to dispense permission and privileges. The selection of the first "It" accentuates this tendency, and the teacher must be careful not to give permission when children ask, "Can I be 'It'?" The best way to respond to this request is by asking the child to ask the other players. The solution other players usually propose is Eeney, Meeney or a similar verse.

It is easy enough to say that when children appeal to the teacher in a conflict, the important principle to remember is to encourage them to come to their own solution. However, it is not easy to figure out the right thing to say in specific situations. Following is an example of an excellent remark which worked out well: When one child (A) insisted on playing Candy Land by the printed rule, and another child (B) insisted on a different way, child A went to the teacher for support. The teacher comforted him and said, "You can't play unless you agree on the rule. . . . Maybe you want to find something else to do." The child thought about this idea, went back to child B, and said, "I'll play your way if you play X (another game) afterwards."

Our adult power is so natural and our empiricist assumptions about learning are so strong and unconscious that we often do things in spite of our intentions. The teacher in Block Race (Chapter 4) who arbitrarily imposed a handicap on Jack and a head start on Anita has already been mentioned. Children accept arbitrary, unilateral commands and usually obey us without protest. We can see that the children were not happy when the teacher imposed the handicap and head start, but they seemed to have learned not to express their opinion honestly in such situations. Alert children notice and say that something is wrong when a child is suddenly singled out for a different treatment.

In Pin the Tail on the Donkey (Chapter 8) we see another example of a teacher who exercised her adult power arbitrarily in spite of her intention not to. She insisted that a paper cutout was the pig's nose and not his eyes, distributed the four body parts to the children rather than inviting them to choose what they wanted, and pronounced whether or not the children were successful in putting each part in the right place.

Sometimes it is impossible for children to resolve their conflict. For example, a bully may constantly change the rule to suit himself and dominate the others. In such a situation, the teacher may have to use his adult power to protect the weak. However, real life is full of bullies, and the teacher needs to keep in mind that children will eventually have to find ways for themselves to deal with those who wield power.

Principles of Teaching

Finally, it is sometimes desirable to violate what has been said above. At the beginning of Tag 2, for example, the teacher proposed a compromise instead of encouraging the children to invent a solution. She said, "OK, kids, the trash can and refrigerator are glue. Richard is 'It,' and he's going to try to catch you." She did this because she felt it would be better to get the game started than to prolong the discussion in an impasse and risk deterioration of interest. The teacher has to apply these principles flexibly, taking into account the many factors involved in a classroom. It is not always possible or desirable to follow these principles, but he should know when he violates them why he is violating a principle that would usually be good.

I would now like to turn to some questions often asked by teachers concerning group games in general. They are listed first and answered in the discussion that follows.

> How do I choose a game?
> Does constructivism imply that games should be introduced in a certain way (to facilitate discovery)?
> How much should I intervene in a game?
> How do I evaluate a game after I try it?
> What should I do when a child does not want to play a game?
> I simply cannot get my children to enforce rules. What can I do?

How do I choose a game?

It does not matter which game a teacher chooses as long as the game promotes the objectives discussed in Chapter 2. For example, children can cooperate with other children and use their intelligence in a hiding game just as well as they can in a chasing game. I would, therefore, not worry about which specific game to choose but, instead, think about the variety of games that are introduced. Each of the eight types presented in Chapter 3 encourages different ways of thinking. It is therefore desirable to begin by considering one from each category. In choosing a game, use the criteria given in Chapter 1.

In the classroom, however, the teacher has to think about practical, specific objectives in addition to the theoretical, general goals. For example, if a group consists mostly of four-year-old beginners but also includes some experienced players who are five, and the teacher cannot divide the group for various reasons, a relatively undesirable game can have merits. Below is a game that we consider generally undesirable because it encourages random guessing rather than intelligent guessing based on pertinent facts.

Dog and Bone

A unit block is placed under a chair which is in the center of a circle of children. One child is the dog who sits in the chair and closes his eyes. The teacher points to another child who must creep up to steal the dog's bone without making any noise. If the dog hears the thief, he "wakes up" and the thief must return to his place in the circle. If the thief succeeds in stealing the bone and gets back to his place without being heard, all the children put their hands behind them, and the dog must try to guess who has the bone. (Tiemersma 1952, p. 38)

Some teachers at Circle Children's Center found this game desirable under the circumstances described above because (a) the beginners quickly catch on to the very idea of a group game, (b) young children tend to take wild guesses anyway, (c) the game moves fast, and (d) the children LOVE it. Hiding games usually work well with beginning players. Dog and Bone has the further advantage of being a circle game, which stays together more easily than one in which children move about [such as Doggy, Doggy, Your Bone Is Gone (p. 49)]. One of the reasons for the popularity of Dog and Bone is that children get a chance to be "It" in the middle of the circle, and each child gets his name called when "It" takes a guess.

The gratification of getting the group's attention is at times in itself a legitimate reason for playing games in the classroom. I am against the playing of a game without thinking about its special good points. If a game can serve a cognitive purpose, the teacher should be aware of this and take advantage of the opportunities it provides. If a game serves primarily a socio-affective purpose, the teacher should know this, too, and play the game accordingly.

Finally, for very young children, the teacher must choose "games" which do not meet all the criteria of games given in Chapter 1. As we saw in Block Race (Chapter 4), young children change competitive games into rituals. For three-year-olds and most four-year-olds, therefore, it is best to choose rituals from the very beginning such as Mulberry Bush, Farmer in the Dell, Looby Lou, Hokey Pokey, In and Out the Window, and finger plays like Two Little Blackbirds.[2] These rituals all involve acting out ideas in ways similar to

[2] Descriptions of Mulberry Bush, Farmer in the Dell, Looby Lou, Hokey Pokey, In and Out the Window, and Two Little Blackbirds follow.

Mulberry Bush

Children form a circle and sing "Here We Go 'Round the Mulberry Bush," performing the actions called for in the song (walking in a circle, pretending to wash clothes, iron clothes, etc.). (Kohl and Young 1953, p. 36)

Farmer in the Dell

Players form a circle around one child who is the farmer, and everyone sings the story about the farmer taking a wife, who takes a child, who takes a nurse, who takes a cat, who takes a rat, who takes the cheese. As the group sings this song, the farmer chooses a child to join him in the circle as the wife. Then the wife chooses a player to be the child, etc. The cheese becomes the farmer for the next game. (Tiemersma 1953, p. 45)

Looby Lou

Players form a circle and sing "Looby Lou," a song describing a Saturday night bath. Players perform the actions of putting their right hand in (the water), taking it out, shaking it, and turning about. Other stanzas repeat the sequence for the left hand, foot, head, and whole self. (Tiemersma 1953, p. 48; Kohl and Young 1953, p. 39)

Hokey Pokey

Children form a circle and sing "Hokey Pokey," as they perform the actions of putting the appropriate body part (right hand, left hand, right foot, left foot, head, whole self) forward, shaking that part, and turning about.

In and Out the Window

Players stand in a circle, holding hands. "It" goes to the center and the others raise their joined hands above their heads. When the music begins, "It" weaves his way in and out under the arched arms, going behind one child and in front of the next. When the music begins again, "It" joins hands with a second child and the two together weave in and out of the circle. The music stops, and a third child joins the weaving chain. The game proceeds in this manner until there is no circle left. (McWhirter 1970, pp. 22-23)

continued on p. 208

Charades (p. 54) and Simon Says (p. 57). Young children play these competitive games noncompetitively anyway. For them, the teacher needs to choose rituals, which are not really games according to the definition given in Chapter 1.

Does constructivism imply that games should be introduced in a certain way (to facilitate discovery)?

Many educators equate Piagetian teaching with the "discovery method," according to which children are believed to learn with better understanding and longer retention when they discover something than when they are instructed directly. This is a misconception. Piaget's theory does imply that learning takes place best when children are mentally active. But it does not imply that everything can be learned by discovery. Piaget makes a distinction between *discovery* and *invention*. Discovery is the finding of what is out there in external reality. Oil was discovered rather than invented. The automobile, on the other hand, was invented and not discovered. The automobile was not out there in external reality before its invention. Rules of games were also invented by people and are an example of social (conventional) knowledge. Rules can eventually be inferred by older children if they can figure out what facts to put into relationships. For young children, however, it is much too hard to figure out the rules of a game, and therefore "discovery" is impossible.

Introduce a game by being as clear and brief as possible. Back-to-Back (Chapter 6) is an example of a good introduction. The teacher in this chapter made her statements clearly as she demonstrated what she meant. She also quickly began playing the game rather than prolonging the verbal description. It is better to clarify the rules as we go along than to try to clarify them verbally before the children have had a chance to experience the game. Children may interpret the rules in their own way, but the initial introduction has to be clear and explicit. Otherwise we cannot know why children do the things they do. If we do not understand the why of their behavior, we cannot decide how to react to children.

Tag 1 (Chapter 5) was an unfortunate introduction for Anita. She would probably not have understood even the clearest description anyway. This, however, does not change the undesirability of not even explaining the game to a beginner. Making Families (Chapter 10) is another example of a game introduced without explicit communication of the rules. The children dealt the cards face up, looked at other players' cards, and put down two or three cards

[2]*continued.*

Finger Play: Two Little Blackbirds

Two little blackbirds (Wiggle two index fingers)
Sitting on a hill (Wiggle two index fingers)
One named Jack (Make one index finger bow)
One named Jill (Make the other index finger bow)
Fly away, Jack! (Wiggle one index finger while moving hand behind back)
Fly away, Jill! (Wiggle the other index finger while moving hand behind back)
Come back, Jack! (Bring wiggling finger back)
Come back, Jill! (Bring other wiggling finger back)
Two little blackbirds (Wiggle two index fingers)
Sitting on a hill (Wiggle two index fingers)
One named Jack (Make one finger bow)
The other named Jill (Make the other finger bow).

---

without waiting to have a set of four. It was impossible to determine exactly why they were doing such peculiar things because the teacher had not communicated explicitly the rules concerning these aspects.

Regarding the clarity of the rules at the time a new game is introduced, it was unfortunate for Anita to be introduced to Tag with a safety area. Tag can be played without a safety area. *Safety* constitutes an exception to the general rule, and this exception complicated the general rule that was impossible for Anita to understand in the first place.

After children have played many games, it is highly desirable to ask them to invent their own. As stated earlier, the teacher in Chapter 7 (Marbles) specifically asked children to invent a game, and they turned out to be prolific inventors.

How much should I intervene in a game?

This question must be answered in two ways: with respect to the management of the game and with respect to stimulating children's thinking. As far as the first aspect is concerned, my answer is "as little as possible." This means a lot of intervention at the beginning and none at all when children have become able to play games on their own. The ultimate goal is to enable children to initiate, organize, and play their own games without any help whatsoever from the teacher. (See Photograph 12.1.) As stated earlier, the teacher intervenes only when it seems necessary and fosters the development of ability to play without the teacher. The adult in Chapter 10 (Making Families) continually told the children whose turn it was, rather than asking who was next. Being asked "Who is next?" stimulates the development of children's ability to keep track of turns. Being told "It's your turn now" reinforces their dependence on the teacher.

In Tag 1 (Chapter 5), when Richard got no response after saying to Anita, "I touched you, Anita," the teacher said to him, "Anita doesn't know what that means. You have to tell her what that means." This intervention showed

12.1. *Pick-Up Sticks. The children initiated their own game without the teacher's presence. A game with only two players is the easiest to organize and keep organized.*

Principles of Teaching

the children how to manage their own game. It would have been easier for the teacher to tell Anita what Richard meant. But she encouraged Richard to talk to Anita to foster the development of their autonomy.

To stimulate children's thinking, the second aspect of the question concerning teacher intervention, my answer is "sparingly, and posing the right question at the right time." In playing The Orchestra Conductor (p. 54), for example, after "It" guessed who the conductor was, a teacher occasionally asked, "How did you guess that so-and-so was the conductor?" Many children naturally replied in the typical way of four-year-olds: "'Cause I guessed," and "'Cause I just knew." Others, however, had a variety of replies that stimulated decentering. One said, "'Cause he put one hand down (abruptly) before everybody else." Another said, "'Cause Johnny said it was Suzy." (Many four-year-olds loudly give the answer away.) A third said, "'Cause he was smiling." Another reply was "'Cause I saw you (the teacher) telling him to do this." (The conductor kept doing the same thing for a long time without showing any sign of any intention to change the action. Thinking that this slow child did not have any idea what to do next, the teacher ended up signaling to him what else he could do.) Still another reply was "'Cause Jeff was the only one who didn't have a turn." (The child deduced this from the teacher's policy that every child is entitled to a turn.)

If the teacher too often asks, "How did you guess?" the question will become boring and will make the game distasteful. If the right question is posed at the right time, however, it will reveal to the others how "It" thinks. Knowing a variety of facts that "It" uses as clues, the group can decenter and play the game at a higher level.

How do I evaluate a game after I try it?

The answer to this question is "by using the same criteria given in Chapter 1 to evaluate the game before trying it out." If the children were interested and mentally active in the game, the game was a good one for that group.

Tag (Chapter 5), Marbles (Chapter 7), Pin the Tail on the Donkey (Chapter 8), and Making Families (Chapter 10) were all judged to be excellent according to the above criterion. Block Race (Chapter 4) could not be considered good because it did not offer enough alternatives for children to think about. The players even expressed the desire to quit after a while. Back-to-Back (Chapter 6) caused a problem by the nature of the game. For groups that can handle the conflict between children who insist on being "It," this game can be said to be a good one. For those who get hopelessly stuck, the game is not suitable. Kitty Wants a Corner (Chapter 9) has been found by many kindergarten teachers to be a good game, although the accounts given in this particular chapter lead to the opposite conclusion. Excellent games can seem poor for certain groups under certain circumstances.

Games that are too easy or too hard are generally not interesting and not conducive to children's being mentally active. For example, by the time children are in the second grade, Tag and Musical Chairs become very easy. When children can organize their own game on the playground and the teacher is no longer needed, it is usually advisable to stop playing them in the classroom. As stated before, however, thinking is not the only objective that is important for a teacher. If social and affective reasons rather than cognitive ones prompted the teacher to choose a particular game in the first place, the same criteria remain pertinent after trying out the game.

It was stated in Chapter 1 that children's inability to play a game generally makes it undesirable. Tom, Tom, Run for Your Supper was cited as being so hard for most four-year-olds that the teacher has to keep telling them what to do. When this happens, children cannot be mentally active and have to depend on the adult to know what to do. This dependence on adults makes the game educationally undesirable. Children can change many games to fit their developmental level, but some games like this one do not seem to lend themselves to such modification.

What do I do when a child does not want to play a game?

Do not require children to play group games. The value of group games vanishes if they are imposed on children. Children can develop toward the goals discussed in Chapter 2 through many other activities.

Certain children consistently stay out of all group games. Others avoid only certain games. Within the same game, some will play a certain role but not another. For example, in a game similar to Cat and Mouse (p. 46) called Fox and Chicken, we found that some boys wanted to be the fox but not the chicken. Finally, there are moments when children want to run around freely and do not feel like being in an organized game.

Fear is one of the common reasons for children's avoidance of games. In Tag, for example, some children get scared if they know that once they are caught, they cannot possibly catch anybody. A three-year-old can also be petrified in a situation like Anita in Tag 1. Anita bounced around in her own world when told to catch someone, but others under the same circumstances can become bewildered and scared by not having any idea what is going on. The teacher must be sensitive to these feelings and prevent traumatic experiences that may lead to children's avoidance of games.

I simply cannot get my children to enforce rules. What can I do?

First of all, it is normal for all young children not to be able to enforce rules. All young children begin by being egocentric and gradually develop the ability to coordinate actions and points of view with others. Development is a slow process, and it takes weeks and months of patient teaching to see the kinds of results we hope to see. Just as the amount of learning achieved in learning experiments depends on the level already attained by the child (Inhelder, Sinclair, and Bovet 1974), the development of autonomy depends on how much autonomy children bring to school in the first place. Those who are used to decision making and negotiations at home quickly become leaders when games are taught in the way discussed in this chapter.

The most common reason for children's inability to learn to govern themselves in games is the general authoritarian practices in the classroom. As can be seen in the Appendix, classrooms are usually run in the empiricist tradition of filling the day with commands and sanctions. In this tradition, children are told not to talk to each other and are told what to say, when to open a book, when to pick up a pencil, when to get in line with their arms folded, etc., etc., etc. These commands reinforce children's heteronomy.

It is impossible to expect children to have initiative in games if the rest of their day is filled with commands. In a card game already mentioned in Chapter 2, when I asked a first grader, "Are YOU going to let so-and-so cheat you like THAT?" he sat there looking at me, as if to say, "Of course, because

YOU are the adult, and YOU are supposed to do something." By observing the way in which the children were forced into obedience all day, I understood why I was totally unable to get any opinion or initiative from these children. They had learned that the teacher takes care of every problem, and that the safe thing to do is to sit and say nothing.

I would now like to add a few remarks about each of the eight types of games presented in Chapter 3. I hope they will help the teacher know generally what to expect and how the first principle applies specifically to different types of games.

Comments About Each Type of Game

Aiming games

Most aiming games and some races involve what we call physical knowledge activities. As discussed in *Physical Knowledge in Preschool Education* (Kamii and DeVries 1978) and the Appendix on p. 236, children learn about the physical world by acting on objects and noticing how objects react. This beginning leads to more precise intentional actions, i.e., acting on objects to produce exactly the desired effect. Most of the activities presented in Part II of *Physical Knowledge* (Kamii and DeVries 1978) were of this type. For example, in Rollers I (Chapter 4), children used rollers to take rides. In Rollers II (Chapter 5), they used rollers and boards to make objects fly up in the air.

Adding the social dimension of group games develops physical knowledge beyond the level described in *Physical Knowledge*.[3] Most of the activities discussed there can be elaborated into group games, and many are found in the sports of older children and adults. Young children often spontaneously develop physical knowledge activities into group games. For example, while watching water or sand run out of containers with holes in them, they exclaim,

[3] I am referring here to the teacher's development of physical knowledge *activities*, and not to the child's development of physical knowledge itself.

12.2.
*Bowling with Rollers.
Another game initiated
spontaneously by children.*

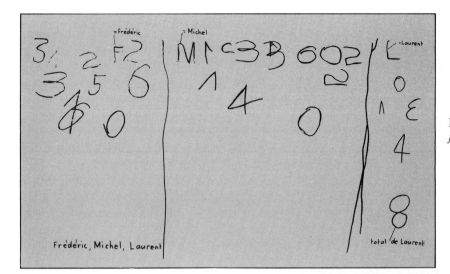

Figure 12.1. *A score sheet from Bowling.*

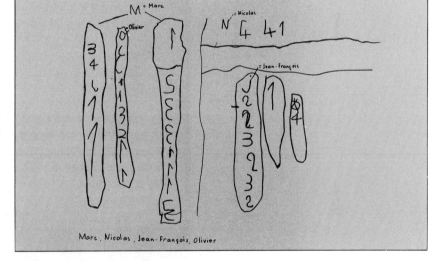

Figure 12.2.
*A score sheet from
Bowling in which temporal
order is represented
spatially.*

"I'll race you." In playing with rollers, they sometimes set them up like bowling pins and knock them down by rolling one from a distance (see Photograph 12.2). Spontaneously, they begin to take turns and try to knock more pins down than anybody else, from a greater distance than anybody else.

Some physical knowledge activities are particularly conducive to numerical reasoning and the representation of numerical ideas. An example can be found in the evolution of Bowling in the last chapter of *Physical Knowledge* (pp. 302-305, which was cited from Capt, Glayre, and Hegyi 1976). Two of the score sheets from this game are reproduced in Figures 12.1 and 12.2. As can be seen in the first figure, Laurent wrote his initial, a 0, 1, 3, and 4, and an 8 at the bottom to represent his total score. Children often have discussions about whether or not a 0 is necessary to enter, as zero means nothing. In these sheets, we can see a gradual structuring of the columns to represent a sequence in time. The numerals in Figure 12.2 are neatly arranged, but in Figure 12.1, only Laurent's column is close to representing a temporal sequence in a straight line.

The following two principles of teaching are also important.

Start aiming games as individual physical knowledge activities and suggest a group game when it will enhance the activity

When children are beginning to roll a roller to knock bowling pins down, or when they are beginning to toss rings to reach a target, the physical action and the object's reaction are so absorbing that it is not possible for them to concentrate on anything except this physical aspect. Therefore, it is unwise to introduce a game before children have played extensively with the material. When a physical knowledge activity becomes well known and boring, the social context of a game often revives interest and purposefulness. This is why Fineberg planned the blowing activity described in *Physical Knowledge* (Kamii and DeVries 1978, p. 51) in the following way: She assembled a variety of junk objects such as a ping-pong ball, paper boat, and orange juice can to blow across the water table (see Photograph 12.3). She planned to give a straw to each child and to suggest that he or she find the things which could be blown with it to the other side. She also planned the following two possibilities to suggest:

a. a race (by asking children to find the object that would get across the fastest)
b. a kind of hockey game in which two children on opposite sides of a water table blow on a ping-pong ball, each trying to make it touch the other side

If the activity seemed absorbing and challenging enough in itself, she planned not to suggest the idea of a game.

Photographs 12.4 through 12.7 show another example of the development of a physical knowledge activity into a group game.

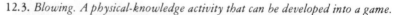

12.3. *Blowing. A physical-knowledge activity that can be developed into a game.*

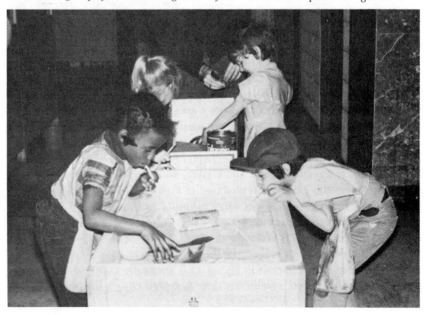

12.4. *Drop the Clothespins. The teacher asks each child to take five clothespins.*

12.5. *When dropping the clothespins into the cylinder became too easy, the teacher suggested, "Do you want to stand on a chair or drop them in some other way?"*

12.7. *Most of the children left the activity, but four of them stayed and thought of a different way to drop the clothespins.*

12.6. *Some children imitated one child who dropped the clothespins with her eyes closed.*

Encourage children to invent games

This point has already been made above with Marbles (Chapter 7) as an example. It therefore requires no further elaboration.

Before concluding this section, I would like to make a few remarks about Ring Toss and Drop the Clothespins. The first game involves the rule of standing behind the line. The second will be discussed with respect to determining who won in an aiming game.

If, from a child's point of view, an aiming game is not competitive, the distance to the target does not need to be exactly the same. If the teacher insists on the children standing behind the line in Ring Toss, they usually obey her. Children who obey the teacher in this way do not relate standing at a particular spot with chances for success. Such an intervention does not lead to any thinking and results only in reinforcing children's heteronomy. In addition, such insistence takes away from children's opportunities to use their initiative by noticing and trying to solve a problem.

As was pointed out in Chapter 3, when a child announces, "I got five," and another says, "I got six," in Drop the Clothespins, these may be parallel announcements of the results of counting, rather than a comparison of quantities. Whether or not to push for a comparison by asking, "Who got more then?" can be answered only with an, "It depends." The answer depends on a number of factors such as children's emotional strength, their cognitive level, and the interpersonal climate of the group. When in doubt, it is best not to suggest making direct comparisons. Scorekeeping will naturally emerge anyway. Although this game provides opportunities for numerical comparison, it is sometimes best to avoid it. In Drop the Clothespins, a five-year-old had agreed to play to see who could get the most into a jug. When the moment came to count the clothespins, however, she refused to count them, and the teacher guessed she knew she was the loser. (This is an example of the inseparability of cognition and affectivity.) As long as the other players do not object, it seems best not to insist on fair play or counting under such circumstances.

Races

Many races such as Spoon Race (p. 41) and Blowing Race (p. 42) involve physical knowledge. Since the development of physical knowledge activities into group games was discussed above, the same principles that apply to races will not be repeated here. The following applies particularly to races.

Encourage children to direct the race themselves as soon as possible

The social organization of races is parallel and simple, and many five-year-olds love to direct them. The teacher can start by asking who wants to say, "Ready, set, go," and gradually give an increasing amount of responsibility to the leader.

I would like to add a few remarks about Musical Chairs, Spoon Race, and Tom, Tom, Run for Your Supper, which were not included in Part II.

Musical Chairs (p. 43) with as many chairs as children makes no sense to adults. For four-year-olds, however, the fun of the game is as a ritual of marching to music with others and running to grab a chair when the music stops. Since each child thinks about *his* fun and what *he* does, the game is more fun for him when he gets a chair.

Some preschool teachers have been playing Musical Chairs for years with the same number of chairs as children. When we ask them why they do this, they usually explain that children's feelings are hurt when they do not get a chair. We agree that emotional bruises are bad for children's development, but from the Piagetian perspective, we have other reasons for preferring to have enough chairs for all the players. From the child's point of view, the game is a ritual and not a competition. A ritual entails the need for enough paraphernalia to complete the activity.

Furthermore, young children have not constructed the logico-mathematical notion of number and cannot understand that if there is one more child than chairs before the music starts, there will necessarily be one child without a chair when the music stops. In spite of the teacher's explanation beforehand that there will be one person who will not get a chair, the loser nevertheless looks for *his* chair. Many three-year-olds cry when they cannot find their chairs. Such bewilderment and trauma are not conducive to affective or cognitive development. Children will eventually learn by empirical generalization that there will be one person without a chair. This ability to anticipate, however, does not make the ritual more sensible to them than when they were surprised not to get a chair. [4]

Number is constructed by reflective abstraction and not by empirical abstraction. (The two kinds of abstraction are discussed in the Appendix.) Chairs are observable, but number is not. Number, according to Piaget, is created by each child by reflective abstraction, i.e., by putting objects into numerical relationships. Relationships do not exist out there in external reality and are not observable. By observing that one of the children did not get a chair, three- and four-year-olds can come to predict this fact by empirical generalization. The numerical relationship of "one more chair" or "as many chairs" as children, however, is not observable and cannot be learned by empirical generalization. For further details on Piaget's theory of number, the reader is referred to Piaget and Szeminska (1941) and Kamii and DeVries (1976).

In one of the day care centers in which we experimented, the teacher had been playing Musical Chairs in the usual way almost every day with a group of four-year-olds. When we asked her what she thought of trying the game with the same number of chairs as children, she laughed and did not even want to consider such an idea. Finally, we persuaded her to try our way once. For our research she agreed to let us videotape the two ways to compare how children run. After playing the game in the usual way, she explained to the children that, for the visitors (us), she wanted to try a new way with enough chairs for everybody. She was surprised to observe that when she stopped the music, the children ran just as fast and excitedly as before to sit in a chair. We then asked her to ask the children which way they preferred, the new way or the old. In unison, they shouted, "The new way!"

In another day care center, an all-Black institution, the teachers objected for different reasons. They insisted (a) that children become lackadaisical when things come too easily to them and (b) that Blacks are losers in this society and, therefore, children should learn from the beginning to accept the idea of being a loser more often than being a winner. This is not just a Black point of view. Many other people hold the belief that insecurity motivates

[4] I said in the preceding chapter on competition that Hildebrand did not go far enough in modifying Musical Chairs. I hope it is clear now that letting a loser join a rhythm band is not much of a modification.

children to make efforts. I think that if children are to become good sports, they have to have feelings of security and confidence built with lots of gratifying experiences in general.

As noted in Chapter 3, the most valuable part of Musical Chairs may be in the preparation of the game, when children decide how many chairs they need and how the chairs should be arranged. Too often, the adult does this work for the children, thereby depriving them of the opportunity to put into relationship the number of players and the number and spatial arrangement of the chairs.

In another room of four-year-olds, the teacher presented Spoon Race by including the rule that if someone drops his ball, he has to begin all over from the starting line. When the children did not go back to the line but, instead, picked up the ball, put it back on the spoon, and continued to run, she enforced the rule by making them go back to the line. When someone held the ball on the spoon with his free hand, she told him to hold this hand behind his back. These examples of "teaching" violate both of the principles discussed at the beginning of this chapter. As noted before, children usually obey adults at such moments, but this obedience does not result in any learning (in relation to our objectives) and serves only to reinforce children's heteronomy. If the point of the game in the child's view is to carry the ball successfully to a certain spot, going back to the line or holding the free hand behind one's back is completely irrelevant.

Group games often elicit unexpected kinds of thinking in children. In Tom, Tom, Run for Your Supper (p. 5) that we observed in a kindergarten room, for example, the circle became deformed at one point as shown in Figure 12.3. When child A noticed this, he complained that the situation was unfair because he would have a longer way to run than child B! That he was alert enough to compare distances is an example of the kind of thinking that can take place in group games. The teacher in this kind of situation should ask the group what they think of this complaint. The best way to foster the development of logico-mathematical knowledge is through the exchange of viewpoints. As was pointed out with evidence from Perret-Clermont's (1976) study cited in Chapter 2, logico-mathematical knowledge develops by the coordination of points of view, rather than by the teaching of the "correct" answer. The best intervention in a situation of this kind is to try to get children to confront each other's ideas.

At another point in the same game, the teacher said to the group, "There are people who have not had a turn. Let's choose only people who have not had a turn." One of the children immediately complained that he would never get a chance to be "It" because he was sitting between two children who had already had their turns. Again, the teacher in this kind of situation should ask the group what they think should be done about this problem.

Chasing games

There are no important principles of teaching to add to those that have already been discussed in Chapters 3 and 5. I would like to make two points concerning Duck, Duck, Goose, probably the most popular chasing game in preschool. The problem of taking turns and the element of symbolic play pertain to many other games.

Children tend to choose their friends to be the goose, and the game

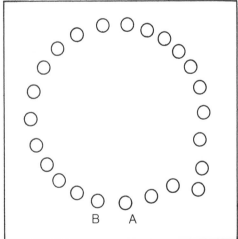

Figure 12.3. *Tom, Tom, Run for Your Supper. The circle became deformed at one point.*

quickly becomes monopolized by a few. When the teacher says that those who have had a turn cannot be chosen any more, those who know they will not get another turn lose interest and become restless. The best solution is for the teacher to say "Try to choose somebody who has not had a turn." The teacher here is admittedly giving an unclear message, and some children interpret it as an order to choose only those who have not had a turn. Some teachers with whom I have discussed this point disagree with me, but others have said that this request works well for them.[5] They say that when "It" feels free to disregard the teacher's request, the players who have had a turn have reason to remain interested and alert.

When children are encouraged to invent games and modify them, they often invent ideas that improve the game by introducing an element of symbolic play. In Duck, Duck, Goose, when the goose catches "It" before "It" sits down, some children have suggested that the old "It" should "go in the duck pond" and sit in the middle of the circle.[6] This clever modification keeps "It" from monopolizing the game by purposely getting caught repeatedly. The symbolic aspect reduces the punitive element of the rule, and the child in the pond may even enjoy pretending to swim. Children thus introduce symbolic play into group games, and the teacher must be ready to make use of this tendency. When the child in the pond asks when he can get out, it is, of course, time for the group to make one more decision.

Hiding games

The first principle discussed at the beginning of this chapter is again applicable when a child calls out "here I am" in Hide and Seek, or when he tells the finder where the object has been hidden. Go along with the children's way as long as it seems to make sense to the group. In Hide and Seek, children at different developmental levels can often play together, each at his own level, with the three- and four-year-olds happy to be found quickly, and the five-year-olds proud to be the last ones found. In a game like Doggy, Doggy, Your Bone Is Gone (p. 49), somebody will eventually object to a hider telling where the bone is.

When the hot-cold clue is used in Doggy, Doggy, Your Bone Is Gone, the teacher often does not decenter enough to make the distinction between the spatial proximity of the finder and the place where he is looking for the object. For example, a finder may be looking at a closet containing the hidden object while standing at the far end of the room. Spatially, the finder is far from the object, but psychologically he is close to it. The teacher may need to help children come to an agreement as to what they mean by hot and cold. There is no absolute meaning conveyed by these terms. It is important that the players agree on their meaning when these words are used.

As stated in Chapter 3, it is good to modify Doggy, Doggy, Your Bone Is Gone by asking for a group to hide the object and a group to find it. This modification increases not only the number of children who can participate in the game but also the need for cooperation. The hiders have to agree on where

[5] Heidi Mounoud has stated with particular conviction that this request has worked for her.

[6] Credit goes to Nancy Fineberg for pointing out that the element of pretend play (symbolic play) has a large part in young children's group games.

to hide the object, and the finders do well to keep track of the spots where others have looked. Using two objects is also a modification that can increase the possibility for more participation.

Guessing games

Very young children cannot keep secrets in games and often give the answer away. The principle to keep in mind again is to let the objection come from the children rather than from the teacher.

Following are a few remarks about two types of guessing games: (a) guessing from tactilo-kinesthetic clues and (b) guessing from visual clues (body movements).

Guessing from tactilo-kinesthetic clues

Mystery Bag (p. 53) is an old game which very young children can play. Occasionally, there are children who do not say anything and will not name an object. For these children and others who have trouble guessing, it may be good to provide a second set of identical objects, visible to all, so that the guesser can point to the one that is the same. The teacher can ask children to make the two sets of objects before playing the game as can be seen in Photograph 12.8.

Guessing from visual clues (body movements)

As stated earlier in the discussion on how to choose a game, the principle to remember is to start the game as a ritual and gradually develop it into a group game. Some four-year-olds cannot play Charades (p. 54) because they cannot imitate an action well enough to serve as a clue. For these children, it is best to do rituals, usually with a song or nursery rhyme such as "Here We Go 'Round the Mulberry Bush." In these rituals, children can copy the teacher and each other, and the imitation soon improves.

When a ritual is first developed into a group game, it is best to introduce the game in a noncompetitive way. For example, children can take turns being

12.8.
Mystery Bag.
The children are making two sets of objects while Professor Piaget watches them (October 1967).

"It" in Charades. The game can later be modified into the competitive version described in Chapter 3.

Games involving verbal commands

As stated in the discussion of Charades, Simon Says is best played non-competitively at first. In this version, there is no attempt to catch the opponent doing the wrong thing. Anyone can make a suggestion such as "touch your nose," and the entire group does what was suggested. When children have mastered this version, the teacher can introduce the rules that modify it into a competitive game.

Card games

Card games differ from every other type of game discussed so far by involving special materials made with a logical organization. As stated in Chapter 3, many card games provide special opportunities for logical reasoning.

Some principles of teaching are given here as answers to the following questions:

How do I choose a game?
What kinds of cards should I use?
How large a group should I begin with?
How many cards should I give to children for a particular game?
What can I do about children's difficulty in holding cards?
When do I correct children, and when do I try to change the rule instead?

How do I choose a game?

In Chapter 3, the various card games were presented generally in order of difficulty. Picture Cards (p. 61) is the easiest, and Rummy (p. 70) and Sevens (or a greater total that can be made with two cards, p. 71) are the hardest.

It was stated in Chapter 3 that in card games, there are elements of chance and elements of decision. Picture Cards is almost totally a game of chance. This makes the game easy and good for four-year-olds who have never before played with cards. It is also what makes the game boring for advanced five-year-olds even in their first experience with a card game.

Making Families (p. 64 and Chapter 10) and Go Fish (p. 64) give the possibility of decision making based on logical reasoning. They are, therefore, good for children in kindergarten and first grade who have had considerable experience with card games.

Some games involve very simple judgments rather than logical reasoning. For example, Slap Jack (p. 61) and Snap (p. 62) require little more than perceptual discrimination. War (p. 68) requires judgment of which card has more (or the most). These games are more challenging than Picture Cards on the one hand, and a lot easier than Making Families and Go Fish on the other. Slap Jack, Snap, and War, plus Concentration (p. 62), are good for beginning card players who are four or five years old.

Another consideration in choosing a game is the number of cards children have to hold. This point will be discussed shortly.

After introducing the game, the teacher can decide only by observing children's play whether or not to continue with it. Certain games offer many more possibilities than the children can use. Chapter 10 (Making Families) is an example of such a situation. With the particular group of three children described in this chapter, I believe that it would have been good to continue playing the same game because the children were learning a great deal from playing it.

What kinds of cards should I use?

It was pointed out in Chapter 3 that all the card games presented there were possible with regular playing cards, and that some of them were possible with picture cards. It was also stated that Concentration seems best with picture cards. In most games, pictures are easier to deal with.

Another consideration concerns the choices that should be available in the classroom at a given time. Although versatility is the beauty of playing cards, the teachers at Circle Children's Center who experimented with card games feel that it may be confusing to introduce too many games with one set of cards. The children of kindergarten age in their class had the following repertoire by the middle of the year. The four games marked with asterisks were played only with playing cards. For all the other games, the children had special cards.

*Picture Cards
*Slap Jack
Concentration
Go Fish
*Bango[7]
War
Piggy Bank
Card Dominoes
*Crazy Cards[8]

For Concentration, the children had a variety of cards such as teacher-made plaques with pictures of fish and sea animals, cards of animals put out by the National Wildlife Federation (no date) and other cards which are widely available. For Go Fish, they had the cards consisting of solid colors put out by Ed-U-Cards and mentioned in Chapter 3 (footnote 22). For War, they had cards made by the teacher having various quantities of circles. For Piggy Bank, they had the cards mentioned in Chapter 3 put out by Ed-U-Cards. For Card Dominoes, they had a printed experimental set which is illustrated in Figure 12.4b. This set represents the following modifications of playing cards to overcome the two problems mentioned in Chapter 3 (footnote 26):

[7] As can be seen below, Bango is similar to Bingo (p. 78):

Bango
Two decks of cards are used. The dealer deals five cards to each player from one deck. Each player spreads his cards face up in front of himself. The caller then turns up cards from the other deck, holding them up and calling them out by denomination and suit (e.g., a four of clubs). The player who has the matching card places the caller's card on top of his own. The player who found a match for each one of his five cards calls "Bango!" and is the winner.

[8] Crazy Cards is a simplification of Crazy Eights (p. 69). It is played in exactly the same way as Crazy Eights, except that there are no wild cards. If a player does not have a card that matches by number or by suit, all he can do is keep taking cards from the deck until he gets one that matches.

1. The series begins with a 1 rather than an ace and goes only up to 10.
2. The 40 cards come in four colors instead of four suits. There are four 1's, four 2's, four 3's, etc., each number in red, black, green, and blue. By using colors, we can inscribe the suit in the numeral, thereby eliminating the need for the small symbol under each numeral. (In regular cards, the small symbol is necessary when the cards are held like a fan as shown in Figure 12.4a.)

When this variety of cards sat on the shelf, the teachers observed that other cards were often used during free play, but not playing cards. We do not know whether this was due to the nature of the four games played with playing cards or to the fact that the playing cards were used for so many games that children could not think of a game when they looked at these cards on the shelf. We hypothesize that for children of kindergarten age it may be best to have a different set of cards for each game. The children played very well with the teacher when she initiated Slap Jack, Bango, and Crazy Cards with playing cards, but if we want children to initiate their own games, it may be best not to present four different games with the same set of cards.

As stated in Chapter 3, picture cards offer almost unlimited possibilities in content. Flowers, animals, occupations, tools, and cars are but a few examples of content that can be used for games in which children make pairs or sets of three or four cards that are the same or alike.

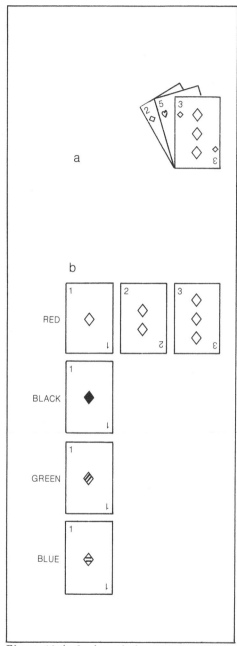

Figure 12.4. *Cards made for young children so that there are only three diamonds to count for "3" (and not five).*

How large a group should I begin with?

The ideal size to begin with depends on the teacher's objective, the children's age, the game chosen, and the number of adults available to play with children. If an extra adult is available in the classroom, four players is ideal for games such as Making Families (Chapter 10). If the teacher is the only adult in the classroom, and his objective is to get children to become able to play on their own as soon as possible, it may be best to play War with a capable leader so that he will then play with another child and thus teach the game to many other children.

As stated earlier, Concentration is a parallel-role game that demands a minimum of social organization. It goes well with four players from the beginning if an adult is present to keep the turns going in cyclic order. The transition from two to three players is hard for young children because the turns switch from simple alternation to a cyclic order. This is why two is the best number for children to begin playing without an adult. As they continue to play, the group often evolves into a larger organization.

How many cards should I give to children for a particular game?

Usually, the greater the number of cards, the harder it is to organize them logically. The ideal number of cards for a game also depends on a number of factors such as the number of children involved, the type of game played, the type of cards used, and the level of the players' development.

In Making Families (Chapter 10), the teacher selected five sets out of the nine that were available. This number seemed right for four players of kindergarten age.

For Concentration, the teacher might begin by selecting eight pairs of cards for four players and put the 16 cards on the floor in a 4×4 arrangement. If this number is too easy, more cards can be added.

Sometimes, it is best to give the entire deck to children and let them figure out which cards to eliminate. It was stated in Chapter 3, for example, that for the game of Elevens, the cards exceeding 10 cannot be used (because it is impossible to make a total of 11 with two cards if one of them exceeds 10). However, it is sometimes more educational to give the entire deck to children and let them find out the problem. In the game of Sevens, for example, many first graders go on turning up cards from the drawing pile when the three cards that are turned up all exceed six (for example, an 8, a 10, and a J)! Sometimes, one of the players ends up announcing that some of the cards have to be set aside because they don't work.

What can I do about children's difficulty in holding cards?

Young children have trouble holding more than a few cards, and this is a serious problem. The three solutions that I can think of are (a) selecting games that do not require the holding of many cards, (b) using a certain kind of cards, and (c) using certain tools. Each one of these solutions is discussed here.

1. Select games that do not require the holding of many cards. The games presented in Chapter 3 can be grouped into the following four categories:

   a. Games that do not require holding any cards
      Picture Cards
      Slap Jack
      Concentration
      Snap
      War
      Sevens
      (Dominoes)

   b. Games that require holding no more than 5 cards
      Go Fish, when there are 3 or 4 players
      Making Families, in the situation described in Chapter 10

   c. Games that require holding 6-10 cards
      Go Fish, when there are only 2 players
      Animal Rummy
      Rummy

   d. Games that require holding more than 10 cards
      Old Maid
      Card Dominoes
      I Doubt It
      Crazy Eights

This first solution, therefore, entails the selection of games in the first two of the preceding categories. However, children whose logic is well developed manage to look through all their cards systematically even if they have trouble holding them. Therefore, this solution seems worth considering when both logic and motor coordination are at a low level.

2. Use a certain kind of cards. As stated in Chapter 3, Go Fish, which is put out by Ed-U-Cards, consists of cards of solid colors (four each of eight different colors). With these cards, it is possible for the child to know which ones he has by glancing at them, even when he is holding them in a very awkward way.

3. Use certain tools. The ideal tool is the card holder shown in Photograph 12.9. This is made with two plastic disks that are held together in the middle with a spring. If these card holders are not available, box tops or inverted egg cartons can also be used as shown in Photograph 12.10.

When do I correct children, and when should I try to change the rule instead?

This question can be answered only by figuring out how children are thinking and why they are doing the "wrong" thing. As stated in Chapter 10, children may be doing the wrong thing simply because they do not know the rule.

12.9. *A card holder.*

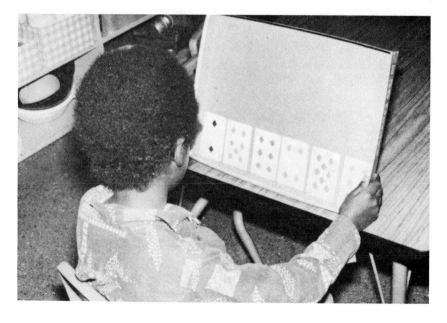

12.10. *A box top used to hold cards.*

A child may know the rule but become careless in his eagerness to put cards down. If he puts down an incomplete family in Making Families, this behavior seems appropriate to correct. If the behavior is not a manifestation of a fundamentally different way of thinking about the rule, the teacher's correction is perfectly acceptable and understandable to the child.

An example of behavior which seems inappropriate to correct in Making Families is Maurice's announcing that he had the card that Eron wanted. This behavior would have been inappropriate to correct for the following three reasons:

1. Maurice had two criteria for winning, one of which was to be the first to get rid of his cards. If this was the motivation for announcing the possession of cards, correcting the surface behavior would have only gone counter to his way of thinking. Besides, when this criterion sooner or later ceased to be important, he would stop wanting to give cards away anyway.

2. Maurice was in transition from being unable to compete to becoming able to do so. As we saw in the chapter on competition, young children want the finder to find the hidden object. If Maurice's reason for announcing the possession of cards was partly due to this kind of motivation, correcting the surface behavior would only have confused him. As he developed, the problem would correct itself without any teaching.

3. Maurice's behavior was not disturbing the rest of the group. It is sometimes necessary to correct the behavior of one child in the interest of the group. In this case, there was absolutely no need to intervene for this reason.

In card games, too, it is best not to correct the child but to interact with him as a fellow player. For example, in Concentration, if a child peeks at one card after another until he finds the one he is looking for, the teacher might ask, "May I do that, too?" If the child replies no, the teacher might insist on peeking in the same way if the child is emotionally strong enough to cope with the teacher's insistence.

Card Dominoes offers the possibility of planning strategies by reasoning logically. To know which card is the most advantageous to play in the version described in Chapter 3, adults usually organize their cards in the following way:

1. They first sort the cards by color (or by suit if they are using regular playing cards).

2. They seriate the cards within each color (or suit).

3. They know that the cards to play first are the ones that come before those in their hand that must be played later. For example, if one has a red 2 without any other red card, and a green 2, 5, and 9, the card to play first is the green 2. Adults also know that it is best to keep the red 2 as long as possible to keep the other players from being able to play their red cards.

Young children do not think of these strategies and usually do not even think of sorting their cards. The teacher is tempted to show the first two of the above steps and explain the reasoning in the third step. However, it is generally more educational to let children invent these strategies or find out about them from friends. If children learn to follow the rules given by adults, they become dependent and lacking in initiative.

The card games as well as other games in Chapter 3 are often described without precision. It is best to give children room to notice the need for a rule. When children are encouraged to come up with rules, they will also take the initiative to modify them as they outgrow them. Following is an example of the way in which kindergarten children modified a rule of Card Dominoes (p. 67) after going from one level of play to another in six months.[9]

The first level we saw consisted of putting only two elements at a time into relationship, in a unidirectional way. For example, when there were only four ones down at the beginning of the game as shown in Figure 12.5a, the child

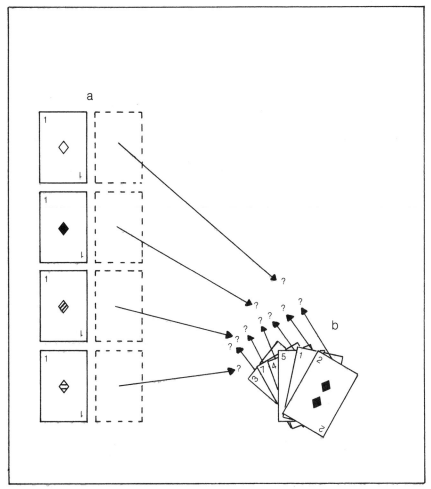

Figure 12.5, *The beginning of Card Dominoes in which four 1's have been put out.*

[9] Credit goes to Nancy Fineberg and Kathleen Harper for making these observations.

at this level looked for the red 2 among his cards. If he did not find it, he went on to look for the green 2 in his hand, then the black 2, and then the blue 2, always starting the relationship unidirectionally from the floor.

The child sometimes started the relationship in the opposite direction, from each card in his hand as shown in Figure 12.5b. If he was systematic, he focused on one card after another in sequence and asked himself, "Can I put this card down? . . . or this one? . . . or this one? . . ." In this process, some children made a dichotomy that I never thought of: They grouped the big numbers and little numbers because only the little numbers can be played at the beginning.

The creation of relationships between only two elements in a unidirectional way is what Piaget calls "functions" (Piaget, Grize, Szeminska, and Bang 1968). This is the limited, small structure that characterizes preoperational thinking. Later, when children's thought becomes more mobile, they become able to put more than two elements into relationships and can think in two directions. This is why they become able to go through their cards only once, looking for one of the four cards that can be played.

After playing this game for a few months, many six-year-olds independently come up with the following modification: "When your turn comes, you put down all the cards you can put down." This evolution is further evidence of children's increasing ability to coordinate many relationships at the same time. When higher-level relationships are possible to establish, children become bored and impatient with the slow, old way of playing.

Children also invent the three modifications presented in Chapter 3: (a) starting with all the 10's and making the matrix in descending order, (b) starting with all the 5's and building the matrix in both descending and ascending order, and (c) letting the first player begin the game by putting down any card he wants.

Finally, children of kindergarten age come up with modifications that show that children want to be active and constructively occupied. When they win the game by being the first to get rid of all their cards, they sometimes say "I can't play any more. Can I have some of your cards?" If the important thing is the fun of playing rather than of winning, it is no fun having to stop playing. Children want to be active and want to go on to ever higher levels. The teacher's task is to foster their natural tendency to construct, and not to teach the "right" way to play.

Board games

Two general points might be made about board games. One concerns "cheating," and the other, levels of play.

"Cheating." Board games often involve chance with throwing a die, spinning a spinner, or drawing a card. In Candy Land (p. 72), for example, children draw cards to know how far they can go toward the finishing line. When young children get a card they do not like, they often go on turning one after another until they get one that is acceptable! (They do the same thing in Concentration, p. 62.) Similarly, they throw the die again, if the number turned up is not to their liking, and push the spinner to the spot they want.

All these behaviors, which look like cheating, are not when viewed from the point of view of young children. I once noticed a young four-year-old playing Candy Land alone, with all the cards facing up in a box. When I asked him if it might be better to turn the cards over, he answered no and offered to pick a card for me if I wanted to play with him. He not only chose a good card for me but also let me have many turns until I caught up with him.

When children select cards, the teacher may want to react as a player (a) by playing by the conventional rule to model the correct way or (b) by asking the child if it is OK for him (the teacher) to do the same thing. If the child says no, as it was stated with regard to card games, the teacher might insist on playing in the same way as the child, arguing that it is not fair if a rule applies only to one player. Alternatively, the teacher may decide that it is best to go along with the child, saying something like "I don't understand why *you* can and I can't, but OK (if you say so). . . ." Under most circumstances, as he becomes less egocentric, the child will come to realize that such rules are unfair.

Levels of play. Some board games lend themselves to distinct levels of play which are useful for the teacher to know. In Chinese Checkers (p. 198), for example, we found the following three levels:[10]

Level I: The use of the material as a physical knowledge activity. The child may put all the marbles in holes (sometimes asking for more because there are not enough to fill all the holes), or he may shake the board trying to get many marbles into the holes.

Level II: The child concentrates on one marble at a time and tries to take one all the way to the end point before advancing the next one. No matter how the adult tries to explain that he has a chance to jump with another marble, he insists on using only one at a time, even to the extent of moving sideways or backward!

Level III: The child can play with many marbles and jumps many times with each one. (This level is preceded by the child's taking only single jumps, beginning by jumping only his own.)

At each level, it is important to encourage the child to think and play in his own way. As a physical knowledge (and logico-mathematical knowledge) activity, Level I is perfectly useful for the child's construction of knowledge and confidence in his ability. Level II is also a necessary step, and we have observed many times the uselessness of trying to center the child's attention on more elements than he can think of.

Piaget's recent twin books, *The Grasp of Consciousness* (1974a) and *Success and Understanding* (1974b) on the relationship between practical intelligence and the conceptualization of what we do in practical intelligence shed much light on the development of every practical field such as education, agriculture, animal science, medicine, engineering, and navigation. Practice, beginning with trial and error, came first in every one of these fields. It is much later that practice became conceptualized and modified by scientific knowledge.

In education, as discussed in the Appendix, scientific research and theory are only beginning to modify old practices. Piaget (1967, Chapter 4) says,

---

[10] Credit goes to Nancy Fineberg and Kathleen Harper for observing these levels.

however, that teaching is both an art and a science because many complex factors must be taken into consideration in teaching, and a large part of the teacher's job is based on guesses. These guesses, however, must be educated based on scientific knowledge about how children learn.

Group games have been around for a long time. Piaget's theory provides new insights into old practices and suggests how they might be changed to increase their educational value.

Figure 1.
Relationships between behaviorism and Piaget's theory.

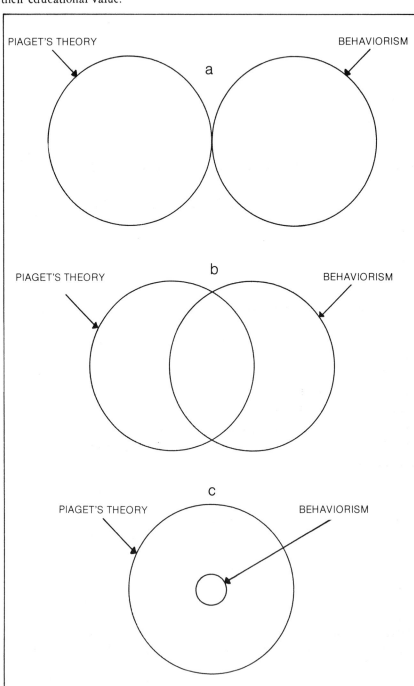

Appendix[*]

Piaget's Theory, Behaviorism, and Other Theories in Education

Constance Kamii

MANY THEORIES or philosophies, such as those of Socrates, St. Augustine, Comenius, Rousseau, and Dewey, have influenced education. The term *theory* in this context refers broadly to "a particular conception or view of something to be done or of the method of doing it" (Barnhart 1963). In recent years, educators have been influenced by different kinds of scientific theories which have been tested and verified empirically all over the world. Examples of scientific theories are behaviorism and Piaget's theory.

Piaget's theory differs from behaviorism, and the two are often discussed as if they were mutually exclusive as shown in Figure 1a. An example of this view follows:

> The cognitive-developmentalist, following Piagetian theory, believes that the process of education is one of building cognitive structures in the mind of the child. The behavior modifier, following the theories of B. F. Skinner, is wont to say that he does not know what cognitive structures are—that he believes these are fictions, myths, invented by the psychologist that serve more to hinder than to help his understanding of how the child learns. The Skinnerian conceives of education as a process of producing changes in observable behavior. . . . The Skinnerian thinks of behavior as being under stimulus control and holds that education consists in bringing specified behavior under the control of specified stimuli. . . . The Skinnerian does not, of course, believe that the child has

*This Appendix is a revision of an article published in the *Journal of Education* 161 (1979): 13-33.

no brain or that nothing goes on inside the head—only that it is not profitable to speculate about these internal processes, since they cannot be directly observed or controlled. . . .

The Piagetian does not conceive of the child as being under stimulus control. On the contrary, to put the issue in the most extreme form, he conceives of stimuli as being under the control of the child. More stimuli are always present in the stimulus complex that surrounds the child than he can respond to. The child . . . not only selects, but interprets what is selected in terms of his previously stored experience. (Maccoby and Zellner 1970, pp. 33-34)

The preceding quote can also be represented as shown in Figure 1b. The intersection in this figure stands for the statement that "the Skinnerian does not, of course, believe that the child has no brain or that nothing goes on inside the head."

How can two scientific theories be so opposed and yet true? In the discussion that follows, I will attempt to answer this question, discuss the epistemological significance of Piaget's theory, and present the educational implications of these theories.

Piaget's Theory and Behaviorism

The relationship between the two theories as I see them is represented in Figure 1c. As can be seen in this figure, behaviorism is much more limited than Piaget's theory and is, in fact, encompassed by it. Piaget's theory is broader and more powerful than behaviorism because it explains every intellectual and moral phenomenon described by behaviorism, while behaviorism cannot explain most of Piaget's findings. For example, behaviorists interpret Pavlov's dog as demonstrating conditioning and extinction. Piaget interprets the same phenomena differently. For him, the bell comes to be a signal for the appearance of food, after the repeated presentation of the bell and meat (Piaget 1947, 1967; Piaget and Inhelder 1966b). If the meat subsequently stops appearing, the dog simply stops anticipating it. Piaget thus explains conditioning and extinction in terms of the organism's ability to attribute meaning to objects and events and to anticipate future happenings, thereby adapting to its environment.

While Piaget's theory explains the phenomena studied by behaviorists, the converse is not the case, for example, the quantification of class inclusion (Inhelder and Piaget 1959). No behaviorist can explain why all children begin by saying that there are more dogs than animals. Neither can behaviorists explain why, without any teaching whatsoever, children later come to say that there are more animals than dogs.

In order to present Piaget's explanation of the quantification of class inclusion, it is necessary to clarify the task. In this task, the child is given six miniature dogs and two cats of the same size, for example, and is asked, "What do you see?" so that the examiner can proceed with whatever word comes from the child's vocabulary. The child is then asked to show "*all* the animals," "*all* the dogs," and "*all* the cats" with the words that came from his vocabulary, e.g., "doggy." Only after ascertaining the child's understanding of these words does the adult ask the following class inclusion question: "Are there more dogs or more animals?"

Four-year-olds typically answer "more dogs"; whereupon the adult asks "than what?" The four-year-old's answer is "than cats." In other words, the question the examiner asks is "Are there more dogs or more animals?" but the one young children "hear" is "Are there more dogs or more cats?" Young children hear a question that is different from the one the adult asked because once they mentally cut the whole into two parts, the only thing they can think about is the two parts. For them, at that moment, the whole no longer exists. They can think about the whole, but not when they are thinking about the parts. In order to compare the whole with a part, the child has to do two opposite mental actions at the same time: cut the whole into two parts and put the parts back together into a whole. This, according to Piaget, is precisely what four-year-olds cannot do.

By eight years of age, Piaget states, most children's thought becomes mobile enough to be reversible. Reversibility refers to the ability mentally to do two opposite actions simultaneously—in this case, separating the whole into two parts and reuniting the parts into a whole. In physical, material action, it is not possible to do two opposite things simultaneously. In our heads, however, this is possible to do when thought has become mobile enough to be reversible. It is only when the parts can be reunited in the mind that a child can "see" that there are more animals than dogs.

Piaget thus explains the attainment of the hierarchical structure of class inclusion by the increasing mobility of children's thought, which culminates in reversibility. In the quantification of class inclusion, furthermore, there is no extinction. Once the child believes that there are more animals than dogs, there is no way of convincing him that he should go back to his earlier way of thinking. This is an example of a cognitive structure alluded to earlier. Behaviorism is too limited to explain how logic develops in the human mind.

Let us take another example from the realm of moral development to explain Figure 1c: In *The Moral Judgment of the Child*, Piaget (1932) spoke of sanctions, which the translator unfortunately changed to punishment. In this book, Piaget stated that adults use sanctions to get children to behave in certain ways, and that in life it is often impossible to avoid sanctions, for example, when we don't want children to touch knobs on the television or stereo set. While he thus acknowledged the inevitability of sanctions (and in this sense agreed with behaviorists), he also insisted that sanctions have the effect of prolonging the child's heteronomy by preventing the development of autonomy. Autonomy, it will be recalled, is a political term that means governing oneself. Heteronomy, by contrast, means being governed by somebody else. Heteronomy can be seen in the example of the seven-year-old who says "no" to the question "would it be bad to tell lies if you were not punished?" Autonomy can be seen in the example of the 12-year-old who said, "Sometimes you almost have to tell lies to a grown-up, but it's rotten to do it to another fellow (p. 173)." Autonomous people have their own criteria for judging what is right or wrong, and their judgments are not based on whether or not they might be punished.

We can limit sanctions to the positive side and practice reward without punishment and approval rather than disapproval. However, all the power of positive sanctions can only result in prolonging the child's heteronomy.

Sanctions explain why most people's behavior can be controlled to a large extent, but they cannot explain the courageous behavior of autonomous people who refuse to go along with the reward system and stand up for what they believe to be morally right. Heteronomy can be explained by behaviorism, but autonomy can be explained only by a broader theory.[1]

The relationship between behaviorism and Piaget's theory is analogous to that between the geocentric theory and the heliocentric theory in astronomy; between Newton's theory and Einstein's in physics; and between Euclidean geometry and non-Euclidean geometry. Many people today have trouble seeing the part-whole relationship shown in Figure 1c because Piaget's theory is revolutionary, and the psychology of learning is in the midst of what Kuhn (1962) calls a scientific revolution. Kuhn points out that each scientific revolution grows out of the inadequacy of the previous theory. For example, the Copernican revolution came after a long period of dissatisfaction with the inaccuracies obtained in calculating the positions of planets and in trying to make the old calendar work within the geocentric theory. Astronomers kept making corrections for these inaccuracies until the geocentric theory became hopelessly complex and incoherent. Just as astronomers introduced corrections in the geocentric theory to make calculations correspond to the actual positions of planets, behaviorists have introduced corrections which only complicate a model that is inadequate to begin with. Hull's (1952) "fractional antedating goal responses" is an example of such corrections.

Copernicus created a new conceptual framework through which he looked at the same planets, thereby increasing the accuracy, simplicity, and coherence of astronomy. Resistance is the first reaction to any revolutionary theory, according to Kuhn. Because all scientists are trained to think about and study nature in a way that fits the conceptual framework supplied by their education, it is natural for them to resist a new framework that subverts the old rules of how to go about trying to get at the truth. Copernicus was laughed at by his fellow scholars, and the ridicule was so strong that for at least 16 years, Galileo pretended that he disagreed with Copernicus (Koestler 1959). Competition between two groups—one committed to the old framework, and one committed to the new one—occurs after the initial resistance. According to Kuhn, competition between segments of the scientific community is the only process that has historically resulted in the rejection of a previously accepted theory.

If there is a tendency today to view behaviorism and Piaget's theory as mutually exclusive as shown in Figure 1a, or as only partially overlapping as shown in Figure 1b, this is so because we are in the midst of a revolution when two segments of the scientific community are in competition. The mutually exclusive relationship implies that educators must choose one and reject the other. Figure 1c shows that Piaget's theory leads not to the rejection of behaviorism but to its inclusion in a larger, more adequate theory. The pedagogical implication of Figure 1c is that behaviorism can still be useful to solve certain problems within certain limits. For example, the logic of multiplication cannot be taught by programmed instruction, but once this logic is constructed by the child, memorization is the only way to learn the

---

[1] In extreme cases, sanctions result in the following three types of outcomes: (a) calculation of risks (or of the cost of getting a reward), (b) blind conformity, and (c) revolt, usually in adolescence. The reader interested in Piaget's ideas about how to foster the development of autonomy is referred to Chapter 3 of *The Moral Judgment of the Child*.

multiplication tables. Behaviorism can be useful within certain limits because immediate feedback is very useful in this kind of memorization. Behaviorism can also be applied effectively with spelling.

The geocentric theory is likewise not entirely false or useless. Within a certain limited point of view, it is still adequate today as can be seen in the terms *sunrise* and *sunset* that we hear in the daily weather forecast. Similarly, Newtonian physics and Euclidean geometry are still entirely adequate to solve most practical problems today. In all these scientific revolutions, the old theory became encompassed in a broader, more adequate theory. Just as Newtonian physics became a particular case of Einstein's theory, Euclidean geometry became a particular case of non-Euclidean geometry.

The evolution of the child's thought from one level to the next is similar to the evolution of scientific theories. For example, when the child becomes a conserver, he does not reject his previous way of thinking. He still thinks that the liquid in the taller, thinner glass is "more" in a certain sense, but he has a different way of apprehending this "fact" when he can coordinate a host of relationships and assimilate the old "fact" into a new system of relationships. Just as preoperational relationships become incorporated into later relationships, behaviorism becomes incorporated into a more complete theory that eliminates the contradictions found in the previous theory.

The revolutionary nature of Piaget's theory was discussed above to show that the adequacy of an educational program can be determined by the adequacy of the theory on which the program is based. To the extent that a theory is scientific, it can be subjected to the same scrutiny as any other scientific theory. I think, therefore, that the competition between behaviorism and Piaget's theory will eventually be resolved.[2] What worries me more is that most educational practices are based not on tightly conceptualized scientific theories but on diffuse, implicit beliefs which are not subjected to rigorous examination. In order to discuss these diffuse beliefs, I would now like to shift from Piaget's theory as a psychological theory to the broader epistemological questions he addressed.

Empiricism, Rationalism, and Piaget's Theory

Piaget is often believed to be a psychologist, but he is actually an epistemologist. Epistemology is the study of the nature and origins of knowledge expressed in questions such as how do we know what we think we know, and how do we know that what we think we know is true? Two main currents developed over the centuries in answer to these questions—the empiricist and rationalist currents.

Empiricists (such as Locke, Berkeley, and Hume) in essence argued that knowledge has its source outside the individual and that it is internalized through the senses. They further argued that the individual at birth is like a

---

[2] I have seen many psychologists who changed from behaviorist or associationist views to a Piagetian outlook. However, I have never known of a Piagetian who later became a behaviorist. Once a person understands a more adequate theory (e.g., the heliocentric theory), he cannot go back to a more limited outlook (e.g., the geocentric theory).

clean slate on which experiences are "written" as he grows up. As Locke expressed in 1690,

> The senses at first let in particular ideas, and furnish the yet empty cabinet, and the mind by degrees growing familiar with some of them, they are lodged in the memory . . . .(p. 22)

Rationalists such as Descartes, Spinoza, and Kant did not deny the importance of sensory experience, but they insisted that reason is more powerful than sensory experience because it enables us to know with certainty many truths which sensory observation can never ascertain. For example, we know that every event has a cause, in spite of the fact that we cannot examine every event in the entire past and future of the universe. Rationalists also pointed out that because our senses often deceive us in perceptual illusions, sensory experience cannot be trusted to give us reliable knowledge. The rigor, precision, and certainty of mathematics, a purely deductive system, remains the rationalist's prime example in support of the power of reason. When they had to explain the origin of this power of reason, rationalists ended up saying that certain knowledge or concepts are innate and that they unfold as a function of maturation.

Piaget saw elements of truth and untruth in both camps. As a scientist trained in biology, he was convinced that the only way to resolve epistemological problems was to study them scientifically rather than by speculation. With this conviction, he decided that the best way to study the nature of empirical knowledge and reason in man was to study the development of knowledge in children. His study of children was thus a means to answer epistemological questions scientifically.

The relationship among empiricism, rationalism, and Piaget's theory is shown in Figure 2. The best way to explain Piaget's position may be by comparing the outer oval of this figure with the overlap between the two circles inside that represent empiricism and rationalism. This overlap refers to the fact that empiricists recognized the importance of reason, and rationalists did not deny the necessity of sensory input. Piaget's theory differs from this overlap in stating that observation and reason are not just important in such a juxtaposed way, but that neither can take place without the other.

What does this statement mean? Piaget makes a fundamental distinction between physical knowledge and logico-mathematical knowledge. Physical knowledge refers to knowledge of objects which are out there and observable in external reality. The source of physical knowledge is mainly in objects. The only way the child can find out the physical properties of objects is by acting on them materially and mentally and finding out how objects react to his actions. For example, by dropping a ball and a glass on the floor, the child finds out how the objects react differently to the same action. Since it is with his senses that the child observes the reactions of objects, physical knowledge is partly empirical knowledge.

An example of logico-mathematical knowledge is knowing that there are more beads than red beads in the world. While the source of physical knowledge is at least partly *in objects*, the source of logico-mathematical knowledge is *in the child*. I would like to clarify this statement by taking the example of the simplest relationship between two objects, such as a red bead and a green one of the same size, both made of wood. The two beads can be

Figure 2. *Piaget's theory in relation to empiricism and rationalism.*

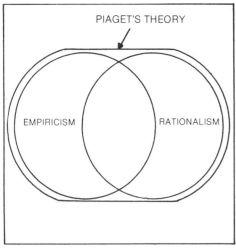

considered "different." In this situation, the relationship "different" exists neither in the red bead nor in the green one, nor anywhere else in external reality. This relationship exists in the head of the person who puts the objects into relationship, and if he did not put the objects into this relationship, the difference would not exist for that person. It is in this sense that the source of logico-mathematical knowledge is in each child. The same beads can also be considered "the same." In this case, the sameness exists neither in one bead nor in the other, but in the head of the person who puts the objects into this relationship. A third example of a relationship created by the child is "two." In this situation, the two-ness again exists nowhere in external reality but in the head of the person who puts the objects into this relationship. Logico-mathematical knowledge is constructed by coordinating these relationships that have their origins in the mental actions of the child. It is by coordinating the relationships of "same," "different," and "more" that the child comes to deduce that there are more beads than red ones.

The above dichotomy is actually an oversimplification of Piaget's theory because, according to him, physical knowledge cannot be constructed outside a logico-mathematical framework, and conversely the logico-mathematical framework could not be constructed if there were no objects in the child's environment to put into relationship. To recognize a bead as being red, for example, the child needs a classificatory scheme of "red" as opposed to "all other colors." To recognize a round wooden object as a bead, likewise, the child needs a classificatory scheme of beads as opposed to "all other objects." If the child did not have this classificatory scheme, or a logico-mathematical framework more broadly, every fact would be an isolated fact, unrelated to the rest of his knowledge. This is why I stated earlier that the source of physical knowledge is *mainly*, rather than *entirely*, in objects. Empirical "facts" cannot be "read" from reality without a classificatory framework.

Piaget's theory can be called interactionist because, according to him, knowledge comes not directly from the environment as claimed by empiricists but, rather, through the interaction between the object in the environment and the knowledge that the subject brings to the situation. For example, a baby bottle is not the same object for 1-month-old subjects and those at age 1, 7, and 25. Likewise, at age 18, a car is usually not the same object for boys and for girls. In Piaget's theory, there is no such thing as a "stimulus" or a "fact" independently of a network of relationships into which "facts" are assimilated. It is not the "stimulus" that automatically stimulates the subject. Rather, it is the subject who acts on the object and transforms it when he observes it.

Piaget's theory is not only interactionist but also constructivist. Obviously the knowledge a subject gets from an object depends on what he already knows. What is not so obvious is that this knowledge got there through a constructive process from the inside rather than through an additive process from the outside. To explain Piaget's constructivism, it is necessary to discuss a third aspect of knowledge, social (conventional) knowledge, in addition to physical and logico-mathematical knowledge. It is also necessary to discuss the logico-arithmetical and spatiotemporal frameworks around which the child constructs knowledge.

Examples of social (conventional) knowledge are that there is no school on Saturdays and Sundays, that December 25 is Christmas Day, that a bead is called *bead*, and that one sometimes shakes hands with another person. These truths have their source in the conventions worked out by people.[3] Because these truths are established by people, the child can only find out about them from other people.

Social knowledge is like physical knowledge in that it is knowledge of content and has its source mainly in external reality. I say mainly again because social knowledge is not constructed directly from external reality but from within, through a logico-mathematical framework in interaction with the environment. Without a logico-mathematical framework, the child would not be able to understand any convention just as he would not be able to recognize a wooden object as a red bead. For example, to understand that certain words are considered bad, the child has to distinguish bad words from those that are OK. To understand that there is no school on Saturdays and Sundays, the child has to structure events into days, dichotomize the days into school days and days when there is no school, and coordinate this dichotomy with the cyclic order of seven different days.

Physical and social knowledge are mainly empirical knowledge. Logico-mathematical knowledge, in contrast, represents the rationalist tradition.

The two examples of logico-mathematical knowledge given so far are knowing that there are more beads than red ones, and that there are more animals than dogs. It is now necessary to clarify the relationship between logico-mathematical knowledge and the logico-mathematical framework that is necessary, for example, to recognize a certain object as a red bead.

Our knowledge is organized around two frameworks—a logico-arithmetical framework and a spatiotemporal framework. When Piaget speaks of the logico-mathematical framework, he is lumping the two frameworks together. (Mathematics includes geometry, which grows out of the spatiotemporal framework.) It has been argued above that a classificatory scheme (part of the logico-arithmetical framework) is necessary to recognize each object in the environment. Objects exist in space and time, and we need a spatiotemporal framework to locate objects and events in space and time. For example, empirical facts such as the Mediterranean Sea, the French Revolution, and the movement of a pendulum could not be understood without an organization of space and time in our minds. While the spatiotemporal framework makes it possible for us to understand certain aspects of empirical facts, the logico-arithmetical framework is also necessary for this understanding. For example, the very idea of sea, revolution, or pendulum would be impossible without a logico-arithmetical organization. Because neither the logico-arthmetical nor the spatiotemporal framework can be reduced to the other, Piaget states that our knowledge is organized around these frameworks.

While many rationalists stated that certain ideas such as those of space, time, causality, and number are innate, Piaget proved that the logico-arithmetical and spatiotemporal frameworks are constructed by each child. The construction of the former has already been alluded to in the example of the classificatory scheme that the child constructs as he learns about every object in his environment, such as bead as opposed to every other kind of

---

[3] Piaget never designated social (conventional) knowledge by a name, but he unmistakably referred to it, especially in *The Moral Judgment of the Child* and his discussion of the "sign" (i.e., language, which is a conventional system).

object and dog as opposed to every other kind of animal. It has also been shown that this classificatory framework evolves into a hierarchical organization as the child coordinates part-whole relationships based on the sameness and differences he sees among objects. To illustrate the child's construction of the spatiotemporal framework, examples follow from *The Child's Conception of Geometry* (Piaget, Inhelder, and Szeminska 1948, Chapter 7) and *The Child's Conception of Time* (Piaget 1946a).

In the task concerning the structuring of space, the child was given two white sheets of paper, one with a dot as shown in Figure 3a. He was also given a variety of instruments such as a pencil, ruler, stick, strips of paper, and bits of string, and was asked to make a point on the blank sheet so that it would look exactly like the other sheet. Four-year-olds (Level I) drew the point by visual inspection of the position without measuring anything. At Level II, children began to use the ruler but made only one diagonal measurement, usually from the closest corner as shown in Figure 3b! At Level IIIB, around age nine, they finally became able to draw the point at the exact spot by making two measurements as shown in Figure 3c. This behavior is evidence of a system of coordinates that the child has constructed. When this system is present, the child knows that it is necessary to measure two distances perpendicularly to the edge of the paper.

Let us look at how four-year-olds read certain "facts" before constructing a coherent, deductive system of time. Piaget asked a typical four-year-old, "Who will be the older of you two when you grow up, you or your baby sister?" The answer was "I don't know." The rest of the conversation went as follows:

> Is your Granny older than your mother? *No.* Are they the same age? *I think so.* Isn't she older than your mother? *Oh no.* Does your Granny grow older every year? *She stays the same.* And your mother? *She stays the same as well.* And you? *No, I get older.* And your little sister? *Yes!*
> (1946a, p. 221)

The above conversation shows that without a coherent system of time, the child is limited to empirical knowledge and cannot deduce that the difference in age between her sister and her will always remain the same. Neither can she

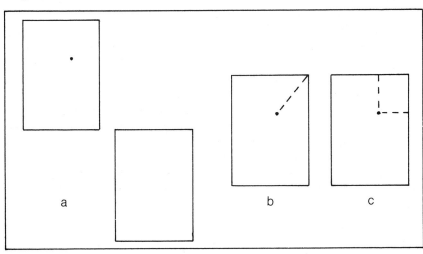

Figure 3.
Children's ways of locating a point on a rectangular surface.

deduce that her grandmother is older than her mother, and that the two get older just as children and babies do.

The logico-arithmetical and spatiotemporal frameworks are created by the child by reflective abstraction (and equilibration). Piaget makes an important distinction between *reflective* and *empirical* (or simple) abstraction. In empirical abstraction, the child focuses on a certain physical property of the object and ignores the others. For example, when he abstracts the color of an object, he simply ignores the other properties such as weight and the material with which it is made. Reflective abstraction, in contrast, involves the creation of relationships between/among objects, such as "the same," "different," and "two." Relationships, as stated earlier, do not have an existence in external reality. The term *constructive* abstraction might thus be better than reflective abstraction in that this term indicates that the abstraction is a veritable construction by the mind.

I would like to cite one example each of physical and social knowledge to illustrate the importance of the logico-arithmetical and spatiotemporal frameworks in the construction of knowledge of content. The first example concerns why a wooden ball floats while a key and nail sink in water.

> DUF (7;6): "That ball?"—*"It stays on top. It's wood; it's light."*— "And this key?"—*"Goes down. It's iron; it's heavy."*—"Which is heavier, the key or the ball?"—*"The ball."*—"Why does the key sink?" —*"Because it is heavy."*—"And then the nail?"—*"It's light but it sinks anyway. It's iron, and iron always goes under."* (Inhelder and Piaget 1955, p. 29)

This child's thinking is full of contradictions. When his thinking becomes better structured, he will become aware of the contradictions and will begin to eliminate them. By thus eliminating every factor except the weight and size of the objects and putting them into relationship as shown in Figure 4, he will realize that, although the larger the object, the heavier it tends to be (the X's in this figure), *some* small objects are heavy and *some* large ones are light.[4] With this realization, he is on his way to constructing the concept of specific gravity. Specific gravity is not observable and must be constructed by the child. Without the structure of class inclusion and seriation, the child cannot possibly construct this concept. Specific gravity is an example of knowledge created by the logico-mathematization of observable facts.

The second example of the importance of the logico-arithmetical and spatiotemporal frameworks in the construction of knowledge concerns children's notions of a country, a town, and nationality. Piaget (1951) found that until seven or eight years of age, children may assert that Geneva is part of Switzerland but think of the two as situated side by side as can be seen in the following interview:

> Claude M. 6;9: What is Switzerland? *It's a country.* And Geneva? *A town.* Where is Geneva? *In Switzerland* (The child draws the two circles side by side but the circle for Geneva is smaller). *I'm drawing the circle for Geneva smaller because Geneva is smaller. Switzerland is very big.* Quite

Figure 4. *The class-inclusion structure involved in the construction of specific gravity.*

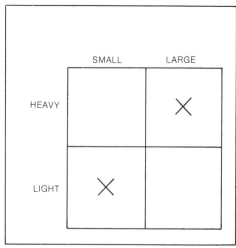

[4] Figure 4 is presented as a double dichotomy to simplify the discussion. Actually, both weight and size must be seriated. The relationship between the weight and size of objects is, therefore, more complex than this double dichotomy implies.

right, but where is Geneva? *In Switzerland.* Are you Swiss? *Yes.* And are you Genevese? *Oh no! I'm Swiss now.* (p. 40)

The child knows the words *country, town,* and *in Switzerland,* but below this surface is poorly structured social knowledge.

Piaget proved that knowledge does not come directly from the outside through the senses as claimed by empiricists (Figure 2). Although his position is on the rationalist side of the fence, he disproved the existence of innate ideas that many rationalists postulated. By demonstrating that each child constructs the basic frameworks of knowledge in interaction with the environment, he proved that reason is not innate in man but the result of his creation. The better these frameworks are structured, the more accurate and elaborate the information is that a person can get from reality. More accurate, elaborate, and well organized information in turn constitutes better structured logico-arithmetical and spatiotemporal frameworks.

As an educator, constructivism is the most fundamental point I get from all the books by Piaget. The view that knowledge is acquired by construction differs radically from the empiricist assumptions on which education has been based for centuries. I would now like to turn to the educational implications of this point.

Implications of Constructivism for Education

Empiricist assumptions are reflected almost everywhere in education. For example, by considering the learner like an empty glass, educators have arranged the classroom into neat rows like rows of empty glasses to be filled and passed on from one grade level to the next in an assembly-line fashion. In each grade, the teacher tries to fill all the glasses up to a certain level before giving them to the next teacher. This pouring of knowledge implies that the teacher is like a giant funnel that has collected all the wisdom of the past and selects out of her repertoire what to teach, with what organization, and in what sequence. The neat rows of desks may have disappeared from many classrooms, but the stuffing of knowledge from the outside continues, or is even intensified, with behavioral objectives, lesson plans, verbalism, and the acceptance only of the ''right'' answer. In the moral realm, obedience is obtained by using privileges, gold stars, citizenship awards, and the detention hall.

Programmed instruction and behavior modification are more recent refinements of the empiricist tradition of compartmentalizing subject matters, presenting them in the ''right'' sequence, and insuring ''correct'' internalization. Behaviorism came out of the empiricist tradition and studies observable behavior in relation to observable independent variables. Behaviorists are interested in the prediction and control of behavior without trying to understand what goes on in the learner's head. Educators who think that programmed instruction and behavior modification are innovative do not realize that these are only technological refinements that intensify old traditions.

Many critics and reformers have come and gone against the background of this tradition. For example, Rousseau (1780) opposed the excessive verbal instruction that he saw. Froebel (1885) insisted that the goal of education cannot be imposed on the student because each person is like a plant that unfolds. Dewey (1902) opposed the fragmentation of the curriculum into subjects and lessons and argued that the curriculum should be rooted in each student's interests. More recently, we have seen a rash of protests from authors such as Dennison (1969), Goodman (1962), Herndon (1968), Holt (1964), Kohl (1967), and Silberman (1970). These authors based their pedagogical beliefs on empathic observation and opinion rather than a scientific theory. Their philosophy can nevertheless be recognized as unmistakably having elements of constructivism.

Most reformers have run small, marginal schools which have not lasted very long. The reason for this marginality is that reformers' convictions have been based on personal opinions rather than a scientific theory, with the result that (a) they could not convince the majority of professional educators, and (b) they could not develop or evaluate their own teaching with theoretical rigor. A notable exception to this statement is the Eight-Year Study (Aiken, 1942).[5] Frequently, disagreements developed among the proponents, especially after the death of the leader. Without a scientific foundation, one opinion is as good as another.

The following is an example of the kind of rationale found in Dewey's writing (1902). The last four sentences particularly reflect a constructivist point of view, but they can hardly be expected to convince the majority of professional educators, who believe that education consists of putting subject matter into more or less empty glasses.

> The child is the starting-point, the center, and the end. His development, his growth, is the ideal. It alone furnishes the standard. To the growth of the child all studies are subservient; they are instruments valued as they serve the needs of growth. Personality, character, is more than subject-matter. Not knowledge or information, but self-realization, is the goal. To possess all the world of knowledge and lose one's own self is as awful a fate in education as in religion. Moreover, subject-matter never can be got into the child from without. Learning is active. It involves reaching out of the mind. It involves organic assimilation starting from within. (p. 9)

Following is an example from the writing of a teacher who also came to a constructivist conclusion. Again, however, such a private view can be taken only as the opinion of an idealist.

---

[5] The purpose of this study was to find out if students could do better in college if they did not take certain high school courses usually required for college entrance and, instead, engaged in more integrated, critical, and in-depth study. The conclusion can be found in the following summary:

> It is quite obvious from these data that the Thirty Schools graduates, as a group, have done a somewhat better job than the comparison group whether success is judged by college standards, by the students' contemporaries, or by the individual students. (Aiken 1942, p. 112)

The unusual features of this experiment were that (a) almost 30 reputable high schools and 25 colleges and universities participated, including Harvard, MIT, and Princeton; and (b) principles of Progressive Education were clearly delineated, and rigorous evaluation took place on a relatively long-term basis (eight years).

After all I have said and written about the need for keeping children under pressure, I find myself coming to realize that what hampers their thinking . . . is a feeling that they must please the grownups at all costs. The really able thinkers in our class turn out to be, without exception, children who don't feel so strongly the need to please grownups. . . . They don't work to please us, but to please themselves. (Holt 1964, pp. 39-40)

I do not want to imply that personal beliefs have no value. On the contrary, I admire the educators who have been autonomous and courageous enough to have convictions that went counter to the prevailing point of view. I am saying that reform must go beyond personal opinions because opinions are not enough to change the minds of those in the overwhelming majority who have empiricist beliefs. Without a scientific foundation, the unconventional opinion of a few idealists can be taken only as a minority opinion or a passing fad. The "back to the basics" and "back to strict discipline" philosophy has always survived in the mainstream of education.

It is well known that public schools have failed and continue to fail, especially in the education of children of low socioeconomic status and certain minority groups. But public education goes on with an incredible array of diffuse, implicit, and contradictory theories. An example of such theories is that when we succeed in teaching something, we attribute this success to our teaching. But when we fail to teach something, we say that it is the child who is not "ready" or "mature." If the cause of our failure is attributed to the child, the cause of our success must also be found in the child.

Educators often cannot see this contradiction because of the relationship between constructivist and empiricist-behaviorist beliefs that remain implicit and diffuse in their thinking. Teaching usually does produce observable changes. But when children seem to be learning, we must ask *which children* are learning, *what* they are learning, and *how*.

Middle- and upper-middle-class children who have already constructed a great deal of knowledge outside of school generally learn easily. Research such as that of Okada, Cohen, and Mayeske (1969) has shown over and over that within each ethnic or racial group at each grade level, higher socioeconomic groups have higher achievement scores.

What do children learn when they seem to be learning? The advanced students tend to learn in the way the teacher intended. Too often, however, children learn only the "right" answer the teacher wants, and the teacher remains under the illusion that teaching has been successful. As quoted earlier from Holt, the most important thing for many children is to please the adult. The learning of "right" answers, motor skills, and specific information that must be memorized (such as the multiplication tables and spelling mentioned earlier) can be explained in part by behaviorism (the inner circle in Figure 1c). Intelligent learning with understanding, as well as the complete absence of learning, can be explained only by constructivism (the outer oval in Figure 1c).

An example of an extreme empiricist-behaviorist view can be seen in Engelmann (1971) and Kamii and Derman (1971).[6] In this study, Engelmann argued that if children do not know something, this is because they have not

---

[6] Engelmann is the principal developer of the well-known DISTAR method (Engelmann, Osborn, and Engelmann 1969), which is used in several Head Start and Follow Through programs.

been taught that fact or concept. He chose to teach the concept of specific gravity, among other things, to a group of six-year-olds, and agreed to let me give the post-test to these children.

According to Piaget (Inhelder and Piaget 1955), as we saw earlier, specific gravity is not possible to understand before the period of formal operations. I was, therefore, not surprised that the children had memorized only an overlay of verbalism. They had been taught to say that if something sinks, it sinks because "it is heavier than a piece of water the same size," and if it floats, it floats because "it is lighter than a piece of water the same size." Underneath the surface was the same kind of preoperational thinking found in any six-year-old. In my opinion, the children were harmed by this teaching because they were taught to say things that contradicted what they honestly believed.[7] Below is an example with a big cake of Ivory soap (which floated the day before) and the little cake of soap (that sank):

Examiner: Did both of these sink yesterday?
Child: Yes.
Examiner: Feel this big one and this little one in your hands.
Child: (Feeling the weight of the two pieces) The big one feels heavier.
Examiner: Will both of them sink?
Child: I think the little one will sink, too. . . .
Examiner: Why?
Child: Because they are both soap.
Examiner: You put them in the water and see what happens.
Child: (Finding out that the big one floated and the little one sank) I forgot yesterday!
Examiner: Remember you said the big one was heavier?
Child: The big one must be lighter, and the little one must be heavier.
(Kamii and Derman 1971, p. 140)

Engelmann agreed completely with the facts obtained in the post-test, but he drew the opposite conclusion. For him, the cause of failure lay in the way he had taught, and he stated that with more time to perfect the program, he could bring the children up to the desired criterion.[8] This type of verbalistic teaching to produce the "right" answer can be found in less extreme form in every school in the nation. For example, if a first grader has difficulty answering $\Box + 2 = 6$ but not $2 + 4 = \Box$, most first-grade teachers engage in the kind of teaching advocated by Engelmann. The actual teaching of the average teacher may be less forceful, but underlying the implicit theory are empiricist-behaviorist beliefs.

Instruction must mesh with and support the natural constructive process. The teaching of specific gravity *can* result in solid learning when the adolescent is already at a certain level of development. Instruction in reading, too, can produce easy learning when a six-year-old is at a certain level.

In the moral realm, schools try to get values internalized from the outside by giving orders and using sanctions. Children are told what to learn and

[7] They also learned to distrust their own thinking. Undermining children's confidence can have detrimental long-range effects.

[8] It has been ten years since Engelmann made this statement. I am still hoping for an opportunity to evaluate another version of his program.

Appendix

when, and the school day is filled with orders and rules to obey—no talking, fold your hands, get in a line for recess, walk with your arms crossed, no ball playing here, no throwing of snow balls, and there will be no recess for Johnny today because he talked in class. Schools use behaviorist techniques that are conducive to obedience or the morality of heteronomy. If some children develop the morality of autonomy, this is because of the social interactions at home that permitted the autonomous construction of values.

Piaget's theory is a descriptive and explanatory one, and, as he has often stated, a pedagogy cannot be deduced directly from this theory. Much theoretical and experimental work, therefore, remains to be done to develop a Piagetian pedagogy for real classrooms in real schools. The details of such work are beyond the scope of this Appendix, and the reader is referred to Kamii (1980), Kamii and DeVries (1978), Kamii and DeVries (1977), and Kamii and DeVries (1976) for examples. Just as all sciences and all children develop by going through one stage after another of being "wrong," a Piagetian pedagogy can develop only by successive approximation. The nation's schools are plagued by enormous problems ranging from illiteracy to apathy, poor discipline, alienation, and vandalism. Obviously, not all the solutions to these problems can come out of Piaget's theory. However, I am convinced that a fundamental reconceptualization of curriculum, methods of teaching, and children's development of autonomy will take us far closer to solutions than any other theory.

References

Aiken, W. M. *The Story of the Eight-Year Study.* New York: Harper, 1942.

Barnhart, C. L., ed. *The American College Dictionary.* New York: Random House, 1963.

Bureau of Curriculum Development, Board of Education, City of New York. *Prekindergarten and Kindergarten Curriculum Guide,* 1970.

Capt, C. L.; Glayre, L.; and Hegyi, A. *Des Activités de Connaissance Physique a l'École Enfantine.* Unpublished memoire de license, University of Geneva, 1976.

Dami, C. *Stratégie Cognitives dans des Jeux Compétitifs á Deux.* Geneve: Éditions Medecine et Hygiene, 1975.

Dennison, G. *The Lives of Children.* New York: Vantage Books, 1969.

DeVries, R. "The Development of Role-Taking as Reflected by Behavior of Bright, Average, and Retarded Children in a Social Guessing Game." *Child Development* 41(1970): 759-770.

Dewey, J. *The Child and the Curriculum* (originally published in 1902) *and the School and Society.* Chicago: University of Chicago Press, 1956.

Engelmann, S. E. "Does the Piagetian Approach Imply Instruction?" In *Measurement and Piaget,* eds. D. R. Green, M. P. Ford, and G. B. Flamer. New York: McGraw-Hill, 1971.

Engelmann, S. E.; Osborn, J.; and Engelmann, T. *DISTAR Language I Teacher's Guide.* Chicago: Science Research Associates, 1969.

The Encyclopedia Americana. New York: Americana Corporation, 1957.

Ferreiro, E. "Vers une Théorie Génétique de l'Apprentissage de la Lecture." *Revue Suisse de Psychologie* 36(1977): 109-130.

Ferreiro, E. "What Is Written in a Written Sentence? A Developmental Answer." *Journal of Education* 160(1978): 25-39.

Froebel, F. *The Education of Man.* New York: Appleton-Century, 1885.

Frostig, M. *The Developmental Program in Visual Perception: Beginning Pictures and Patterns.* Chicago: Follett Publishing Co., 1966.

Giannoni, J. *Card Games for Kids.* Racine, Wisc.: Western Publishing Co., 1974.

Goodman, P. *Compulsory Mis-Education* and *The Community of Scholars.* New York: Vantage Books, 1962.

Gove, P. B., ed. *Webster's Third New International Dictionary.* Springfield, Mass.: G. & C. Merriam Co., 1961.

Herndon, J. *The Way It Spozed to Be.* New York: Simon and Schuster, 1968.

Hildebrand, V. *Introduction to Early Childhood Education.* New York: Macmillan, 1976.

Holt, J. *How Children Fail.* New York: Pitman, 1964.

Hull, C. L. *A Behavior System.* New Haven, Conn.: Yale University Press, 1952.

Inhelder, B., and Piaget, J. *The Growth of Logic from Childhood to Adolescence.* New York: Basic Books, 1958 (first published in 1955).

Inhelder, B., and Piaget, J. *The Early Growth of Logic in the Child.* London: Routledge & Kegan Paul, 1964 (first published in 1959).

Inhelder, B., Sinclair, H., and Bovet, M. *Learning and the Development of Cognition.* Cambridge, Mass.: Harvard University Press, 1974.

Kamii, C. "Evaluation of Learning in Preschool Education: Socio-Emotional, Perceptual-Motor, Cognitive Development." In *Handbook on Formative and Summative Evaluation of Student Learning,* eds. B. S. Bloom, J. T. Hastings, and G. F. Madaus. New York: McGraw-Hill, 1971.

Kamii, C. "An Application of Piaget's Theory to the Conceptualization of a Preschool Curriculum." In *The Preschool in Action,* ed. R. K. Parker. Boston: Allyn and Bacon, 1972a.

Kamii, C. "A Sketch of the Piaget-Derived Preschool Curriculum Developed by the Ypsilanti Early Education Program." In *History and Theory of Early Childhood Education,* eds. S. J. Braun and E. P. Edwards. Worthington, Ohio: Jones, 1972b.

Kamii, C. "A Sketch of the Piaget-Derived Preschool Curriculum Developed by the Ypsilanti Early Education Program." In *Revisiting Early Childhood Education,* ed. J. L. Frost. New York: Holt, Rinehart and Winston, 1973a.

Kamii, C. "A Sketch of the Piaget-Derived Preschool Curriculum Developed by the Ypsilanti Early Education Program." In *Early Childhood Education,* ed. B. Spodek. Englewood Cliffs, N.J.: Prentice-Hall, 1973b.

Kamii, C. "Piaget's Theory, Behaviorism, and Other Theories in Education." *Journal of Education* 161(1979): 13-33.

Kamii, C. "Application of Piaget's Theory to Education: The Preoperational Level." In *Piagetian Theory and Research: New Directions and Applications,* eds. I. E. Sigel, R. M. Golinkoff, and D. Brodzinsky. Hillsdale, N.J.: Erlbaum Associates, 1980.

Kamii, C., and Derman, L. "The Engelmann Approach to Teaching Logical Thinking: Findings from the Administration of Some Piagetian Tasks." In *Measurement and Piaget,* eds. D. R. Green, M. P. Ford, and G. B. Flamer. New York: McGraw-Hill, 1971.

Kamii, C., and DeVries, R. *Piaget, Children, and Number: Applying Piaget's Theory to the Teaching of Elementary Number.* Washington, D.C.: National Association for the Education of Young Children, 1976.

Kamii, C., and DeVries, R. "Piaget for Early Education." In *The Preschool in Action* (2nd ed.), eds. M. C. Day and R. K. Parker. Boston: Allyn and Bacon, 1977.

Kamii, C., and DeVries, R. *Physical Knowledge in Preschool Education: Implications of Piaget's Theory.* Englewood Cliffs, N.J.: Prentice-Hall, 1978.

Kamii, C., and Radin, N. "A Framework for a Preschool Curriculum Based on Some Piagetian Concepts." *Journal of Creative Behavior* 1(1967): 314-324.

Kamii, C., and Radin, N. "Framework for a Preschool Curriculum Based on Some Piagetian Concepts." In *Educational Implications of Piaget's Theory,* eds. I. J. Athey and D. O. Rubadeau. Waltham, Mass.: Xerox College Publishers, 1970.

Koestler, A. *The Sleepwalkers.* London: Hutchinson, 1959.

Kohl, H. *36 Children.* New York: New American Library, 1967.

Kohl, M., and Young, F. *Games for Children.* New York: Cornerstone Library, 1953.

Kohlberg, L., and Mayer, R. "Development as the Aim of Education." *Harvard Educational Review* 42(1972): 449-498.

Kuhn, T. S. *The Structure of Scientific Revolutions.* Chicago: University of Chicago Press, 1962.

Leeper, S. H.; Dales, R. J.; Skipper, D. S.; and Witherspoon, R. L. *Good Schools for Young Children.* New York: Macmillan, 1974.

Locke, J. *Essay Concerning Human Understanding.* Oxford, England: Oxford University Press, 1947 (first published in 1690).

Maccoby, E. E., and Zellner, M. *Experiments in Primary Education: Aspects of Project Follow-Through.* New York: Harcourt Brace Jovanovich, 1970.

McKinnon, J. W., and Renner, J. W. "Are Colleges Concerned with Intellectual Development?" *American Journal of Physics* 39(1971): 1047-1052.

McWhirter, M. E., ed. *Games Enjoyed by Children Around the World.* Philadelphia: American Friends Service Committee, Inc., 1970.

Morris, W., ed. *The American Heritage Dictionary of the English Language.* Boston: American Heritage Publishing Co., Inc., and Houghton Mifflin, 1973.

Murray, A.; Bradley, H.; Craigie, W.; and Onions, C. eds. *The Oxford English Dictionary.* London: Oxford University Press, 1970.

Okada, T.; Cohen, W. M.; and Mayeske, G. W. *Growth in Achievement for Different Racial, Regional, and Socio-Economic Groupings of Students.* U.S. Office of Education, 1969.

Opie, I., and Opie, P. *Children's Games in Street and Playground.* Oxford, England: Clarendon Press, 1969.

Palmer, M. W. ed. *Day Care Aides: A Guide for In-Service Training.* New York: National Federation of Settlements and Neighborhood Centers, 1968.

References

Perret-Clermont, A. N. *L'Interaction Sociale Comme Facteur du Developpment Cognitif.* Ph.D. thesis, University of Geneva, 1976.

Piaget, J. *Language and Thought in the Child.* London: Kegan Paul, 1926 (first published in 1923).

Piaget, J. *The Child's Conception of the World.* New York: Harcourt and Brace, 1929 (first published in 1926).

Piaget, J. *The Moral Judgment of the Child.* New York: Free Press, 1965 (first published in 1932).

Piaget, J. *The Origins of Intelligence.* New York: Norton, 1963 (first published in 1936).

Piaget, J. *The Construction of Reality in the Child.* New York: Basic Books, 1954 (first published in 1937).

Piaget, J. *The Child's Conception of Time.* London: Routledge & Kegan Paul, 1969 (first published in 1946a).

Piaget, J. *Play, Dreams, and Imitation in Childhood.* New York: Norton, 1962 (first published in 1946b).

Piaget, J. *The Psychology of Intelligence.* London: Routledge & Kegan Paul, 1950 (first published in 1947).

Piaget, J. *To Understand Is to Invent.* New York: Grossman, 1973 (first published in 1948).

Piaget, J. "The Development in Children of the Idea of the Homeland and Relations with Other Countries." In *Piaget Sampler,* ed. S. F. Campbell. New York: Wiley, 1976 (first published in 1951).

Piaget, J. *Biology and Knowledge.* Chicago: University of Chicago Press, 1971 (first published in 1967).

Piaget, J. *The Grasp of Consciousness.* Cambridge, Mass.: Harvard University Press, 1978 (first published in 1974a).

Piaget, J. *Success and Understanding.* Cambridge, Mass.: Harvard University Press, 1978 (first published in 1974b).

Piaget, J. *Recherches sur la Contradiction /1.* Paris: Presses Universitaires de France, 1974c.

Piaget, J. *Recherches sur la Contradiction /2.* Paris: Presses Universitaires de France, 1974d.

Piaget, J.; Grize, J. B.; Szeminska, A.; and Bang, V. *Epistémologie et Psychologie de la Fonction.* Paris: Presses Universitaires de France, 1968.

Piaget, J., and Inhelder, B. *The Child's Construction of Quantities.* London: Routledge & Kegan Paul, 1974 (first published in 1941).

Piaget, J., and Inhelder, B. *The Child's Conception of Space.* New York: Norton, 1956 (first published in 1948).

Piaget, J., and Inhelder, B. *The Origin of the Idea of Chance in Children.* New York: Norton, 1975 (first published in 1951).

Piaget, J., and Inhelder, B. *Mental Imagery in the Child.* New York: Basic Books, 1971 (first published in 1966a).

Piaget, J., and Inhelder, B. *The Psychology of the Child.* New York: Basic Books, 1969 (first published in 1966b).

Piaget, J.; Inhelder, B.; and Szeminska, A. *The Child's Conception of Geometry.* London: Routledge & Kegan Paul, 1960 (first published in 1948).

Piaget, J., and Szeminska, A. *The Child's Conception of Number.* London: Routledge & Kegan Paul, 1952 (first published in 1941).

Rousseau, J. J. *Emile.* New York: Appleton, 1914 (first published in 1780).

Sastre, G., and Moreno, M. "Représentation Graphique de la Quantité." *Bulletin de Psychologie* 30(1977): 346-355.

Schwebel, M. "Formal Operations in First-Year College Students." *The Journal of Psychology* 91(1975): 133-141.

Silberman, C. *Crisis in the Classroom.* New York: Random House, 1970.

Sinclair, A.; Sinclair, H.; and de Marcellus, O. "Young Children's Comprehension and Production of Passive Sentences." *Archives de Psychologie* 41(1971): 1-22.

Sonquist, H., and Kamii, C. "Applying Some Piagetian Concepts in the Classroom for the Disadvantaged." *Young Children* 22(1967): 231-246.

Sonquist, H.; Kamii, C.; and Derman, L. "A Piaget-Derived Preschool Curriculum." In *Educational Implications of Piaget's Theory,* ed. I. J. Athey and D. O. Rubadeau. Waltham, Mass.: Xerox College Publishers, 1970.

Tiemersma, K. J. *What Shall We Play? A Handbook of Games for the Elementary Grades.* Grand Rapids, Mich.: Wm. B. Eerdmans Publishing Co., 1952.

Board Games

"Candy Land." Springfield, Mass.: Milton Bradley, 1978.

"Cat and Mouse." Salem, Mass.: Parker Brothers, 1964.

"Chinese Checkers." Lafayette, Ind.: Warren Paper Products Co. (no date).

"Chutes and Ladders." Springfield, Mass.: Milton Bradley, 1956.

"56 Games." Racine, Wisc.: Western Publishing Co., 1975.

"Hi-Ho! Cherry-O." Racine, Wisc.: Western Publishing Co., 1975.

"Treasure Hunt." Minneapolis: Judy Co., 1973.

Card Games

"Animal Rummy." Lafayette, Ind.: Warren Paper Products Co. (no date).

"Go Fish." New York: Ed-U-Cards, 1951.

"Piggy Bank." New York: Ed-U-Cards, 1965.

"Concentration." Washington, D.C.: National Wildlife Federation (no date).

Index

abstraction
  constructive 240
  empirical 217, 240
  reflective 39, 82, 217, 240
academic subjects 21
activity
  blowing 214
  group 2
  mental 8, 9, 30, 35
  perceptual 132, 139
  physical 8, 30, 35
  physical-knowledge 127, 142, 170, 212, 213, 214, 216, 229
  political 28
  representational 140
  role of, 35
  tactile 140
addition 60, 71, 79
adult
  authority 7, 54, 85, 137, 201
  attention 191
  -child interactions 17
  evaluation 7
  power 12, 13, 15–17, 22, 86, 104, 109, 110, 159, 201, 204, 205
agreements
  exchange 147
  mutual 168
alertness 14, 21
All Gone 81
analysis
  behavior 6
  content 6
angle of incidence and reflection 40
Animal Charades 54, 55
animalism 26
Animal Rummy **65**, 66, 67, 70, 224
arithmetic xi, 13, 70, 117
arrangement
  linear 4
  spatial 218
Arranging Colored Balls **4**, 7
artificialism 26
autonomy 12, 15–17, 29, 85, 114, 117, 118, 128, 134, 166, 199, 201, 233, 234
  development of, 24, 29, 32, 86, 89, 90, 91, 93, 104, 107, 109, 198, 204, 205, 210, 211, 245

intellectual 18, 21, 22, 29, 111
moral 15, 17, 22, 29, 111, 245
political 29

Back-to-Back 29, 32, **57**, 58, **111–118**, 203, 204, 208 210
back to basics 243
Bango **222**, 223
Basketball 37
basketball net 37
behavior
  modification 16, 231, 241
  techniques 245
behaviorism xiii, 241, 243
  and Piaget's theory 230–235
Billiards **38**, 41
Bingo 72, 77, **78**, 79
block building 1, 2
Block Race 85, 86, **87–93**, 147, 191, 195, 202, 205, 207, 210
  Race 1 88
  Race 2 89
  Race 3 89–90, 203
  Race 4 90–91
  Race 5 91–92
Blowing Race **42**, 43, 216
boredom 8
bowling xii, 22
  pins 213, 214
Bowling 37, **38**, 40, 41, 213
bridge 22
"Bubblegum" 125
Bull's-eye 7, **37**
Button, Button **49**, 52

Candy Land **72**, 76, 205, 228, 229
Card Dominoes **67**, 222, 224, 226, 227
card holders 225
cards
  holding 224–225
  number of, 223
  picture 61, 222, 223
  playing 60, 222, 223
  recognizing 61
  sorting 226
  special 60, 222
  teacher-made 222
  wild 69

Cat and Mouse 45, **46**, 74–75, 211
categorization 60
causality 200
centration
  tactile 140
  visual 140
Chair Ring Toss 6, **37**
chance 32, 76, 79, 82
  games of, 199–200, 221, 228
Charades 6, 53, **54**, 55, 208, 220–221
cheating 176, 177, 228
Checkers 22, 72, **82**, 83, 84, 198, 199
chess 22
children
  first grade 32
  five-year-old 24, 37, 44, 79, 83
  four-year-old 36, 48, 53, 55–56, 81, 87, 191, 202, 228
  kindergarten 32, 190
  six-year-old 40, 83
  three-year-old 50, 52, 65–66, 81
Chinese Checkers, 83, 84, 198, 229
Chutes and Ladders 22, 72, **73**, 76, 83, 200
classification 26, 60–61, 67, 192, 200
class inclusion 202, 233, 240
  hierarchical structure of, 233
  quantification of, 232–233
Climb the Ladder **78**
clues
  auditory 53
  hot-cold 51, 219
  tactilo-kinesthetic 53, 220
  verbal 54–55, 56, 221
  visual 54, 220
coercion 15
cognition 28, 29
collaboration 48
commands 211
  and "cheating" 57
  games involving 35, 36, 56–60
  tricky 57
  verbal 58, 221
communication 25

competition xiii, 1, 24, 43, 92, 154, 159, 165, 183, 201, 217
  facing 199
  in school 196
  issue of, **189–200**
  principles of teaching 199–200
  socioeconomic 195–196
complementarity 57
Concentration **62**, 63, 65, 66, 221, 222, 223, 224, 226, 228
conditioning 232
confrontation
  physical 147
conservation 192, 200
constructivism xi–xii, 13, 14, 19–22, 197, 206, 208, 237, 242, 243
conversation 25
cooperation 9, 16, 18, 24, 48, 203, 204, 219
  group 190
  incipient 23, 24, 192
coordination
  interindividual 104
  motor 44, 224
  of collaborative actions 160, 161, 163
  of complementary intentions 103
  of different points of view 12, 26, 28, 192, 193, 195, 200, 202, 211
  of opposite intentions 45, 160, 161, 163
  perceptual-motor 39, 79
correspondence
  serial 43, 51
counting 80, 185, 216
Crazy Cards 222, 223
Crazy Eights 29, **69**, 70, 222, 224
curiosity 14, 21
curriculum xii, 245

dancing 1, 2
darts 37
decentration 12, 16, 18, 23, 24, 44, 47, 50, 51, 55, 58, 66, 79, 192, 193, 195, 199, 200, 202, 210
development 8, 27–33, 211, 217

affective 13, 217
cognitive vii, 13, 33, 72, 198, 201, 217
conceptual 139
emotional 29, 30, 32, 33, 118, 198, 201
intellectual 4, 18, 22, 35
language 12, 13, 25, 51, 58
levels of, 3, 4, 8, 44
moral 11, 18, 22, 33, 198, 233
of initiative 199
of logic 184
political 33
social 13, 18, 33, 35, 104, 198, 201
dice 73, 74, 77, 228
discovery 208
discrimination
perceptual 65, 79, 198
Dodge Ball **37**, 38, 40
Dog and Bone 8, **206**, 207
Doggy, Doggy, Your Bone Is Gone **49**, 51, 207, 219
Dominoes 62, **63**, 65-66, 224
"Don't Get Hit by the Ball" 38, 40
Dot-to-Dot **79**, 80
Dragon's Tail **46**, 47, 48
Drop the Clothespins 3, 6, 9, **36**, 37, 216
Drop the Handkerchief **45**, 46, 47, 48
Duck, Duck, Goose 8, 31, 45, **46**, 47, 48, 202, 218, 219
Ducks Fly **57**, 58

education 27, 241-243
early 12, 204
objectives of, 11, 12-22, 33
empiricist-behaviorist view of, 243-244
public 243
science xi
theories of, 230-245
traditional 15
Eeney Meeney 120, 122, 124, 175, 205
egocentrism 23, 24, 26, 193, 195, 200, 211
Elevens 71, 224
empiricism xiii, 235-236
empiricist 21, 235, 237, 241
assumptions 205
tradition 93, 211, 241
epistemology 235
evaluation
natural 144

of games 210-211
self- 144
exercises 27
exploration
tactual 132, 137, 138, 140, 143
visual 139
extinction 232, 233

fairness 168, 216
falsehood 133
The Farmer in the Dell 190, **207**
Forward and Backward 73, **75**, 77
Fourteen, Stand Still 52, **53**, 55
Fox and Chicken 211
Fox and Geese **83**

games
aiming xi, 9, 30, 35, **36-41**, 43, 53, 59, 212-216
avoidance of, 211
board 36, **72-84**, 228, 230
card xi, 4, 27, 28, 29, 31, 32, 36, 59, **60-72**, 76, 184, 211, 221-228, 229
chasing 30, 31, 35, 36, **44-48**, 206, 218-219
collaborative 163
collective 9
competitive 189, 190, 195, 197, 198, 200, 202, 203, 207, 208, 221
complementary role 36, 37, 44, 75, 79, 83, 104, 190, 193, 195, 203
criteria for, 3-9
defined 1-2
guessing 30, 35, 36, **52-56**, 202, 220-221
hiding 30, 31, 35, 36, **48-52**, 206, 207, 219-220
in preschool 35
involving verbal commands 35, 36, **56-60**, 111
noncompetitive 203
of chance 199-200, 221
parallel-role 36, 59, 75, 193, 195, 203, 223
regulation of, 155, 159, 163, 180
significance of, for children 23-27
street 22
types of, 35-84
value of, 22-33
generalization

empirical 217
geometry 234, 235, 238
Giant Steps **57**, 58
Go Fish xi, 62, **64**, 66, 67, 221, 222, 224
Golden Rule 28
golf 22
guessing
games 30, 35, 36, 52-56
pattern of, 193
Guess Which Hand the Penny Is In 191, **192-195**, 198

Here We Go 'Round the Mulberry Bush 190, **207**, 220
heteronomy 15, 17, 54, 201, 211, 216, 218, 233, 234
morality of, 15-16, 245
Hide and Seek 2, 6, 31, **48**, 50, 52, 96, 202, 219
Hi-Ho! Cherry-O 72, **80**, 81, 82
hints
see clues
hobbies 27
hockey 214
Hockey 36, **38**
Hokey Pokey **207**
honesty 16
Hoppity Scoot **83**
Hopscotch 36, **59**, 60
Hyena and Sheep 46

I Doubt It **68**, 224
image
mental 41, 55, 145, 146
spatial 146
visual 132, 137, 139, 142, 143, 144
In and Out the Window **207**
independence 15
instruction
group xii
individual xii
intelligence 145, 146
evolution of, 146
practical 229
intentions
collaborative 147, 161, 163
opposed 147, 159, 160, 161, 163, 194-195
reciprocal 166
interactions
adult-child 17
social 18, 19
with peers 18
interdependence 9
internalization 14

inventing 84
strategies 227
invention 208
of games 216, 219
I Saw 7, 53, **54**, 55
I Say Stoop **57**, 58
It Is I **53**, 55

kinesthetic exploration 55
Kitty Wants a Corner 36, **59**, 60, **147-171**, 195, 210
Game 1 148-153
Game 2 153-157
knowledge 14, 17, 22
conceptual 143
empirical 236, 238, 239
logico-mathematical 32, 44, 72, 127, 217, 218, 229, 236, 237, 238-240
perceptual 143
physical 3, 40, 41, 43, 44, 127, 129, 212, 216, 229, 236, 237, 238-240
practical 143
scientific 229
social 208, 237, 238, 240, 241

language 13, 192, 200
learning 12, 21, 27, 208, 243
empiricist-associationist view of, 14
Piagetian view of, 14
legislation 28
lessons 27, 31
levels of development 3, 4, 8, 81, 179, 190, 211, 219
formal operations 40
preoperational 18
lie 133
logic 65, 185, 224
development of, 184
Looby Loo 190, **207**
losing 196, 199, 200
Lotto **77**, 78, 79, 186

Making Families 62, **64**, 66, 67, 86, **173-187**, 195, 203, 204, 208, 210, 221, 222, 223, 224, 226
Marbles vii, 23, 24, 28, **38**, 41, **119-129**, 191-192, 193, 195, 198, 203, 204, 209, 210, 216
marbles 23, 38, 83, 120, 229
math clubs 27
mathematics 27, 236, 238
matrix 67-68, 79, 184
memorization 234
memory 4, 65

minority
   groups 243
   rights 28
monologue 25
   collective 25
moral
   judgment 200
   values 14, 28
Mother Goose 55
Mother Hen **49**, 52
multiplication 234, 243
   tables 235
Musical Chairs 6, 8, 28, 41, **34, 43,** 44, 190, 210, 216, 217–218
Mystery Bag 52, **53**, 55, 220

number 76, 82
   construction of, 3, 217
   lottos 79
Number Recognition **2**
numerical
   comparisons 185, 216
   problems 162
   quantification xi, 40, 41, 117

objectification 26
objectives
   affective 13
   cognitive 13
   of early education 12–22
   social 13
Old Maid 62, **63**, 66, 186, 224
Old Mother Cat **49**
One Potato 95
operations
   formal 11, 40
operativity vii
opposition 8
The Orchestra Conductor 53, **54**, 55, 210
order
   cyclic 223
   temporal 66

Parcheesi **74**, 77
participation
   active 8–9
   passivity 8, 28
Peanut Race **43**, 44
perception
   tactile 132, 139, 140
   tactilo-kinesthetic 41
   tactual 131
   visual 41, 140
physical properties of objects 14, 42
physics xi, 27

Piaget's theory xi–xiii, 11, 12, 14, 28, 35, 86, 197, 200, 201, 208, 217, 245
   and behaviorism 230–235
   educational implications of, 232
   epistemological significance of, 232
Pick-Up Sticks 29, 30
Picture Cards **61**, 62, 199, 221, 224
Piggy Bank **71**, 72, 222
ping-pong ball 41, 214
Pin the Tail on the Donkey **39**, 41, 53, 85, 86, **131–146**, 191, 203, 204, 205, 210
play vii, 26, 27
   classroom 22
   competitive xiii, 184
   conflict-free 161
   egocentric 23, 25, 192
   individual 23, 192
   levels of, 23, 102, 192, 229
   low-level 165
   motor 23, 192
   noncompetitive xiii, 184
   parallel 165
   pretend 2
   socialized 192
   symbolic 152, 218, 219
Poison Seat **43**, 44, 58
Police Officer 53, **54**, 56
pool 28, 203
probability 200
punishment 15, 233
   physical 17

races 35, 36, **41–44**, 199, 202, 214, 216–218
   nonparallel 147
rationalist 236, 238, 241
reading 13, 84
reasoning
   logical 221
   logico-mathematical 146
   numerical 40, 44, 83, 128, 213
   spatial 3, 30, 40, 47, 55, 60, 79, 83, 84, 117, 127, 135, 140, 146
   spatiotemporal 6, 162
reciprocity 160
   of attitudes 166
   social 163
recreation 22
relations
   logico-mathematical 3
   spatial 139, 144
relationships
   collaborative 161

conventional 79
   logical 62, 128
   logico-arithmetical 79
   numerical 44, 217
   opposed 161
   part-part 144
   part-whole 60, 144, 200, 239
   preoperational 235
   spatial 26, 39, 41, 66, 79, 131, 142, 192
   temporal 26, 192
relays 41, 44
reversibility 233
reward 16
Ring Toss 30, 37, 40, 216
rituals 202, 204, 207, 216, 217, 220
   jeering 154
role
   authoritarian 167
   collaborative 2, 9
   interdependent 2
   of mental imagery 145
   opposed 2, 160
   player's 124
   teacher's 92–93, 104, 124
Rollers I and II 212
rowing 27
rules 2, 24, 245
   abiding by, 198
   applying 29
   arbitrary 2, 81
   clarification of, 167
   codification of, 23, 24, 192
   common 24, 184
   conventional 2, 186
   enforcement of, 28, 29, 204, 211–212
   introduction of, 167
   making 27, 28, 197–198
   modification of, 27, 29, 203, 225–228
   moral 16, 17, 22
   mutually agreed upon 24
   social 17
Rummy xi, **70**, 186, 221, 224

safety 95, 197, 205, 209
   glue 105, 106
sanctions 16, 211, 233, 244
   by exclusion 17
   invention of, 28
   positive 233
scheme
   classificatory 43, 47
   seriation 43
school
   curricula 27
   public 243

"success" 12
science
   education xi
   history of, 26
scoring 2, 41
self-concept 13
selfishness 23
sequence
   patterned 176
   spatial 59
   temporal 213
seriation 26, 60–61, 192, 202, 240
set partitioning 31, 60, 71, 72
Sevens **31**, 32, **71**, 221, 224
Shadow Tag 45
Shuffleboard **38**, 40
signals 156
Simon Says **57**, 58, 208, 221
singing 1, 2
skiing 27
Skipping Stones 72, **73**
ski trips 27
Slap Jack **61**, 62, 65, 221, 223, 224
Snake Dice 77, **78**
Snap **62**, 63, 65, 198, 221, 224
specific gravity 240, 244
speech
   egocentric 25
spelling 235, 243
spinner 73, 74, 81
Spoon Race **41**, 43, 44, 198, 216, 218
sports 27, 212
   "good" 218
Squirrel with a Nut **46**
strategy 2, 68, 76, 77, 79, 138, 147, 156, 158, 164, 198, 226
   invention 227
   planning 83
   tactual 137
subtraction 79
symbolization 81
system
   conventional 79
   decimal 79
   deductive 239
Tag 8, **45**, 47, **95–110**, 155, 190, 195, 204, 208, 209, 210, 211
   Tag 1 29, 95–104, 203, 204, 211
   Tag 2 104–110, 197, 204, 205, 206
target 36, 214
teacher

dominance 168
evaluation 7
intervention 166-169, 204, 209-210, 216
role of,
   in Block Race 92-93
   in Kitty Wants a Corner 166-170
   in Making Families 186-187
   in Tag 1 104
teaching 17, 230, 243
   constructivist view of, 15
   principles xii, **201-230**
   verbalistic 244
Teapot 53, **55**, 56
teasing 166

function of, 154
tennis 22, 27
theory
   Einstein's 235
   geocentric 234, 235
   heliocentric 234
   Newton's 234
   psychological 235
   scientific 229, 231, 232
   see also Piaget's theory
thought
   classificatory 56
   competitive 184
   human 26
   independent 128
   logical vii, xi, 11, 18, 28, 67
   noncompetitive 184

operational 146
   preoperational 228, 244
   scientific 26, 192
Three-Legged Race **42**, 44
Tic-Tac-Toe 78, **79**
tinkering 27
Tinker Toys 120
Tom, Tom, Run for Your Supper **5**, **43**, 211, 216, 218
Track Meet **74**, 76
training
   inservice 85
Treasure Hunt 74
trust 13
Tug O'War 73, **75**, 76, 77
Twenty Questions 56

Two Little Blackbirds 207, **208**

War 28, 29, 32, **68**, 69, 76, 221, 222, 224
Wheelbarrow Race **42**, 44
winning 36, 148, 183, 191, 196, 198, 199, 200, 228
   criteria of, 184
Wolf **45**, 47
work 26, 27
worksheets 30, 31, 32, 72
   Frostig's 80
writing 13, 84

Zoo **53**, 55

Index

Ideas for Using This Book in a Workshop or Class

In a Workshop

The best way to use this book in workshops held in several sessions is to have the participants read parts of it first for an overview, discuss them in small groups, try out the ideas with children, and then go back for a deeper examination. The leader may want to begin by asking the participants to read Chapters 1 (Good Group Games: What Are They?) and 2 (Why Use Group Games?), and to skim Chapter 3 (Types of Group Games). Two simple chapters in Part II such as Chapters 4 (Block Race) and 5 (Tag) may then be good before going on to Chapter 11 (The Issue of Competition) and the first part of Chapter 12 (Principles of Teaching). Questions such as the following in preparation for the small group discussion will orient the reader: What points remain unclear to you, and with what points do you agree or disagree? (If the workshop is brief, the leader needs to summarize the highlights of the theoretical chapters and ask the participants to do the reading afterwards.)

After the small group discussion, each member or a few volunteers should try out a game and videotape it if possible. If videotaping is not possible, observation by other participants would be the next best thing, to be able to discuss the activity afterwards. (In a one-day workshop, it may be necessary to use a "canned" videotape.) To choose the game to try out and think about its possibilities, read parts of Chapter 3 carefully. One of the easiest games to play is Doggie, Doggie, Your Bone Is Gone (p. 49). A teacher trying Tag should not expect the game to come out as described in Chapter 5. As can be seen in the difference between Tag 1 and Tag 2, each activity comes out differently with a different group of children.

Ask the teacher participant to put his plan on paper before trying out a game. Such a plan may include the following headings:

1. age and number of children
2. objectives: (a) for the teacher and (b) for the children
3. the way I plan to introduce the game (and alternatives)
4. expectations of how the game will go

The teacher often ends up throwing out his plan, but the thinking he did while putting the plan on paper will be useful in making the best of any unexpected situation.

A discussion after the activity or after viewing the videotape is then essential. Following are two basic questions to address:

Was this game appropriate for this particular group of children?
What did the teacher do well or poorly?

As stated at the end of Chapter 4, it is natural for teachers to direct children too much to make the game go smoothly. Some go to the other extreme of giving too much freedom and responsibility to the children to run the game. Every teacher must experiment with each group of children, and fellow teachers can help in finding the right medium between these extremes. Much depends on the relationship between the teacher and children. The kind of discussion among children found in Tag 2 and Back-to-Back (Chapter 6) takes months of cultivation before it can happen.

For many teachers, it is threatening to be observed, videotaped, or discussed by others. Avoid such obvious stress. If a private viewing of the teacher himself on videotape is possible, this is an excellent means of facilitating decentering. All of us are surprised to observe ourselves even on audiotape. To the extent that the teacher is helped to have a more objective view of himself, he will become a better teacher. The teachers we have worked with greatly appreciated the opportunity to observe themselves on videotape.

The rest is more of the same—trying out other games and/or the same ones and reflecting on what one did well or poorly. Just as children need time and experience to develop, adults, too, cannot develop in one workshop. Constructivism and autonomy are basic principles to keep in mind for both children's and teacher's development. Each teacher must construct his own way of teaching by reflecting on what he does. It is hoped that reading the rest of Part II and experimenting with a variety of games found in Chapter 3 will give new ideas and experience for teachers to discuss with each other. In Chapter 12 are pointers that apply to each category presented in Chapter 3.

In a Class

This book is for teachers who are past the "survival stage" in running group games. While the preceding ideas are also applicable in a class, a class permits the deeper exploration of specific issues. Among those issues we have frequently encountered are the following:

Can competition in games really be harmless?
What does it mean in the reality of the classroom to reduce adult power "as much as possible"?
Is it true that social interaction among children is essential for children's moral and intellectual development?

Information about NAEYC

NAEYC is . . .

. . . a membership-supported organization of people committed to fostering the growth and development of children from birth through age 8. Membership is open to all who share a desire to serve and act on behalf of the needs and rights of young children.

NAEYC provides . . .

. . . educational services and resources to adults who work with and for children, including

- *Young Children, the* journal for early childhood educators
- **Books, posters, brochures, and videos** to expand professional knowledge and commitment to young children, with topics including infants, curriculum, research, discipline, teacher education, and parent involvement
- An **Annual Conference** that brings people from all over the country to share their expertise and advocate on behalf of children and families
- **Week of the Young Child** celebrations sponsored by NAEYC Affiliate Groups across the nation to call public attention to the needs and rights of children and families
- **Insurance plans** for individuals and programs
- **Public affairs information** for knowledgeable advocacy efforts at all levels of government and through the media
- The **National Academy of Early Childhood Programs,** a voluntary accreditation system for high-quality programs for children
- The **National Institute for Early Childhood Professional Development,** providing resources and services to improve professional preparation and development of early childhood educators
- The **Information Service,** a centralized source of information sharing, distribution, and collaboration

For free information about membership, publications, or other NAEYC services . . .
. . . call NAEYC at 202-232-8777 or 800-424-2460.

Or write to **NAEYC, 1834 Connecticut Avenue, N.W., Washington, DC 20009-5786.**